T0230033

Lecture Notes in Computer Science 1306

Edited by G. Goos, J. Hartmanis and J. van Leeuwen

Advisory Board: W. Brauer   D. Gries   J. Stoer

Springer

Berlin
Heidelberg
New York
Barcelona
Budapest
Hong Kong
London
Milan
Paris
Santa Clara
Singapore
Tokyo

Clement Leung (Ed.)

Visual
Information Systems

 Springer

Series Editors

Gerhard Goos, Karlsruhe University, Germany

Juris Hartmanis, Cornell University, NY, USA

Jan van Leeuwen, Utrecht University, The Netherlands

Volume Editor

Clement Leung
Victoria University of Technology
Department of Computer and Mathematical Sciences
PO Box 14428, MCMC
Victoria 8001, Melbourne, Australia
E-mail: clement@matilda.vut.edu.au

Cataloging-in-Publication data applied for

Die Deutsche Bibliothek - CIP-Einheitsaufnahme

Visual information systems / Clement Leung (ed.). - Berlin ;
Heidelberg ; New York ; Barcelona ; Budapest ; Hong Kong ;
London ; Milan ; Paris ; Santa Clara ; Singapore ; Tokyo : Springer,
1997
    (Lecture notes in computer science ; Vol. 1306)
    ISBN 3-540-63636-6

CR Subject Classification (1991). H.2, H.3, H.4, H.5, I.3.7, I.6.8

ISSN 0302-9743
ISBN 3-540-63636-6 Springer-Verlag Berlin Heidelberg New York

This work is subject to copyright. All rights are reserved, whether the whole or part of the material is
concerned, specifically the rights of translation, reprinting, re-use of illustrations, recitation, broadcasting,
reproduction on microfilms or in any other way, and storage in data banks. Duplication of this publication
or parts thereof is permitted only under the provisions of the German Copyright Law of September 9, 1965,
in its current version, and permission for use must always be obtained from Springer -Verlag. Violations are
liable for prosecution under the German Copyright Law.

© Springer-Verlag Berlin Heidelberg 1997
Printed in Germany

Typesetting: Camera-ready by author
SPIN 10545890   06/3142 – 5 4 3 2 1 0   Printed on acid-free paper

Preface

Human information processing often involves the recognition, storage, processing and retrieval of visual and multimedia information. Although vast amounts of multimedia information are being continuously generated in a variety of applications, current information systems are incapable of dealing with them effectively, as these systems are primarily designed to function with symbolic and structured data. While there is no difficulty for humans to flexibly recognise and retrieve the contents in multimedia data, this presents severe difficulties for current information systems.

Present day information systems are mainly based on alphanumeric information, sometimes augmented by graphical RAD (Rapid Application Development) tools together with simple diagrammatic and charting techniques. The effective use of visual information for organisational applications has been limited and is mostly confined to highly specialised applications. Recent trends in the development of computer technology have resulted in endowing machines with abilities to operate more like humans, and future information systems will be required to have the capability to process and retrieve visual information in a routine and efficient manner.

Next generation information systems will have a high visual content, and there will be a shift in emphasis from a paradigm of pre-dominantly alphanumeric data processing to one of visual information processing. This will lead to the development of a new kind of information system: Visual Information Systems (VIS). While there has always been a demand for visual information, the technology for such systems was either immature or unavailable in the past. VIS is now becoming increasingly feasible because of a number of factors.

1. Advances in multimedia hardware for the efficient capture, storage, processing and delivery of visual information, which now pervades all categories of computer usage and is not just confined to certain specialised applications.

2. Ongoing improvement in software methodology and the development of standards for the effective handling of visual data.

3. Advances in digital communication such as FDDI, ATM and other high speed networking equipment, which by providing a significantly higher bandwidth, will enable the efficient transmission and delivery of visual information.

4. Widespread adoption of multimedia chips and general-purpose chips with multimedia functions.

It is expected that VIS will supersede existing information systems, while maintaining all the strengths and fulfilling all the functions of the latter.

Visual information systems are not just about the incorporation of new data types into existing information systems; rather, they require completely new ways of managing, using and interacting with information. Visual information systems will not only substantially enhance the value and usability of existing information, but will also open up a new horizon of previously untapped information sources which will greatly increase the effectiveness of an organisation.

The origin of this volume may be traced back to February 1996 when the First International Conference on Visual Information Systems was held. The conference received enthusiastic support from the international research community and provided a timely meeting point between two groups of researchers: those working on image processing, and those working on database and information systems. A steering committee was established consisting of Shi-kuo Chang (University of Pittsburgh), Ramesh Jain (University of California, San Diego), Tosiyasu Kunii (University of Aizu), Clement Leung (Victoria University of Technology), and Arnold Smeulders (University of Amsterdam). It is recognised that visual information systems will permeate all aspects of computing in the future, and their design and construction will require a new approach significantly different from that used to build conventional computing applications systems.

This volume consists of a cross section of papers from the First International Conference on Visual Information Systems. They have been especially selected to furnish an informative and representative perspective on this important new discipline. All the papers were fully revised, updated and expanded subsequent to the conference. The papers here deal with the main strands of visual information systems, covering the areas of:

- Design and architecture

- Database management and modelling

- Content-based search and retrieval

- Feature extraction and indexing

- Query model and interface

- Object recognition and content organisation

In addition, an introductory chapter on the principal characteristics and architectural components of visual information systems is provided. The two keynote papers included here are fully updated and rewritten versions especially prepared for this volume after the conference.

July 1997   Clement H. C. Leung

CONTENTS

Introduction

Keynote Papers

Design and Architecture

Database Management and Modelling

Content-Based Search and Retrieval

Feature Extraction and Indexing

Query Model and Interface

Object Recognition and Content Organisation

Characteristics and Architectural Components of Visual Information Systems

Clement H. C. Leung and W. W. S. So
Victoria University of Technology, Ballarat Road,
P.O. Box 14428, MCMC, Melbourne 3001, Victoria, Australia
Email: {clement, simon}@matilda.vut.edu.au   Fax: +61 3 9688 4050

Abstract

A Visual Information System represents a radical departure from the rigid text-in/text out paradigm of conventional Information Systems. It significantly enlarges the applications scope of information systems and typically sits on top of a general purpose multimedia operating system supported by multimedia hardware and a high bandwidth network. Unlike a conventional Information System, the types of storage and I/O devices required to support a Visual Information System generally include a much greater variety of facilities for efficient visual information presentation and visualisation. Apart from providing multi-mode delivery, the effective correlation between information of the same media type and information belonging to different media types forms an integral part of such systems. The essential building blocks of a Visual Information System are described, and the management of different types of information contents are discussed.

1. Basic Features of a Visual Information System

An *Information System* (IS) may be defined as an integrated, user-machine system for providing information to support the operations, management and decision-making functions in an organisation [Davi85]. At the structural level, it is made up of a set of components or subsystems that captures, processes, stores, analyses, condenses, and disseminates information in various forms. Traditionally, information systems (Figure 1) are text-oriented which provide reports, documents, and decision-making information for all levels of the hierarchy within an organisation [Senn90]. It is characterised by a text-in/text-out mode of operation, focusing primarily on structured fields and free text. However, this style of IS is becoming obsolete since information is no longer text-based, but instead it is based on a combination of text, audio, video, image together with the semantic and spatio-temporal relationships among them.

A *Visual Information System* can be defined as an integrated, user-machine system for providing *inter-related visual and multimedia information* to support the operations, management and decision-making functions in an organisation. The inter-relationships between different multimedia data may signify relationships between the same media type (intra-media relationships) or between different media types (inter-media relationships). A distinction may be sometimes made between a VIS and a Multimedia System, where the latter tends to be more concerned with the system and support aspects (Figure 2). A VIS, on the other hand, is concerned with the semantics, and possibly pragmatics, of multimedia information which occurs at a higher level much closer to the user. Figure 2 shows a distinction between the low-level support layer, and the high-level application layer. A multimedia system may refer primarily to the hardware/software support environment without reference to the applications running on them. These applications can be quite diverse and may represent different facets of the operations and business functions of an organisation.

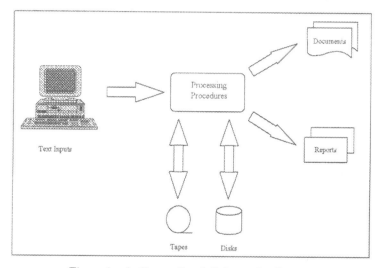

Figure 1. A Conventional Information System

Figure 3 illustrates the functionalities of a Visual Information System. Many of the existing visual-based information systems are either model-based [Gros92] or application specific and can accept only a limited number of information sources. In order to be a general-purpose VIS, the system must be able to handle a variety of information sources such as text, sound, graphics, images and video. In particularly, the contents of these sources ought to be properly indexed and easily accessible. Some of the main characteristics of VIS are the following.

1. The use of multimedia platforms equipped with audio and video facilities, large memory, large disk storage and fast I/O for the effective handling of multimedia data, possibly based on multimedia chips or general-purpose chips with rich multimedia instructions,

coupled with the use of high performance parallel servers and high bandwidth networks.

2. Such systems will incorporate the strengths of traditional information systems components, including Management Information System (MIS), Executive Support System (ESS), Decision Support System (DSS) and data warehouses, and integrates them into a unified VIS architectural environment. As some of these components do not always support a high degree of visual interaction (e.g. an ESS making use of externally produced data) a *visual interface filter* may be used to enhance their visual impact and information delivery.

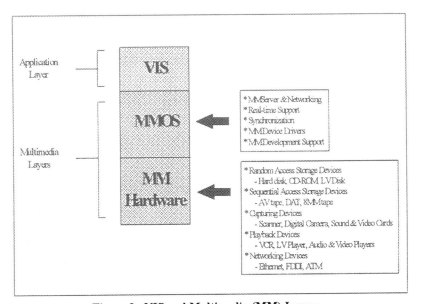

Figure 2. VIS and Multimedia (MM) Layers

3. The use of flexible hypermedia links between multi-type information is a salient feature of VIS. Such links may exist between structured information, unstructured information, still images, sounds, and video clips as well as between information of the same type.

4. Flexible image and pictorial information analysis and synthesis tools incorporating techniques in image understanding and image processing will be available routinely to the users of VIS. This will assist the users in formulating and refining visual queries for processing and information matching by the system.

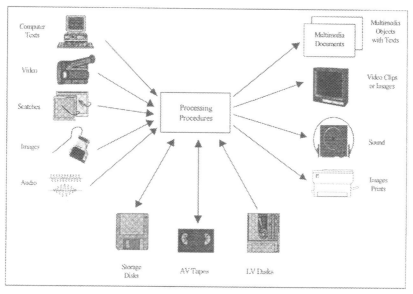

Figure 3. A Visual Information System

5. The presentation and delivery of information is highly graphical and pictorial. This in itself do not guarantee a system to be a VIS, as some conventional systems are also able to do this. Such presentation will involve the extensive use of *visualisation techniques*, and will significantly enhance the value and usability of the underlying information.

6. A flexible query model involving different modes of input which supports both *visual information recovery* and *visual information discovery* will also be used. In addition to the common relational operators, a new set of spatial, temporal, and dynamic operators [Chan96] are needed in composing queries.

7. The use of object-oriented methodology in their design, analysis, programming and implementation, coupled with the deployment of visual RAD (rapid application development) tools, supporting a range of display and modelling functions.

2. An Example Visual Information System

We use a law enforcement application where a collection of visual and textual data for criminals are maintained. This provides a particularly appropriate example to highlight the effectiveness of VIS because of the tight coupling relationships among different data sources. Without the use of an integrated visual information system, the inter-relationship between different types of information will be difficult to manage and maintain.

There are many sources of information that need to be managed in a visual information system for storing data on criminals. Personal details, criminal history, fingerprints, for example, are some of the essential components. Table 1 shows some of the media types of a criminal profile to be used in building the visual information system.

Relevant Data	Media Type
Personal Details	Structured Information
Fingerprints	Images or Graphics
Mug shots	Images
Photofits	Graphics
Voice Samples	Audio
Photo / Video Clips	Images / Video
Permanently Identifiable Features	Text or Images
Personal / Family History	Text
Psychiatric History	Text
Criminal History	Text

Table 1. The Data Types in a Criminal Profile VIS

To use the system effectively, a number of paradigms may be adopted:

- Personal details can be retrieved using conventional database and conventional query language such as SQL
- Personal, psychiatric, and criminal historical information can be indexed using free text indexing together with standard information retrieval techniques
- Techniques from content-based image retrieval and content-based video retrieval will need to be employed for the indexing and retrieval of mug shots and video clips of the criminal
- Graphics contents can be scaled and modified numerically for similarity search
- Automatic extraction of primitive contents such as moustaches, spectacles, contours of faces, voice features and other features of the criminal
- Fingerprint information may be matched and retrieved using a combination of signature schemes
- Voice characteristics may be matched and edited graphically
- Complex contents from photos can be extracted and indexed with human assistance

Managing fingerprint information is a typical component application requiring VIS techniques. There are 200 million Americans who have their fingerprints on file; with such a large number of prints, comparing and retrieving them is non-trivial. Fingerprints are classified into groups such as arch, loop, whorl and composite; they are generally composed of line segments, but may contain complex noises and disconnected virtual lines. Hence, it is often advantageous to use image enhancement techniques to improve their quality and connectivity before classifying them based on the main types and then indexing them using an appropriate signature scheme for rapid identification.

The effectiveness of this system is evident when an integrated query is performed. For example, a police detective may query the Criminal Profile System for "a male criminal who is classified as extremely dangerous, has a tattoo of an eagle on his back and his left-thumb fingerprint is whorl ". This query exploits the *inter-media* relationship among personal details (e.g. male), psychiatric history (e.g. extremely dangerous) and permanently identifiable features (e.g. tattoo and fingerprint), which are represented as structured information, free text and images respectively. The *intra-media* relationship of similarity search in tattoos (e.g. eagle) and fingerprint (e.g. whorl) will also be required, which may be identified using image-based QBE (Query By Example) techniques.

3. Building Blocks of a Visual Information System

The key components and organisation of a VIS is shown in Figure 4. Such visual components will tend to permeate all information systems and in time will not be regarded as a distinct element, but will form an essential part of any information system, working alongside and in harmony with structured information processing components. Here we primarily focus on the processing of visual information, although it is to be understood that all the conventional functions are also being carried out. The main building blocks consist of the following four main subsystems.

1. *Feature Extraction and Indexing.* After the visual information has been entered into the system, their use will be limited unless they are appropriately indexed. With conventional approach, a visual data object may be organised as a record, and structured information about it (e.g. frame number, title, date, originator) may be regarded as properties of the object and entered into a relational database tuple. With this approach, only limited search on contents is possible using the caption field (assuming one is available) within the structured record. In situations where the visual contents are central to user queries, however, then such an approach is inadequate, and different data modelling and design structures have to be used. This subsystem will be responsible for the automatic and semi-automatic feature extraction and indexing of images [Zhen96], together with routines which will suitably place the resultant information in a structured

database management subsystem for later access. Moreover, this subsystem will also support incremental indexing subsequent to the initial entry of the visual information. Such *continuous indexing* may take two forms. The first may relate to the background execution of relatively processor intensive algorithms required for image understanding and feature recognition, while the second may relate to index refinement as a result of evolving usage, arising from the diverse non-unique ways of indexing visual information.

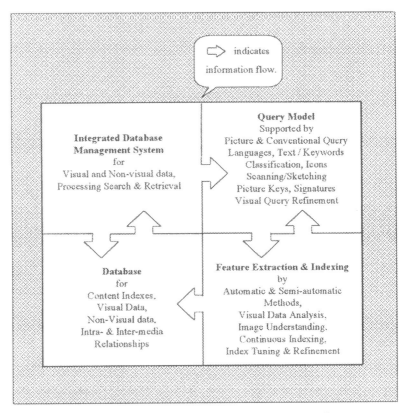

Figure 4. Principal Components of a Visual Information System

2. *Database.* In addition to the raw visual data, which may form the object of retrieval queries, content indexes are also stored to facilitate flexible and rapid access. Unlike in a conventional database, the indexes here typically consists of both structured tables as well as visual-based information such as compressed images [Leun95]. In an integrated system, both visual and conventional data are also stored, although they may be physically separate. Links between different kinds of media data signifying their relationships (e.g. intra- and inter-media relationships) will also been represented, and suitable

storage structures and file organisations are adopted to facilitate their speedy traversal and processing.

3. *Integrated Database Management System.* This includes modules for the management of content indexes, storage structures, search identification and image retrieval. Depending on the data model, information related to the content of images may be organised into conventional databases or, more likely, using an ORDBMS (object-relational database management system). It also provides a level of abstraction above the physical data store so that the users are shielded from implementation issues such as parallel access to the visual data, the data compression techniques, the image file formats, and the organisation of associated retrieval keys.

4. *Query Model.* Unlike in a conventional information system where queries may generally be accurately specified by means of a syntactically well-defined, alphanumeric-based query language, the query interface for VIS will be richer and more diverse. It will not confine to any particular method, but will support a number of query paradigms: classification schemes, icons, visual query language, QBE (Query By Example based on image similarity), text/keywords, scanning/sketching, picture keys, signatures, as well as SQL style specifications. Classification schemes together with thesauri such as AAT, ICONCLASS or TELCLASS are particularly useful in supporting ambiguous queries. Users can also provide sketches or scanned images as part of the query model for similarity search. Colour, texture, picture signature and other lower level primitives can be used to formulate the query. A mechanism is normally included to enable the users to provide feedback to the indexing subsystem so that retrieval performance may improve with usage.

4. The Information Contents in a Visual Information System

The need for using a multi-paradigm approach is closely related to the different types of visual information contents. Although principally geared to the processing of visual information, a VIS should also be able to cater for the following types of contents.

4.1 Text-based Content

Text-based content is the most widely used in traditional IS and comes in a variety of forms. It can be represented using keywords, free text, structured records etc. Keywords and structured text can be indexed using established automatic indexing algorithms [Salt89]. Relational and object-oriented databases are the basic models for representing structured records. Although object-oriented databases offer greater scope for accommodating multimedia objects, they do not in general provide tools for their manipulation and identification. Free text such as the annotation of images and stratification of videos can be indexed using free text oriented databases. The ambiguity inherent in English can be minimised by using a thesaurus and classification methods.

4.2 Audio-based Content

Audio-based content is the least researched area in content-based retrieval. It can be stand-alone content or tied to video-based content. Parsing of audio content can be done by signal processing and spectrum analysis. For musical data, the MIDI file format (SMF) has become a de facto standard which can represent good quality sound at about 3.5 Kbits/second. Although it is unlikely that automatic extraction is possible due to the multiplexing of different sources of sound in real-life scenario, some simple sound patterns such as door bells, hand clapping or engine vibration can be detected using model-based approaches if the background noise can be minimised. Speech or voice analysis can be done to locate the "signature" of any individual voice. Audio content may be used in conjunction with visual-based content to identify target image sets or video clips.

4.3 Graphics-based Content

Line arts, synthetic images and computer animation may be described by their geometrical properties. VRML modelling and the Synthetic-Natural Hybrid Coding (SNHC) scheme in MPEG-4 for creating models of inanimate objects will clearly be useful in the representation of synthetically generated contents. The line, polygon, surface patches and many mathematical entities can be indexed numerically, and this form of content can be easily manipulated and computed. The motion of objects in computer animation can be traced and the sequences of events can be indexed. In some situations, it may be more efficient to index the characteristics of the underlying graphics generation algorithms, since fast searching and identification may be done using text-based pattern matching procedures.

4.4 Image-based Content

Image-based content is the most researched area in content-based retrieval [Jain93, Gudi95]. Image content such as colour, texture, object shape, and sketch-based feature can be indexed [Nibl93]. Proximity among objects can also be represented. Colour histogram, moment/centroid, segmentation, and other primitive features can be used to form the *signatures* of the images. The signatures can then be indexed for similarity retrieval. Image compression techniques [Furh94] are useful not only for transmission and size reduction, but can also be used for indexing and identification. Visual queries, sketches and fuzzy matches are some of the techniques that can be used for query formulation. Due to the imprecise nature of queries, browsing through miniature icons, compressed images or picture keys would seem to be indispensable operations in image retrieval systems [So96].

Image-based contents can be categorised into complex contents and primitive contents [Leun95] with different methods for their extraction. Primitive contents are low-level contents which can usually be extracted automatically (e.g. textures, colours, boundaries, and shapes). Complex contents are extracted manually or semi-automatically, and corresponds to patterns within a picture which are considered as meaningful by human users and may be applications dependent or applications independent. They cannot normally be automatically identified and are often qualitative in character (e.g. a class room, a bride, a sports car).

4.5 Video-based Content

Video-based content retrieval has been attracting substantial research interests, possibly due to the demands arising from consumer electronics. The use of a flexible arbitrary shape Video Object Plane (VOP) are being supported as part of the MPEG-4 standard. In-house shopping, electronic kiosk, and video-on-demand are some of the commercial driving forces. Motion vectors, salient video stills, annotations and video partitioning [Furh95] are some of the methods employed for their indexing and retrieval. The spatio-temporal aspect of objects between frames is an important property that needs to be indexed. A sufficiently fast index to support real-time retrieval and playback of video-based content appears to pose a considerable challenge [Gemm95].

5. Discussion

The increasingly widespread adoption of multimedia platforms has made visual information more available. This also highlights the limitations of current information systems, which are primarily based on a GUI-assisted alphanumeric paradigm. Although certain forms of visual information processing systems already exist, they tend to be restricted to highly specialised applications such as medical imaging and engineering design. As human end users form an important part of an information system, and as they often prefer non-alphanumeric multimedia interaction, traditional information systems are expected to be superseded by visual information systems. VIS will not only allow more natural interaction between human and machine, but will pervade all applications areas and substantially increase the functionality and effectiveness of information systems, opening up a new horizon of previously untapped information sources. Due to the diverse nature of the information contents, the construction of VIS will require a multi-paradigm approach.

The proper construction of a VIS will be dependent on the underpinning technologies, many of which are still in their infancy. For example, MPEG clearly recognises this need, and the project MPEG-7 will aim to address the issues of content search, standardised descriptions and feature extraction. In a conventional IS, one of the indispensable components is a database management system responsible for the management, updating and querying of structured information. Although there are many research issues that need to be addressed in relation to the design of VIS, analogous to a conventional IS, the key ones would appear to be content-based indexing and retrieval of visual information, and the design of a multi-paradigm query model to support the flexible specification, input, and refinement of visual information queries. Although such technology will take time to mature, any incremental advances is likely to offer substantial advantages over the current situation.

References

[Chan96]   S. K. Chang, "Extending visual languages for multimedia", *IEEE Multimedia*, Fall 1996, pp. 18-26.

[Davi85]   G. B. Davis, and M. H. Olson, *Management Information Systems: Conceptual Foundations, Structure, and Development*, 2nd Edition, NY: McGraw-Hill, 1985.

[Furh94]   B. Furht, "Multimedia Systems: An Overview", *IEEE Multimedia*, Spring 1994, pp. 47-59.

[Furh95]   B. Furht, S. W. Smoliar, and H. J. Zhang, *Video and Image Processing in Multimedia Systems*, Boston: Kluwer Academic Publishers, 1995.

[Gemm95]   D. J. Gemmell, H. M. Vin, D. D. Kandlur, R. V. Rangan, and L. A. Rowe, "Multimedia storage servers: a tutorial", *IEEE Computer*, May 1995, pp. 40-49.

[Gros92]   W. Grosky, and R. Mehrotra, "Image database management", in M.C. Yovits (ed), *Advances in Computers*, Vol. 34, San Diego, CA: Academic Press, 1992.

[Gudi95]   V. N. Gudivada, and V.V. Raghavan, "Content-based image retrieval systems," *IEEE Computer*, Vol. 28, No. 9, September 1995.

[Jain93]   R. Jain (ed), *NSF Workshop on Visual Information Management Systems*, ACM SIGMOD RECORD, Vol. 22, No. 3, September 1993, pp. 57-75.

[Leun95]   C. H. C. Leung, and Z .J. Zheng, "Image data modelling for efficient content indexing," *Proc. IEEE International Workshop on Multimedia Database Management Systems*, New York, August 1995, IEEE Computer Society Press, pp. 143-150.

[Nibl93]   W. Niblack (et al.), "The QBIC project: querying images by content using color, texture, and shape," *IS&T/SPIE Proc. Storage and Retrieval for Image and Video Databases*, San Jose, CA, Vol. 1908, February 1993, pp. 173-187.

[Salt89]   G. Salton, *Automatic Text Processing*, Reading, MA: Addison-Wesley, 1989.

[Senn90]   J. A. Senn, *Information Systems in Management*, 4th Edition, Belmont, CA: Wadsworth, 1990.

[So96]   W. W. S. So, C. H. C. Leung, and Z. J. Zheng, "Picture coding for image database retrieval," *Proc. International Picture Coding Symposium*, Melbourne, March 1996, pp. 69-74

[Zhen96]   Z. J. Zheng and C. H. C. Leung, "Automatic image indexing for rapid content-based retrieval," *Proc. IEEE International Workshop on Multimedia Database Management Systems*, New York, August 1996, IEEE Computer Society Press, pp. 38-45.

Active Visual Information Systems

Shi-Kuo Chang
Visual Computer Laboratory, Department of Computer Science
University of Pittsburgh, Pittsburgh, PA 15260 USA
(Email: chang@cs.pitt.edu)

Abstract: To accomplish the discovery, fusion and retrieval of visual/multimedia information from diversified sources, *active visual information systems* capable of processing and filtering visual/multimedia information, checking for semantic consistency, and structuring the relevant information for distribution are needed. We describe a framework for the human- and system-directed discovery and fusion of visual/multimedia information, which is based upon the observation that a significant event often manifests itself in different media over time. Therefore if we can index such manifestations and dynamically link them, then we can check for consistency and discover important and relevant visual/multimedia information. This dynamic indexing technique is based upon the theory of active index. An approach for rapid prototyping of active visual information systems using Tele-Action Objects, TAO_HTML Interpretor and active index system is then presented.

1. Introduction

The discovery, retrieval and fusion of visual/multimedia information from diversified sources in a heterogeneous information system is a challenging research topic of great practical significance. With the rapid expansion of the wired and wireless networks, a large number of soft real-time, hard real-time and non-real-time sources of information need to be quickly processed, checked for consistency, structured and distributed to the various agencies and people involved in visual/multimedia information handling. In addition to visual/multimedia databases, it is also anticipated that numerous web sites on the World Wide Web will become rich sources of visual/multimedia information.

However, since too much information is available, visual/multimedia information related to an important event could be missed because people are unable to track the manifestations of an unfolding event across diversified sources over time. What is needed, from the information technology viewpoint, is an *active visual information system* capable of processing and filtering visual/multimedia information, checking for semantic consistency, discovering important events, and structuring the relevant visual/multimedia information for distribution.

We describe a framework for the human- and system-directed discovery, fusion and retrieval of visual/multimedia information so that important events can be discovered and relevant visual/multimedia information retrieved. The framework is based upon the observation that a significant event often manifests itself in different media over time. Therefore, if we can index such manifestations and dynamically link them to one another, then we can check for consistency and discover relevant information. This dynamic indexing technique is based upon the theory of active index [1].

The paper is organized as follows. A framework for information discovery and fusion is described in Section 2. Section 3 presents the formal definition of semantic consistency and gives an example. Section 4 introduces the concept of horizontal reasoning and vertical reasoning which can be applied to consistency checking. Section 5 presents the active index and explains how it is applied to dynamic information linking. Section 6 describes how we can prototype visual information systems using Tele-Action Objects (TAO), the TAO_HTML Interpretor and the active index system. Section 7 discusses further research.

2. Visual/Multimedia Information Discovery and Fusion

The framework for human- and system-directed visual/multimedia information discovery and fusion [7] is best illustrated by Figure 1 and Figure 2. As shown in Figure 1, we envision a three-level model for information: **data, abstracted information, and fused knowledge**.

Information sources such as camera, sensors or computers usually provide continuous streams of data, which are collected and stored in visual/multimedia databases. Such data need to be abstracted into various forms of abstractions, so that the processing, consistency analysis and combination of abstracted information becomes possible. Finally, the abstracted information needs to be integrated and transformed into fused knowledge. These three levels of information form a hierarchy, but at any given moment there is the continuous transformation of data into abstracted information and then into fused knowledge. This transformation is effected by the coordinated efforts of the **user**, the **query processor**, the **reasoners**, and the **active index system**.

As shown in Figure 1, the user is capable of controlling the sources to influence the type of data being collected. For example, the user may turn on or turn off the video camera or manually control the positioning of the camera. Data are then transformed into abstracted information through the use of the active indices which also serve as filters to weed out unwanted data. As to be described in more detail in Section 5, the active index system is a message-based system. It receives input data as messages, processes them, and sends abstracted information as its output to storage (the Blackboard). At the same time, it also sends messages to the reasoners, so that the reasoners can perform spatial/temporal reasoning [6, 7] based upon the abstracted information to generate fused knowledge or updated abstracted information in the form of assertions. The query processor then uses data, abstracted information and fused knowledge, to answer user's queries.

The above description proceeds in the "bottom-up" fashion, although the coordination among the user, query processor, reasoners and active index system is not merely hierarchical. The query processor can send messages to the active index system so that it knows what index cells to activate as the appropriate agents to collect abstracted information. The query processor can also interact with the reasoners to process the user's queries. Such interactions are illustrated by dotted lines in Figure 1.

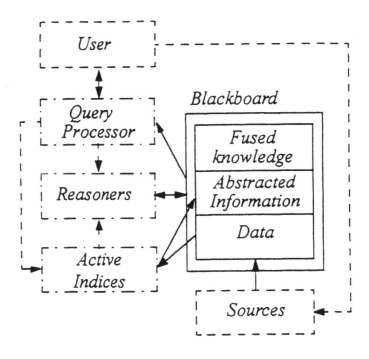

Figure 1. Information discovery and fusion from multiple sources.

Figure 2 illustrates the relationships among data sources, data, abstracted information and fused knowledge, with emphasis on diversity of data sources and multiplicity of abstracted representations. For example, a video camera is a data source that generates video data. Such video data can be transformed into various forms of abstracted representations:

o text (video-to-text abstraction by human agent or computer)
o keyword (video-to-keyword abstraction by human agent or computer)
o assertions (logical representation of abstracted facts)
o time sequences of frames (both spatial and temporal relations are preserved)
o qualitative spatial description QSD (for the most essential contents of video)
o frame strings (the video is abstracted into a sequence of strings)
o projection strings (each frame is abstracted into symbolic projection strings)

In Figure 2, a potentially viable transformation from data to abstracted representation is indicated by a black dot. Thus, from video it is possible to transform into almost all kinds of abstractions. A supported transformation is indicated by a large circle in Figure 2. Thus the image data will be transformed into keywords, assertions, qualitative spatial description (QSD) and projection strings. It should be emphasized that there are more types of abstracted representations than are shown in Figure 2. Conversely, certain information systems may only support assertions, keywords and texts as the only allowable types of abstractions.

The information sources in Figure 2 may include hard real-time sources (such as the signals captured by sensors), soft real-time sources (such as pre-stored video), and non-real-time sources (such as text, images and graphics from a visual database or a web site). The framework can be used to study the discovery, fusion and retrieval of information from these diversified sources.

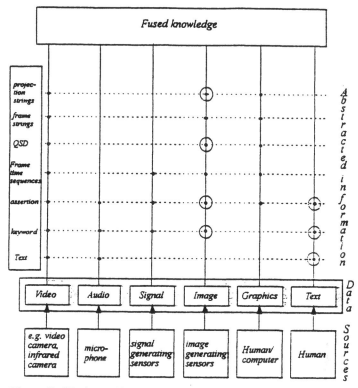

Figure 2. Horizontal/vertical reasoning for information fusion.

3. Formal Definition and Example of Semantic Consistency

In order to address the problem of information discovery and fusion, a clear definition of semantic consistency is necessary. Our definition of semantic consistency is based upon the transformational approach illustrated by the framework of Figure 2. It is different from the usual definitions of semantic consistency in database theory or in AI theory, because we believe the problem of consistency for information discovery and fusion must be first addressed at the level of characteristic patterns detected in visual/multimedia objects. This is where the active visual information system can make the most impact in drastically reducing the amount of visual/multimedia information that ultimately must be handled by human operators.

We define consistency functions to check the consistency among media objects of the *same* media type, by concentrating on their characteristic patterns. For example, two assertions "there is a tank in the target area" and "there is no tank in the target area" can be checked for consistency, and two images of the same target area can also be checked for consistency. These consistency functions are media-specific and domain-specific. For example, to check whether two aerial photographic images are consistent, the consistency function will verify whether the two images contain similar *characteristic patterns* such as buildings, bridges and other landmarks. For different application domains, different consistency functions are needed.

To check whether media objects of *different* media types are consistent, they need to be transformed into media objects of the same media type so that the media-specific, domain-specific consistency function can be applied. Our viewpoint is that each object is characterized by some characteristic patterns that can be transformed into characteristic patterns in different media type. For example, the characteristic pattern is a tank pattern in the image media, which is transformed into the word "tank" in the keyword media. The consistency function can then be applied to the characteristic patterns of objects of the same media type.

Let $o^i{}_j$ be the jth object of media type M^i. Let $c^i{}_k$ be the kth characteristic pattern detected in an object $o^i{}_j$ of media type M^i. Let C^i denote the set of all such characteristic patterns of media type M^i. Let $\phi_{1,2}$ be the transformation that maps characteristic patterns detected in objects of media type M^1 to characteristic patterns of media type M^2.

For each media type M^i there is a consistency function K_i which is a mapping from 2^C (the space of all subsets of characteristic patterns in media type M^i) to $\{T, F\}$. In other words it verifies that a set of characteristic patterns of media type M^i are consistent.

A characteristic pattern $c^1{}_k$ of media type M^1 is consistent with respect to media type M^2 if the transformed characteristic pattern $\phi_{1,2}(c^1{}_k)$ is consistent with the set C^2 of all characteristic patterns of media type M^2, i.e. $K_2(\{\phi_{1,2}(c^1{}_k)\} \cup C^2) = T$. A characteristic pattern $c^i{}_k$ is consistent if it is consistent with respect to all media types M^j.

Finally, a multimedia information space is consistent at time t if every characteristic pattern of every media type is consistent at time t, and a multimedia information space is consistent if it is consistent at all times.

As an example, an aerial photograph of media type M^1 is examined and a possible tank object is detected. This is a characteristic pattern $c^1{}_1$. The keywords describing findings for the intelligence officer is of media type M^2. The transformation $\phi_{1,2}$ maps characteristic pattern $c^1{}_1$ to $\phi_{1,2}(c^1{}_1)$, which could be the keyword "tank". If the consistency function K_2 verifies that the finding "tank" is consistent with other findings, then the characteristic pattern $c^1{}_1$ is consistent with respect to media type M^2. If we can also verify that $c^1{}_1$ is consistent with other patterns detected in media M^1, and suppose the information space contains only objects of these two media types, then we have verified that $c^1{}_1$ is consistent.

The information space is consistent if all such findings are consistent at all times. This of course can be verified only after we run the entire surveillance procedure.

In this example the transformation function is simply the labeling of characteristic patterns. The "tank" characteristic pattern is the pattern detected by a pattern recognizer. There are image processing algorithms which will produce characteristic patterns. As for the consistency function, we can use similarity functions which accept as inputs the characteristic patterns in some media space (the simplest being keywords) and produce the output to verify whether the inputs are consistent [8]. In other words, we can use similarity functions to determine whether the inputs are all within a certain distance. We can also use fuzzy predicates or artificial neural networks as consistency functions. For different media, we need to investigate the most suitable consistency functions.

4. Consistency Checking by Horizontal/Vertical Reasoning

As illustrated in Figure 2, knowledge discovery and fusion can be accomplished when there are several circles in the same horizontal row. For example the current system may only support the transformation of image and text into assertions and keywords, so that consistency checking of assertions, or consistency checking of keywords, become feasible. We call such reasoning the **horizontal reasoning** because it can combine information along horizontal rows.

Another type of reasoning works with different abstracted representations so that they can be combined and checked for consistency. We call such reasoning the **vertical reasoning** because it must combine information along vertical columns.

The active index to be described in Section 5 can be used by the reasoner in vertical reasoning for consistency checking. For example, using active index, we can link an image to a keyword to an assertion. Special algorithms can then be applied to check their consistency. The active index is a dynamic collection of live index cells to exchange messages with one another as well as with the external environment. New index cells are activated by messages, and current index cells can be de-activated due to unuse. Unlike an artificial neural network, an active index does not have a fixed topology, and new cells can be instantiated any time from index cell types. Since the index cells are activated only as needed, the index is compact and efficiently organized. Thus the active index is a dynamic data structure that can evolve, grow and shrink. The active index has been applied to medical image prefetching [4], emergency management and medical multimedia information retrieval [2]. We are currently applying this approach to knowledge-based dynamic information linking for vertical reasoning.

Vertical reasoning requires the combination of information in different representations. An artificial neural network with fixed connections is not as appropriate as an active index with flexible connections. Horizontal reasoning may be more effectively accomplished with the help of artificial neural networks. Horizontal reasoning requires the combination of information abstracted from different media but encoded in the same uniform representation. Therefore, artificial neural network will be a viable approach.

Once a horizontally uniform representation is achieved, a consistency checking reasoner can check for semantic consistency. Thus, we can fuse information and check for consistency in this framework. To speed up processing, the reasoners, the artificial neural networks and active indices can all be working in parallel on a parallel processing computer.

5. Active Index for Dynamic Information Linking

In our approach of human- and system-directed information discovery and fusion, the human can define index cells for the discovery of significant events. The system can generate additional index cells (based upon the artificial neural networks) to monitor significant events. We now describe in detail the index cell, which is the fundamental building block of an active index.

An *index cell* (ic) accepts input messages and performs some actions. It then posts an output message to a group of output index cells. Depending upon the internal state of the index cell and the input messages, the index cell can post different messages to different groups of output index cells. Therefore the connection between an index cell and its output cells is not static, but dynamic. This is the first characteristic of the index cell: *the interconnection among cells is dynamically changing.*

An index cell can be either *live* or *dead*. If the cell is in a special internal state called the *dead state*, it is considered dead. If the cell is in any other state, it is considered live. The entire collection of index cells, either live or dead, forms the *index cell base* (ICB). This index cell base ICB may consist of infinitely many cells, but the set of live cells is finite and forms the *active index* (IX). This is the second characteristic of the index cell: *only a finite number of cells are live at any time.*

When an index cell posts an output message to a group of output index cells, these output index cells are activated. If an output index cell is in a dead state, it will transit to the initial state and become a live cell, and its timer will be initialized (see below). On the other hand, if the output index cell is already a live cell, its current state will not be affected, but its timer will be re-initialized. This is the third characteristic of the index cell: *posting an output message to the output index cells will activate these cells.*

The output index cells, once activated, may or may not accept the posted output message. The first output index cell that accepts the output message will remove this message from the output list of the current cell. (In case of a race, the outcome is nondeterministic.) If no output index cell accepts the posted output message, this message will stay indefinitely in the output list of the current cell. This is the fourth characteristic of the index cell: *an index cell does not always accept the input messages.*

After its computation, the index cell may remain active (live) or de-activate itself (dead). An index cell may also become dead, if no other index cells (including itself) post messages to it. There is a built-in timer, and the cell will de-activate itself if the remaining time is used up before any message is received. This parameter - the time for the cell to remain live- is re-initialized each time it receives a new message and thus is once more activated. (Naturally, if this parameter is set to infinity, then the index cell becomes perennial and can remain live forever.) This is the fifth, and last, characteristic of the index cell: *a cell may become dead if it does not receive any message after a prespecified time.*

Although there can be many index cells, these cells may be all similar. For example, we may want to attach an index cell to an image, so that when a certain feature is detected, a message is sent to the index cell which will perform predetermined actions such as prefetching other images. If there are ten such images, then there can be ten such index cells, but they are all similar. These similar index cells can be specified by an *index cell type*, and the individual cells are the instances of the index cell type. We developed a tool called the *IC_Builder*, which helps the designer construct index cell types using a graphical user interface. The *IC_Builder* can run on a Unix workstation or on any PC with Windows.

To describe precisely the behavior of the active index, we will formally define an index cell.

Definition 1: An *index cell* is described by ic = $(X,Y,S,s_o,A,t_{max},f,g)$ where:

X is the (possibly infinite) set of input messages including dummy input d.
Y is the (possibly infinite) set of output messages including dummy output d.
S is the (possibly infinite) set of states. S includes a
set of ordinary states S and a special state s_{dead} called the dead state. If
an index cell is in the dead state, it is a dead index cell. Otherwise it
is a live index cell.
s_o in S is the initial state of the index cell ic.
A is the set of action sequences that can be performed by this index cell.
t_{max} is the maximum time for the cell to remain live, without receiving
any messages. If t_{max} is infinite, the cell is perennial.

f is a function: 2^X x S -> [0,1] where 2^X is the power set of input X. If
$f(\{x_1,...,x_m\}, s) \geq \theta$, then the cell accepts the input set $\{x_1,...,x_m\}$ and
$x_1,...,x_m$ are removed from the output lists of those cells that produce these
output messages. The removal of messages is an atomic action which will occur
simultaneously. If $f(\{x_1,...,x_m\}, s) < \theta$, the input messages are not accepted.
When several input sets can be accepted, one is chosen non-deterministically.

g is a function: 2^X x S -> 2^{ICB} x Y x S x A such that given input messages
$\{x_1,...,x_m\}$ which have been accepted, i.e., $f(\{x_1,...,x_m\},s) \geq \theta$, and
current state s, $g(x,s)$ is a quadruple (Ic, y, s', u) where

(1) Ic is a set of output index cells to be activated. If an output index cell is in
the dead state, it is changed to the initial state so that it becomes a live cell,
and the clock t is initialized to be t_{max}. If an output index cell is already live,
its current state remains unchanged, but its clock t is re-initialized to be t_{max}.
If an output index cell is the special symbol *nil*, no output index cell is actually activated.

(2) y is the output message for the output index cells in Ic. The output could
be the dummy message d, when there is no real output to the output index
cells. The first output index cell that accepts this output message y will remove it from the output list of ic.

(3) s' is the computed next state of ic. The true next state s" of ic is the dead state if clock time t becomes zero or negative, and s' otherwise. If the next state s' is the dead state, the index cell becomes dead.

(4) a is the action-sequence performed by this index cell, which can be regarded as the output of the cell to the external environment.

Definition 2: The *output list* oL of an ic is of the following form: $[(Ic_1, y_1), (Ic_2, y_2), ..., (Ic_m, y_m)]$, where y_i is the output message posted to the ic's in the set Ic_i. If any ic in Ic_i accepts y_i, the tuple (Ic_i, y_i) is removed from the output list.

Definition 3: An *index cell base* ICB is a (possibly infinite) collection of index cells. Given an index cell base ICB, an *active index* IX is a finite subset of ICB with n index cells, denoted by an n-place ic vector $<ic> = (ic_1, ic_2, ..., ic_n)$, where the ic's are ordered by their (arbitrary) subscripts in ICB.

Definition 4: The *instantaneous description* id of an an active index IX is denoted by $id = (<ic>, <s>, <oL>)$, where $<ic>$ is the ic vector, $<s>$ is the corresponding state vector, and $<oL>$ is the corresponding output list vector.

Definition 5: The *trace* of an active index IX with respect to $(<ic_0>, <s_0>, <oL_0>)$ is:
$(<ic_0>, <s_0>, <oL_0>) =>$
$(<ic_1>, <s_1>, <oL_1>) =>$

.....

$(<ic_n>, <s_n>, <oL_n>)$
where $(<ic_i>, <s_i>, <oL_i>) => (<ic_{i+1}>, <s_{i+1}>, <oL_{i+1}>)$ due to the acceptance of input messages by an index cell. The => symbol reads as "*is transformed into*". Such transformations may occur in any arbitrary order. Each transformation step in the trace takes exactly one clock cycle. If the trace is finite, the active index IX is *terminating* with respect to $(<ic_0>, <s_0>, <oL_0>)$; otherwise it is *nonterminating*.

Therefore, an active index is initially specified by $(<ic_0>, <s_0>, <oL_0>)$ where $<ic_0>$ is the initial ic vector, $<s_0>$ is the initial state vector and $<oL_0>$ is the initial output list vector.

In [1] it was shown that an index cell ic can be modified to post n messages individually to n output index cells. An active index is a dynamically changing net. As shown in [1] the active index can be used to realize Petri nets, generalized Petri nets (G-nets), B-trees, etc. But its primary purpose is to serve as a dynamic index. One application of this model is to improve the efficiency of on-line information retrieval in hyperspace by *prefetching*. In [5] we defined a smart web page as a web page with associated knowledge. The active index technique is used to describe the associated knowledge and to support automatic knowledge-based information retrieval. Experimental results show that a greater retrieval and navigation efficiency can be obtained.

The dynamic information linking proceeds as follows. Referring to Figure 1, the input data can be regarded as input messages to the active index and processed by the actions (such as pattern recognition routines) associated with the first-level index cells. If no significant characteristic patterns are discovered, the processed abstracted information will be stored. If, on the other hand, some significant characteristic patterns are discovered, the second-level index cells will be activated to perform horizontal reasoning. If the horizontal reasoner (possibly an artificial neural network) reports that the new finding is consistent with other findings, these consistent findings can be fused into knowledge by activating the third-level index cells. The simplest form of fusion is the generation of a report listing all the consistent findings, which may be quite adequate for such media as keywords or assertions. Since three levels of index cells are now activated and dynamically linked together, they constitute a vertical reasoner to efficiently process future findings of a similar nature. Another viewpoint is to regard the dynamically linked active index cells as an *active filter* to report on similar findings efficiently.

6. Prototyping Active Visual Information Systems

In this section we describe an approach to prototype active visual information systems. This approach is based upon the concept of Tele-Action Objects or TAOs, which are *active index cells with a visual appearance*. TAOs can be realized as TAO-enhanced html pages. We can then use a TAO_HTML Interpretor to translate the TAO-enhanced html pages into regular html pages. Since these html pages can be interfaced with the active index system, the rapid prototyping of active visual information systems is accomplished.

A. Tele-Action Objects

Tele-Action Objects [2] or TAOs are created by attaching knowledge structure (active index) to the multimedia object which is a complex object that comprises some combination of text, image, graphics, video, and audio objects. TAOs are valuable because they can improve the selective access and presentation of relevant multimedia information. In the Virtual Library BookMan [3], for example, each book or multimedia document is a TAO because the user can not only access the book, browse its table of contents, read its abstract, and decide whether to check it out, but also be informed about related books, or find out who has a similar interest in this subject. The user can indicate an intention by incrementally modifying the physical appearance of the TAO, usually with just a few clicks of the mouse.

TAO can be realized as TAO enhanced html page (see below). The physical appearance of a TAO is described by a multidimensional sentence [3]. The syntactic structure derived from this multidimensional sentence is a hypergraph, which also controls the TAO's dynamic multimedia presentation. The TAO also has a knowledge structure (the active index) that controls its event-driven or message-driven behavior. The multidimensional sentence may be location-sensitive, time-sensitive or content-sensitive. Thus, an incremental change in a TAO's physical appearance is an event that causes the active index to react. To summarize, the TAO's syntactic structure controls its presentation; and the knowledge structure its dynamic behavior.

A Tele-Action Object TAO has the following attributes: tao_name, tao_type, ic, p_part, links, where tao_name is the name of the TAO, tao_type is the media type of TAO such as image, text, audio, motion graphics, video or mixed, ic is the associated index cell, p_part is the physical part of TAO (the actual image, text, audio, motion graphics, video, or a multidimensional sentence for mixed media type), and link is the link to another TAO (there may be none or multiple links).

A TAO can have multiple links. A link has attributes link_type, link_rel and link_obj, where link_type is either relational (spatial or temporal) or structural (composed_of), link_rel is either the structural relation composed_of or a relational expression involving spatial operators or temporal operators but not both, and link_obj is the linked TAO.

Whenever the physical part of TAO is changed, such as the modification of the image or the multidimensional sentence, message(s) are sent to the TAO(s) and associated index cell(s). Sometimes no specific index cell is associated with the TAO, i.e., the attribute ic is null, in which case message(s) are sent to all cells so that those who can respond to the message(s) may be activated. The change of physical appearance of a TAO may be due to (1) manual input, (2) external input, or (3) automatic input from the active index system. Thus a TAO can react to manual or external inputs, and perform actions and change its own appearance automatically. For example, the user clicks on a book TAO, and all related book TAOs change their color.

B. TAO_HTML Interpretor

To prototype an active visual information system, each active component can be realized as an ic associated with a TAO-enhanced html page. Given a TAO-enhanced html page, we can construct an interpretor to read this page first. This interpretor will abstract the necessary TAO data structure and generate the normal html page for the browser. Therefore no matter which browser is used, the application program can run if this TAO_HTML interpretor is installed in advance. This can give some security guarantee. The user can also choose a favorite browser. Furthermore if in the future HTML is out of fashion, the user just needs to update the interpretor and change it into another language. The other parts of application will not be affected.

In order to use TAO_HTML to define a TAO, the data structure of a TAO is extended. A TAO has the following attributes: tao_name, tao_type, p_part, links, ics and sensitivity.

o 'tao_name' is the name of the TAO, which is a unique identifier of each TAO.

o 'tao_type' is the media type of TAO, such as image, text, audio, motion graphs, video or mixed.

o 'p_part' is the physical part of TAO. To implement it in the context of TAO_HTML, 'p_part' here can be denoted by a template which indicates how a HTML page looks like. Templates are some independent HTML pages to define the fundamental display element and location arrangement. For example, if the TAO is of image type, the template will just contain a HTML statement to intrigue an image. If the TAO is of mixed type, the template will define some common parts and leave some space to insert the elements that is specific to this TAO.

o 'links' is the link to another TAO. A link has attributes 'link_type', (COMPOSED OF). in the context of TAO_HTML, a spatial link describes visible relationship between sub_objects inside one mixed object. For example, a mixed tao1 contains an image TAO2 and a text TAO3, then TAO1 has spatial link with both TAO2 and TAO3. A temporal link usually refers to an invisible object which is not a display element, but its activation time is influenced by the other. A structural link relates one TAO with another dynamically via user input or external input. For example, the user clicks a button in TAO1 will invoke another page TAO2, then there's a structural link from TAO1 to TAO2.

o 'ic' is the associated index cell.

o 'sensitivity' indicates whether this object is location-sensitive, time- sensitive, content-sensitive or none-sensitive. Then the same object can have different appearance or different functionality according to the sensitivity. For example, if TAO1 is content-sensitive, it is red when being contained in TAO2 while it is green when being activated by TAO3 via a button. The detailed meaning of sensitivity should be defined by user according to the requirement of applications.

The formal definition of TAO_HTML language can be described in BNF form:

```
TAO_HTML ::= <TAO> TAO_BODY </TAO>
TAO_BODY  ::= NAME_PART TYPE_PART P_PART LINK_PART
IC_PART SENSI_PART
NAME_PART ::= <TAO_NAME> "name" </TAO_NAME>
TYPE_PART ::= <TAO_TYPE> TYPE_SET </TAO_TYPE>
TYPE_SET ::= [image, text, audio, motion_graph, video, mixed]
P_PART ::= <TAO_TEMPLATE> "template_name" </TAO_TEMPLATE>
LINK_PART ::= empty | <TAO_LINKS> LINK_BODY </TAO_LINKS>
LINK_PART
LINK_BODY ::= name="link_name", type = LINK_TYPE, obj = "link_obj"
LINK_TYPE ::= [spatial, temporal, structural]
IC_PART ::= empty | <TAO_IC> "ic_name" </TAO_IC>
SENSI_PART ::= empty | <TAO_SENSI> SENSITIVITY </TAO_SENSI>
SENSITIVITY ::= [location, content, time]
```

In the template of a TAO, in addition to the normal HTML tags and definitions, there's a special TAO tag for link relation with other TAOs. It is defined as:

```
<TAO_REL> "link_name" </TAO_REL>
```

The TAO_HTML Interpretor can now be presented in pseudo-codes:

```
procedure interpretor(char *TAOname)
{
  open TAO definition file
  call TAO_parser() to construct the
    TAO data structure TAO_struct
  call template_parser(TAO_struct)
    to print out HTML file
}
```

```
procedure TAO_parser(file_handle,link_type)
{
  while (not end of file)
  {
    read one line from the file
    distinguish tag and get information
      and store in data structure
  }
}

procedure template_parser(TAO_structure)
{
  open template file
  while (not end of file)
  {
    read one line from the file
    if (not <TAO_rel> tag)
      print out html text
    else
    {
      get link_name from the <TAO_rel> tag
      search in the TAO_structure with link_name
      if (a link structure is found with
        the same link_name)
      {
        get link_type and link_TAO_name
        switch (link_type)
          case structural:
            insert <a href..> link in template
              to link with link_TAO_name
              case spatial
        call procedure interpretor(link_TAO_name)
          to insert template of link_TAO_name
      }
    }
  }
}
```

The *IC_Manager* can run on a Unix workstation or on any PC with Windows to manage the active index system and to support Tele-Action Objects. The realization of active visual information system components as TAOML pages associated with active index cells has the added advantage that the user can easily enter information to experiment with the prototype system. Moreover, whenever the user accesses an html page, an associated ic can be instantiated to collect information to be forwarded to the ic's, so that flexible on-line interaction can be supported.

7. Discussion

In this paper we presented both a general framework for the human- and system-directed discovery and fusion of visual/multimedia information, and a specific rapid prototyping tool for active visual information system design. The general framework is for the sake of conceptualization and discussion. A practical active visual information system covers only a part of the matrix presented in Figure 2. The horizontal and vertical reasoners, in particular, present challenges to researchers in computer vision, pattern recognition, information retrieval, and visual information systems. Artificial neural networks, fuzzy logic, and active index, etc. are among the possible approaches for reasoning, but need to be further explored.

The rapid prototyping tool enables the designer to quickly construct a web-savvy prototype active visual information system. The TAO_HTML Interpretor, IC_Builder and IC_Manager constitute the core of the rapid prototyping tool. We are experimenting with this rapid prototyping tool and at the same time improving it, so that it can be more flexible and user friendly. We are also developing a distributed IC_Manager so that distributed active visual information systems can be prototyped.

References

[1] S. K. Chang, "Towards a Theory of Active Index", Journal of Visual Languages and Computing, Vol. 6, No. 1, March 1995, 101-118.

[2] H. Chang, T. Hou, A. Hsu and S. K. Chang, "The Management and Applications of Tele-Action Objects", ACM Journal of Multimedia Systems, Springer Verlag, Volume 3, Issue 5-6, 1995, 204-216.

[3] S. K. Chang, "Extending Visual Languages for Multimedia", IEEE Multimedia Magazine, Fall 1996, Vol. 3, No. 3, 18-26.

[4] S. K. Chang, "Active Index for Content-Based Medical Image Retrieval", *Journal of Computerized Medical Imaging and Graphics*, Special Issue on Medical Image Databases (S. Wong and H. K. Huang, eds.), Elsevier Science Ltd., 1996, 219-229.

[5] P. W. Chen, G. Barry and S. K. Chang, "A Smart WWW Page Model and its Application to On-Line Information Retrieval in Hyperspace", Proc. of Pacific Workshop on Distributed Multimedia Systems, DMS'96, Hong Kong, June 27-28, 1996, 220-227.

[6] S. Dutta, "Qualitative Spatial Reasoning: A Semi-Quantitative Approach Using Fuzzy Logic", Conference Proceedings on Very Large Spatial Databases, Santa Barbara, July 17-19, 1989.

[7] E. Jungert and S. K. Chang, "Human- and System-Directed Fusion of Multimedia and Multimodal Information using the Sigma-Tree Data Model", Tech Report, Univ. of Pittsburgh, May 1996.

[8] S. Santini and R. Jain, "The Graphical Specification of Similarity Queries", Journal of Visual Languages and Computing, Vol. 7, No. 4, December 1996, 403-421.

Towards Direct Mapping between Visual Information Worlds and Real Worlds

Tosiyasu L. Kunii
Jianhua Ma and Runhe Huang

The University of Aizu, Aizu-Wakamatsu, 965-80 Japan

Abstract. Without supports of effective modeling in visual worlds, even if the visual information can be displayed in real worlds, it is difficult to recognize and extract its features and to confirm or verify the identities and the characteristics. Direct mappings target at refining and abstracting multimedia information by cognitive technology and differential technology to efficiently improve our human performance and actively control the real worlds we live. The modeling of visual worlds includes modeling and assembling 3D objects. An assemblability discriminating method and an assembling sequence generating method named SYDEM, which can reduce component match steps from the order of $O(2^n)$ by compositive assembly to the order of $O(n^2)$, is explained by giving an example of CIM assembly process. The three other examples of an effective guide-map generation method, of a hierarchical description of surfaces, and of a conceptual visual human algorithm for skiing, are given to show the drastic efficiency and exactness increase.

1 Introduction

Animals including human beings have, by nature, sensors dealing with various types of information as multimedia. The information which animals can deal with includes sight (or the sense of vision), hearing, touch, smell, and taste. Current computers can handle only audio and visual information among a variety of multimedia information that animals can process. However, during the last two decades, the evolution of multimedia technology has been contributing to the significant extension of the coverge of information science.

At the emergence of the era of information superhighways, current visual information in computers is already extremely massive. And research on visual information ranges from presentation, transmission, storage and processing of low-level bits and bytes, to representation, indexing, interaction and retrieval of high-level contents [12]. People manage, access and navigate visual information worlds interactively to support learning, entertainment, shopping and so on in daily life, or to perform operations, management and decision-making functions for an organization. Such visual information is massive and most commonly passively stored, transmitted and processed in the digital forms. Even if the visual information can be displayed in the real worlds, it is difficult to recognize and extract its features and to confirm or verify the identities and the validity. Therefore information worlds exist only as assistants of real worlds, and cannot, actively and physically, act on or manipulate real worlds. A bridge is so called direct mappings between information worlds and real worlds, and it should be established so as to understand and control real worlds from visual information worlds efficiently and exactly.

By the direct mappings, connections between information worlds and real worlds become closer and closer. The combinations of these worlds form a new world called as *a hyperworld*. In this hyperworld we can, not only get passive visual information but also, sense and control real worlds directly and actively. The direct mapping is the basic characteristic of a hyperworld. The applications of the direct mapping are unlimited. We are just starting to identify some cases such as telemedicines utilizing a set of direct control micro-machines, factories employing direct control robots, and sporting equipped with direct human motion capture devices for high speed analysis, modeling and visualization of human performance. In the following, we will discuss the features and modeling approaches of the directing mapping, and give several examples to show the drastic efficiency and exactness increase by the direct mappings.

2 The Features and Modeling of the Directing Mapping

The direct mappings are beyond getting passive information from visual information worlds, and target at refining and abstracting multimedia information to efficiently improve our human performance and actively control real worlds around us. The direct mapping means what we or computers are thinking and conceptualizing are realized directly. Drastic efficiency and exactness increase is the primary feature of the direct mappings in general. For example, for a martial art learner to master one expert technique, the conventional approach is the trial-and-error which is known as an extremely inefficient method. With the help of video recorded expert's performance, the learning process can be relatively speeded up and the learner's performance can be relatively improved but not too much because it is difficult for the learner to master the key features of the expert techniques from watching video images. In contrast, if we can directly capture and reconstruct 3 dimensional (3D) body motion of expert performance, and analyze and extract key features by using a dynamic human body model, then it is more efficient and exact to understand the key mechanisms of the expert technique so as to directly instruct the learner to master the technique and improve the performance. By the direct mappings, the learning process can be shorten to 30 minutes from 3 years with 50 thousand times efficiency increase [5].

The drastic efficiency and exactness increase by the direct mappings is based on cognitive technology and differential technology that abstract the key features of visual information, and let knowledge, either inside computers or accessible through information superhighways, match the level of human cognition through abstraction, to control the flood of information as well as to make full of use of expert knowledge in modeling visual worlds. The modeling of visual worlds includes modeling 3D objects in visual worlds and assembling them.

Assembling a visual world requires a particular care since the number of the components n is usually extremely large. Given n components, component match steps are in the order of 2^n, namely $O(2^n)$, for compositive assembly. Even for a small n value $n = 50$ and the component match step time of 1 micro second, the compositive assembly design requires 30 years in the worst case. While by an assemblability discriminating method and an assembling sequence generating method based on decompositive assembly and named SYDEM [6], the component match steps can be reduced to $O(n^2)$ and hence the assembly design requires only 3 milli seconds in the worst case. The detailed example of CIM assembly process using SYDEM will be described in the next section.

For the modeling of 3D objects, shape modeling in particular, the conventional modeling methods such as triangulation and mesh control suffer from information loss both on differentiability and singularity, and are not suited for human cognition and the direct mappings. The desirable model is actually based on homotopic modeling which can be an information lossless representation. Suppose we have two maps f_0 and f_1 such that

$f_0, f_1 \colon X \to Y$ where X and Y are metric space.
f_0 is defined to be homotopic to f_1 and denoted by $f_0 \simeq f_1$ if there exists a continuous map H, such that
$H \colon X \times I \to$ and $H(x, 0) = f_0$, $H(x, 1) = f_1$.
H is called a homotopy from f_0 to f_1.

One approach to the characterization of complex shapes such as visual worlds is based on the Morse theory and Reeb graph [11]. The topology of complex objects are represented by using singular points of a function defined on the object surface, in place of the vertices, edges, faces and holes. The critical points are peaks, pits, and saddles. These singular points play significant roles in characterizing objects. According to the Morse theory [10], a one-to-one correspondence exists between the non-degenerating singular points and cells, and we can construct the object surface by pasting the cells that correspond to the singular points. The critical points and the Reeb graph not only greatly save data space but also directly match human memory and cognition for some applications such as a mountaineering guide and walk-through in a human body.

Another approach to the characterization of complex shapes is based on the concept of wrinkles which widely exist in the world, from the human body to the cosmic space, and from the cloth to the market of financial trading [9]. The wrinkles are commonly abstracted as "signs of singularity" carrying more information than critical points, including critical lines, where critical points are degenerate. Singularity signs are also direction invariant, such as in the case of ridges, ravines and their combinations [7]. Hence, the concept of wrinkles ranges over a wider area of more general applicability than Morse theory does. The theory of singularity signs is called "singularity theory". Other closely related areas of research are homotopy theory, CW-complexes, catastrophe theory and semiotics. All these theories belong to modern differential topology, which is among the fastest growing research area in mathematics with incredibly wide applicability [4].

One of the top levels of shape modeling is mental shape modeling. Mental shape modeling means how a designer models a shape mentally, and remember it. The conceptual design is the most critical phase. Conceptual visual algorithms make mental design processes and design results explicitly represented in a computer executable form after interactive machine translation [8]. The conceptual visual algorithms are closer to human understanding. Therefore, they can exactly instruct learning and efficiently improve human performance.

Three examples of an efficient mountaineering guide-map generation by using the Reeb graph and Morse theory, of a hierarchic description of surfaces by the concepts of ridges, ravines and R-skeleton, and of the conceptual visual human algorithm for recreational skiing, are given in Sect.4, 5, and 6 respectively.

3 Assemblability Discrimination and Assembling Sequence Generation in the SYDEM

Recently, more and more robots are used at various locations within a factory in combination with numerically controlled machines. Current CAD systems are concentrated around computational geometry and especially on solid modeling which aims at defining the shapes of mechanical parts. A mechanical object assembled from a plurality of parts is called an assembly. Although the assembly is essential to the product manufacturing, research on the designing of assembling is less active when compared to research related to solid modeling. Efficient assembling mapping is a very important step in the direct mapping because the most of learning processes in education and even electronic commerce procedures can be mastered very efficiently by the same method.

The assemblability discriminating method and assembling sequence generating method proposed in the SYDEM [6] are as follows. When a set of machine parts is denoted by P based on inputting information from the CAD system, an assembly process of the machines can be described by an assembly process graph $G - (N, A)$ which satisfies the following conditions (1) and (2), where N denotes a set of nodes and A denotes a set of arcs,

$$N = \{(P_1, ..., P_m); P_i \in P, m \geq 1\} \tag{1}$$

$$A = (\{P_1, ..., P_k\}, \{P_1, ..., P_k, P_{k+1}\}) \tag{2}$$

Each node in the assembly process graph G describes one part, a semi-completed or completed product. Each arc connects two nodes. An arc ($\{P_1, ..., P_k\}, \{P_1, ..., P_k, P_{k+1}\}$) of the assembly process G is called a "valid arc" when the part P_{k+1} is assemblable on the semi-completed product which is made up of the parts $P_1, ..., P_k$ via a collision-free path. The arc is otherwise an "invalid arc". Determining the validity of each arc starts from a node which corresponds to the completed product and continuing sequence priority on a depth of the assembly process G. The completed product is determined to assemblable when there exists at least one path of valid arc connecting a node which corresponds to one part to the node which corresponds the completed product, and otherwise the completed product is non-assemblable. The above valid path is called an assembling sequence. When the completed product is assemblable, the decision and the related assembling sequence are output to a computer integrated manufacturing (CIM) device to finish the assembly.

Figure 1(a) is an assembly process graph for explaining an example of an assemblability discriminating method and an assembling sequence generating method according to what described in the above. Figure 1(b) is a side view of parts for explaining the above example. In the example it is assumed that a completed product $\{A, B, C\}$ shown in Fig.1(b) is to be assembled from parts A, B and C. In Fig.1(a), the assembly process graph G has seven nodes and nine arcs, and a valid arc is indicated by a solid line while an invalid arc is indicated by a broken line. Generally, a search with priority on the depth (depth-first search) involves a back-tracking. When it is noted that the assembling environment which mainly affects the validity of the arc is interference or collision, it is possible to avoid the back-tracking. In fact, the back-tracking does not occur when a search start of the top of with the assembly process graph, that is, from the node of the completed product.

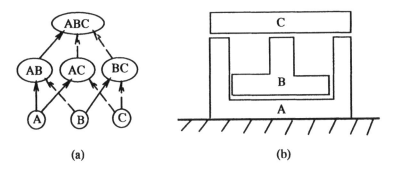

(a)   (b)

Fig. 1. An example of assembability discrimination and assembling sequence generation

When total number of parts is denoted by n and the search with the priority on the depth is carried out from top of the assembly process graph in the disassembling sequence, a number of discriminations to determine the assemblability, that is, a number of arcs applied with the path-detection technique for generating one kind of assembling sequence is $O(n^2)$ in the worst case. The number of discrimination which must made in the conventional case where the search from the bottom of the assembly process graph in the assembling sequence is $O(2^n)$ in the worst case. It can be seen that the efficiency of assemblability discrimination and assembling sequence generation is increased drastically as the value of n increases.

4 Efficient Mountaineering Guide by Using Reeb Graph and Morse Theory

One existing problem in our information era is a situation of information flooding. In this situation, multimedia itself may just end up with more confusion by bringing in multiple types of information. One of the challenging task is the effective utilization of massive amounts of information. Of course, many technological advances in computing, such as very large-scale integration(VLSI), storage capacity, parallel software, user interface, compressing algorithms and networking, have been showing dramatic progress. However, the direct mapping between multimedia information worlds and real worlds are opening up completely new dimensions of a hyperworld. Drastic exactness and efficiency increase can be obtained by the direct mappings in general. The direct mapping is based on the advances in information controlled active devices and domain specific expert knowledge that enables us to extract minimum efficient information and construct effective data structures from real worlds.

Let us assume that a mountaineer, who has sufficient data of a mountainous terrain as shown in Fig.2(a), is going to send information about it to other mountaineers. One simple and straight way is for the mountaineer to send the whole and large amounts of terrain data. It is, however, very inefficient and expensive. Instead of sending the whole terrain data, one of the alternative ways is to obtain sufficient geometric data and a topological graph from the large amounts of terrain data. Here, critical points and their associated Reeb graph of the terrain data are important topological and geometric information such that the feature of the surface of the terrain is able to be reconstructed.

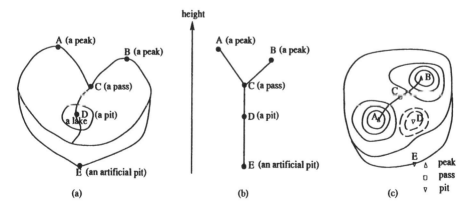

Fig. 2. (a) A mountainous terrain with critical points; (b) Its Reeb graph; (c) Its contour lines

In the following, we give the mathematical definitions of the critical points and Reeb graph.

Critical points: The point x_0 on the manifold M^n is called critical for the function f if grad $f(x_0) = 0$ [4].

Non-degenerate critical points: The critical point x_0 of the function f is called non-degenerate if the matrix $d^2 f$ is non-singular at the point x_0 [4].

Reeb graph: let f: $M \rightarrow R$ be a real value function on a manifold M. The Reeb graph of f is the quotient space of the graph of f in M x R by the equivalence relation given below: $(X_1, y_1) \sim (X_2, y_2)$ holds if and only if $y_1 = y_2$ and $X_1 = X_2$ are in the same connected component of $f^{-1}(y_1)$ where $y_1 = f(X_1)$ and $y_2 = f(X_2)$ [3] [11] [13].

Based on the definitions of critical points and the Reeb graph above, in Fig.2(a), peaks A and B, pass C, pit D, and artificial pit E are critical points of the mountainous terrain and they are non-degenerate. Figure 2(b) is the Reeb graph of the mountainous terrain. Figure 2(c) is the contour lines (the equihight lines) of the mountainous terrain. The contours are closed curves and they are homeomorphic to each other, where solid closed lines are normal contours and dotted closed lines are reverse contours. Reeb graph is one of the topological graph of the height function and represents the splitting and merging of equiheight contours at the critical points. The nodes of the Reeb graph represent the cross sectional planes that include the critical points. Thus, navigated by the Reeb graph, the exact reconstruction of the surfaces of a mountainous terrain can be conducted from a series of continuous lines using continuous deformation represented by homotopy.

The information including the critical points, the Reeb graph, and the contour lines is many orders of magnitude less than the whole terrain data. The amount of information sent to multimedia information worlds from real worlds is significantly reduced and also the critical points representing the peaks, pits, and passes are exactly identified, so that the drastic efficiency and exactness increase can be obtained by the direct inverse mapping from the real world to the multimedia world. And from the multimedia world it becomes possible to directly guide mountaineers in the real world by the direct control of active devices such as navigating devices. The terrain can be a human body and a mountaineer a surgeon. It can also be a factory and a group of direct control robots. This example also shows the importance of reducing excess information by using domain specific expert knowledge and advanced technologies so as to utilize flooding information to our advantage in the information era.

5 A Hierarchic Description of Surfaces by Ridges, Ravines and R-skeleton

In the above example, when the mountainous geographical terrain has a plateau, Morse theory is no longer applicable, because the top of the plateau is, by definition, flat and hence equivalent to having an innumerable number of degenerate peaks. A similar situation occurs when the terrain includes ridges and ravines. Another problem is that Morse theory depends on the direction of the height function being predetermined; when the direction of the function changes, Morse

theory loses its validity. Hence, the concept of wrinkles is important and necessary. Wrinkles are commonly abstracted as "signs of singularity" carrying more
information than critical points, including critical lines, where critical points are
degenerate. Singularity signs are also direction invariant, such as in the case of
ridges, ravines and their combinations [7]. The concept of ridges, ravines and
related structures (skeletons) associated with surfaces in a three-dimensional
space is based on singularity theory and involves both local and global geometric properties of the surface; it is invariant with respect to the translations and
rotations of the surface. It leads to a method of hierarchic description of surfaces
and yields new approaches to shape coding, rendering and design.

Let us consider a piecewise smooth oriented hypersurface M in the Euclidean
space R^d. Let us introduce the distance function from a point x of the Euclidean
space to M by

$$dist(x, M) = \inf_{y \in M} ||x - y||.$$

The distance function to a piecewise smooth hypersurface is continuous, but
not necessarily smooth, even if the initial hypersurface is smooth. Let us consider
the set of all singular points of the distance function to the hypersurface. It turns
out that this set of singular points is a curvilinear polyhedron (hence admitting
a CW-complex structure), whose dimension in a general position is equal to dim
M. We call this polyhedron the R-skeleton for M.

The R-skeleton of a given hypersurface M is the set of all singular points of
the mapping

$$dist(\cdot, M) : \mathbf{R^d} \to \mathbf{R}.$$

Let M be endowed with an orientation $\mathbf{n}(\mathbf{p})$, where $\mathbf{n}(\mathbf{p})$ is the unit normal
vector at the point $\mathbf{p}$ of M.

The ridge-skeleton of a given hypersurface M is the connected component of
the R-skeleton pointed at by the normal $\mathbf{n}(\mathbf{p})$. The ravine-skeleton of a given
hypersurface M is the connected component of the R-skeleton pointed at by the
normal $-\mathbf{n}(\mathbf{p})$.

A ridge (ravine) of a piecewise smooth hypersurface M in the Euclidean space
R^d is the set of all points of M that realize the infimum of the distance function
at the points in the pseudoridge (pseudoravine).

Figure 3 demonstrates the relations between boundary singular points of the
R-skeleton and the ridge (ravine) lines; we also show here possible location of
neighborhoods of the typical points of the R-skeleton.

Let k_{max} and k_{min} be the principal curvatures ($k_{max} > k_{min}$), and $\mathbf{v}_{max}$ and
$\mathbf{v}_{min}$ the corresponding principal directions. An extreme ridge point is a point
where k_{max} has a local positive maximum. An extreme ravine point is a point
where k_{min} has a local negative minimum.

The ridge-skeletons and ravine-skeletons introduced as above may be used
for coding surfaces in the following manner. Suppose a surface M is encoded by
the R-skeleton R, with the function r representing the distance; thus r is the
radius of the sphere with the center at the given point of R, tangent to M at

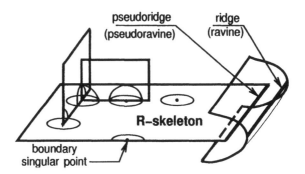

Fig. 3. *R*-skeleton and relative objects

two points. Thus, the surface M must be tangent to each sphere in the family of spheres with centers in R of radii r. Surface features can be classified as follows:

1. Global features, which describe global surface geometry and topology. Among them, it is necessary to mention the Euler characteristics [1], the Reeb graph, the R-skeleton and other.
2. Local features, which are determined by the local properties of the surface. They may be further classified into
   (a) Surface features, such as mean and Gaussian curvatures.
   (b) Line features. A wide variety of such features can be found, for example, in [2]. Here the ridge and ravine lines introduced are added into.
   (c) Point features. Among these, it is necessary to distinguish pits, passes, peaks (if there is a distinguished direction and a height function along it), extreme ridge and ravine points.

Thus, the approach leads us to a natural hierarchical classification: *R-skeleton, ridge and ravine skeletons → ridge and ravine lines → extreme ridge and ravine points*. Terrain feature recognition, dental shape reconstruction and medical imagery are a partial list of applications.

6 Conceptual Visual Human Algorithms for Recreational Skiing

Human performance goes across almost everything including daily life, manufacturing and art such as sporting, crafting, painting, and musical instrument play. Learning and mastering one expert technique in human performance may take a person lots of time, from several months to several years, and even a whole life, by a conventional try-and-error learning approach. Can we synthesize learning processes in visual information worlds and then turn them into real world to improve human performance learning with drastic efficiency? Let us focus on the case of sporting performance, recreational skiing in particular [8].

Learning processes consist, generally, of two steps: mental designing and physical body practicing. The mental designing can be shown clearly by so called conceptual visual human algorithms, a type of algorithms that specify in skier's mind the mental images of the sequences of skiing techniques as the processes of moving both skier's body and ski equipment on varieties of snow fields. Conceptual visual algorithms make mental design processes and design results explicitly represented in a computer executable form after interactive machine translation. The initial stage of any designs is requirement specification. The requirement specification made wrong usually destroys the entire design life cycle. The requirement of recreational skiing are specified as follows:

1. Anyone can enjoy skiing a whole day.
   "Anyone" implies without much special training and hence, employing only most used muscles in daily life, namely using only the muscles for standing and walking.
2. Varieties of snow fields can be enjoyed for skiing.
   "Varieties" means three thing: varieties of snow, varieties of slope shapes, and varieties of environments.

The requirement 1 specifies the skier's posture such that it is vertical to the ski surface. Such vertical posture, namely the upright body posture, uses only the muscles for standing. However, the usual skiing instruction assumes ski control by snow plowing either in a scissors position or a parallel position of a pair of skies, and a lean forward body posture. Such snow plowing forces recreational skiers to get their legs worn out through the extreme use of muscles other than those for daily walking and standing. The lean forward body posture limits the knee lifting range to the 60% of the upright body posture for a walking as shown in Fig.4. The lean forward body posture results in tragedy when skiing on a bumpy slope since the limit in knee lifting can cause throwing up of the whole body into the air at the bump.

Fig. 4. The limit of knee lifting in a upright body posture and a lean forward posture

 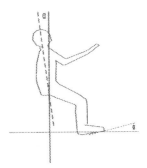

Fig. 5. A lean back posture and its solid model of increasing α

Relative to the snow field surface, ski position is defined by three parameters: the angle α between the sliding surface of a ski along the longitudinal direction and the snow field surface, the angle β between the sliding surface of ski vertical to the longitudinal direction and the snow field surface, and the sideways angle γ from the straight down direction. When snow is varied or a skier wants to decelerate, the requirement 1 derives a lean back posture of the whole body slightly to increase the angle α as in Fig.5. While leaning back, a walking motion to stretch legs forward and touch the ground by heels keeping the posture vertical to the ski surface causes the effect of increased deceleration, then the succeeding walking motion of retracting legs in the same body posture causes the effect of decreased deceleration. The increased α frees the most top portions of a pair of skies from the snow resistance, and as a skier directs the body to wherever the skier wants to go, a pair of skies moves freely and instantly towards the body direction with any sideways angle γ, as the skier wishes. The varieties of snow in the requirement 2 can be enjoyed for recreational purposes. Hence, the requirement 2 drives the identical conceptual visual human algorithms to increase the angle α by lean back posture of the whole body slightly. The walking posture gives a recreational skier a joy of panoramic view that is the key factor to avoid any danger of falling into a hazardous situation such as colliding with obstacles or the other skiers.

After the mental designing is carried out by the above conceptual visual human algorithms, the physical body practicing can be directly instructed by generating computational visual algorithms from the conceptual visual human algorithms. The generating computational visual algorithms is most efficiently done by the SYDEM method as presented in Sect.3. Consider an assembly of the steps of skiing movements leading a stopping posture from a certain starting posture. It is far more efficient to specify the computational steps of the segment movements directly from the steps of the conceptual visual human algorithm as the top level design, rather than randomly computing the movements of the segments until computed movements coincide with the conceptual visual human algorithm. The computational steps thus obtained are the computational visual human algorithm of the stopping. It is possible in this course of generating computational visual human algorithms to go through the physical human body performance algorithms, first, of satisfactory plays meeting all the requirements for use as the reference algorithms of computational visual human algorithms, and second, of lesson plays for diagnosis to identify and correct the erroneous portions of the plays that do not meet the requirements. The correction is based on comparing the difference between the computational visual algorithm that satisfies the requirement and the solid modeled human body movements through capturing and analyzing the physical human body performance algorithm by video cameras from various directions.

A visual human algorithm can be abstracted to a structure of signs based on semiotis or semiology. For example, a skiing algorithm is generally a sequence of signs such as: start, downhill, left turn, downhill, righturn, uphill, stop. The requirement-driven conceptual visual human algorithm to implement the above sequence: start, increase α, left γ, $\gamma = 0$, right $\gamma > 90$ degrees, stop. Neither complicated control of β nor knee operations exist. This means the conceptual simplicity of requirement-driven conceptual visual algorithm, resulting in 2 to 3 days for a complete new skier to master deep snow parallel skiing.

7 Conclusions

In this paper, the concept of a hyperworld is proposed and direct mapping as the basic characteristics of a hyperworld is addressed. In a hyperworld, we can not only get passive multimedia information but also sense and control real worlds by the direct mappings. The direct mappings means what we or computers are thinking and concepturizing are realized directly, and target at refining and abstracting multimedia information to efficiently improve our human performance and actively control real worlds. The drastic efficiency and exactness increase by the direct mappings are based on cognitive technology and differential technology that abstract the key features of visual information and let knowledge match the level of human cognition through abstraction. The modeling of visual worlds includes modeling 3D objects and assembling visual scenes. Although several cases of modeling techniques in visual worlds are presented in this paper, the future applications of the direct mappings are unlimited. Challenging tasks in future are to find good models of various direct mappings between multimedia information worlds and real worlds.

References

1. Chiokura, H.: Solid modelling with DESIGNBASE, Addison-Wesley, 1988.
2. Hosaka, M.: Modeling of curves and surfaces in CAD/CAM, Springer-Verlag, 1992.
3. Ikeda, T., Kunii, T. L., Shinagawa, Y., Ueda, M.: A geographical database system based on the homotopy model, In T. L. Kunii and Y. Shinagawa, editors, Modern Geometric Computing for Visualization, pp193-205, Springer-Verlag, Tokyo, 1992.

4. Fomeko, A. T., Kunii, T. L.: Topological modeling for visualization, Springer-Verlag, 1997.

5. Kunii, T. L., Sun, L.: dynamic analysis-based human animation, T. S. Chua and T. L. Kunii, editors, Computer Graphics Around the World, CG International'90, Springer-Verlag, pp3-15, 1990.

6. Kunii, T. L., et al: Assemblability discriminating method and assembling sequence generating method, US Patent, No.5058026, Oct. 1991.

7. Kunii, T. L., Belyaev, A. G., Anoshkina, E. V., Takahashi, S., Huang, R., Okunev, O. G.: Hierarchic shape description via singularity and multiscaling, in Proceeding of the 8th IEEE Annual International Computer Software and Applications Conference (COMPSAC), Taipei, pp242-251, November 1994.

8. Kunii, T. L.: Conceptual visual human algorithms: a requirement-driven skiing algorithm design, Proc. Computer Graphics International'96, Korea, June, 1996, published by IEEE Computer Society Press, Los Alamitos, California, pp2-8, 1996.

9. Kunii, T. L.: The philosophy of synthetic worlds - digital genesis for communicating synthetic worlds and real world, Technical Report, the University of Aizu, 1996.

10. Morse, M.: The calculus of variations in the large, American Mathematical Society Colloquium Publication, No. 18, Providence, Rhode Island, 1934.

11. Shinagawa, Y., Kunii, T. L.: Surface coding based on Morse theory, IEEE CG and A, Vol.11, No5., pp66-78, Sept. 1991.

12. Steinmetz, R., Nahrstedt, K.: Multimedia: computing, communications and applications, ISBN 0-13-324435-0, Prentice Hall PTR, 1995.

13. Takahashi, Ikeda, T., Shinagawa, Y., Kunii, T. L., Ueda, M.: Algorithms for extracting correct critical points and constructing topological graphs from discrete geographical elevation data, In Proc. of Eurographics'95, 1995

Visual Data Processing in Multimedia Systems

Jesse S. Jin[1], Heather Greenfield[2] and Ruth Kurniawati[1]
[1]School of Computer Science & Engineering
[2]Department of Food Science and Technology
University of New South Wales, Sydney 2052, Australia
E-mail: jesse@cse.unsw.edu.au

Abstract. This paper presents a comprehensive model for visual data processing in multimedia systems. Images are represented as objects in a hierarchical structure. Several issues in processing images in multimedia systems are addressed, e.g. multimedia object composition including spatial and temporal composition. We introduce an object-oriented compression scheme and discuss combining feature extraction with compression. Hierarchical storage, which possesses good properties for image retrieval, display and composition, will be presented. The image is segmented into homogeneous regions. A content-based retrieval scheme (CBIR-VU) using shape, texture and colour information, and a two-stage retrieval method are presented.

1 Introduction

Multimedia systems deal with a variety of information sources, such as text, photographs, audio, graphics, mechanical drawings, statistics charts, tables, numerical data, and full-motion video. Images, in a general sense, include natural images, such as photographs, medical images, and satellite images; artificial images, such as computer graphics, paintings, and drawings; and scientific pictures, such as statistics charts, and visualization patches. There are a large number of operations involved in dealing with these images, such as display, scaling, storage, prescreen manipulation, art-effects processing, etc. However, images themselves are in different formats. The requirements of using images vary significantly and new demands come in an ever-increasing tide making conventional programming of multimedia systems very difficult. Some processes may even be impossible to implement.

Current image database systems can be classified according to the types and natures of the features used for indexing and retrieval as attribute-based systems, text-based systems and content-based systems. Different semantic representations for the features would generally lead to different indexing methods. Attribute-based systems are the legacy of conventional database management system (DBMS) in using a set of structured attributes in accessing the objects, so that the object handling capability can be extended to cope with voluminous and gigantic image objects. Since little special development is required in organizing and retrieving image objects in these systems, many image or pictorial databases in early years are attribute-based (Chang and Fu, 1981). Indexing methods used in these systems are usually B^+-trees (Comer, 1979) or inverted files (Salton and McGill, 1983). Chang and Kunii (1981) surveyed a variety of attribute-based pictorial database systems. The main problem in attribute-based systems is that the adoption of a fixed set of attributes cannot take advantage of the rich content in the images. Moreover, these attributes limit the scope of the application of the database and provide little room for future and unforeseen usage of the images. There are a few commercial text-based image databases such as the Kodak Picture Exchange (KPX) (Larish, 1995) and the PressLink Image Library (Martucci, 1995). In text-based systems, each database object is annotated with free-text and structured fields. Keywords or free-text are associated with each image by visual inspection of the content of the images. To carry out a query, the user issues a query keyword and this is compared with the keywords of the images in the database. Indexing methods for text-based image systems include full text scanning access methods, inverted file and signature file methods (Feichtinger and Gröchenig, 1992). Both attribute-based and text-based methods fail to reflect the rich content of images completely. The indexer may concentrate on and annotate major features of the images, but pay little heed to minor details in the images. Some features in images are extremely difficult, if not impossible, to describe in text. For example, irregular shapes and jumbled textures are not easily conveyed in words. In fact, the indexer's annotations limit the scope for searching the image, since it can only be retrieved using these free-text keywords, leaving no means for the image to be used in future contexts for which it may be appropriate (Jin et al., 1995). Many workers have tried content-based methods (Chua et al., 1994; Niblack et al., 1993; Nagasaka and Tanaka, 1992). The most commonly used content features are shape, colour and texture (Caelli and Reye, 1993).

This paper presents a comprehensive model for image processing in multimedia systems. This scheme represents images as objects in a hierarchical structure and provides a simple representation for processing images. We address several issues in processing images in multimedia systems, such as multimedia object composition including spatial and temporal composition. An object-oriented compression scheme is introduced and combining feature extraction with compression is discussed. Hierarchical storage, which possesses good properties for image retrieval, display and composition, is presented. Other multimedia database issues, such as data integrity, location transparency and consistency are also discussed. The image retrieval issue and the development a content-based retrieval scheme using shape, texture and colour information are addressed. The image retrieval takes two stages: the first stage retrieval is based on the user's query and the second stage retrieval uses the knowledge from the first stage results. Finally, we discuss object-oriented manipulation, such as scaling, display, art-effects and high performance line-art processing, superimposing and projection, custom filtering and prescreen manipulation. Because images are stored in a compressed format, performing normal operations, such as scaling and transformation, without decompressing is also discussed.

The techniques have been practised in developing a prototype multimedia version of NUTTAB 95[1] (Lewis *et al.*, 1995), the Australian food composition database, with the assistance of ARC grants. The multimedia database developed may include photographs, cartoons, text, numerical tables, statistics charts, and drawings. The functions include information retrieval, document composition, slide production, image analysis, survey presentation and computer-aided learning.

2 Data Structure and Document Composition

There are two problems in dealing with multimedia data in multimedia systems. One is the variety of formats. For example, images can be black/white images or colour images. The black/white images include binary images and grey-scale images. The colour images include different shade levels. Images may be in different resolutions. The other problem is duplication of data during storage. Almost all images need a thumbnail for icon display. Some images are part of other images. To store them again creates duplication in the database. Images are also stored in a compressed format. The compression format, such as JPEG (Wallace, 1991), is not usually consistent with image analysis. The images must be decompressed first and then subjected to various analysis processes. The gain in storage space is at the expense of extra computation.

We propose a compression scheme using Gabor functions which allow certain tasks to be performed over compressed data. To apply Gabor functions in image representation we have to construct series expansions with respect to basis functions (Faloutsos and Christodoulakis, 1984). This means that all basis functions are derived from a single function by elementary operations such as translation, modulation, scaling, dilation, or rotation. An image is divided into subband signals, convolved with the set of basis functions, and then encoded as coefficients. Each subband signal encodes a particular portion of the frequency spectrum, corresponding to information occurring at a particular spatial scale. The encoded signals still contain the spatial information, which makes it possible to perform certain tasks such as pattern matching and recognition over the coefficients. To reconstruct the signal, the subband signals are up-sampled, filtered, and then combined additively.

To accommodate multimedia object composition which includes spatial composition and temporal composition we propose a hierarchical data structure for multimedia, as shown in Figure 1. The document can be stored in a hierarchical way, which possesses good properties for image retrieval, display and composition. The hierarchical storage avoids duplication by using a link to the original data. Any

---

[1] Permission was granted by the National Food Authority for the use of NUTTAB 95 for this purpose.

variation can be defined by an attribute attached to the data item. The advantage of this approach is that it retains data integrity, location transparency, and consistency, which is necessary for a database.

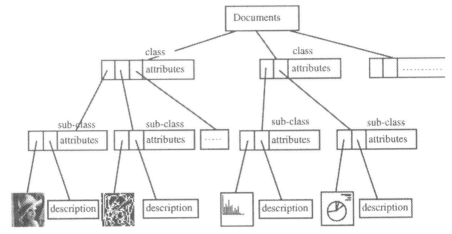

Figure 1. Data structure for multimedia representation

3 Content-based Image Retrieval

Advances in image technology have enabled widespread application of images for more effective representation of visual information and human-machine interface. This can be demonstrated by the fact that NASA's Earth Observing System (Asrar and Dokken, 1993) will transmit a terabyte of satellite imagery per day and medical centres receive gigabytes of patient visual data per day. It is therefore reasonable to expect that most future information systems will require efficient methods for archiving and managing large volumes of images and thus advanced imagery databases are desirable. A more sophisticated method for image indexing and retrieval is content-based. The commonly used content features for image retrieval include shape, colour and texture. Retrieval can be requested directly by submitting a query feature value, or a user-constructed query image which can be in the form of a query colour chosen from a colour palette, a texture selected from a menu of texture patterns, a free-sketch drawn by the user, or a combination of them (Lee *et al.*, 1994a; Lee *et al.*, 1994b).

We have developed a content-based retrieval system, CBIR-VU (Content-Based Image Retrieval at the Visual Information Processing laboratory at the University of New South Wales) using shape, texture and colour information. The image is segmented into homogeneous regions. Each region is associated with three features for indexing and retrieval. We aim to combine content-based retrieval with text-based retrieval to form a sophisticated retrieval method.

3.1 Image retrieval using shape information

We propose a signature using the smallest enclosing circle (SEC). The basis of this method is the transformation which maps a shape from its boundary into an n-dimensional shape-space. The SEC centre of the circle is chosen as the reference point. The SEC of a shape is unique and this uniqueness provides translation invariant. The vector from the SEC centre through the centroid of the shape defines the unique orientation of the shape, which provides rotation invariance. Scale invariance is obtained by dividing the SEC by n radial lines with equal angles, starting at the orientation vector (see solid lines in Figure 2a). The distance from the centre of the SEC to where the boundary of the shape crosses a radial line can be calculated. The ratios of these distances to the SEC radius are scale invariant. The shape is thus represented by n ratios starting from the orientation vector in a counterclockwise order. This n-tuple of ratios can be observed as a point in an n-dimensional space, called the shape space. Segmentation in the SEC can be done in a hierarchical way. Four segments are taken from the first level and two segments are taken from the remaining levels; only sections with large variance need to be further segmented as shown in dashed lines in Figure 2a. We apply the Huffman coding procedure (Huffman, 1952) on the variation of $\Delta r/\Delta s$, where r is radius and s is the length of perimeter. The ratio $\Delta r/\Delta s$ is invariant to scaling. If we take the total $\Delta r/\Delta s$ as a unit, partial $\Delta r/\Delta s$ is an indication for Huffman coding. Since the partial $\Delta r/\Delta s$ over half circle is definitely large enough to go to the second level in the coding procedure, we combine the first two levels to form the four segments in our coding. Figure 2b shows the coding tree.

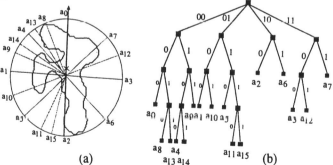

(a)

(b)

Figure 2. Signature using SEC (a), and its hierarchical coding scheme (b)

There are several properties of this signature. First, the SEC can be calculated in linear time, thus the signature has an order $O(n)$ in computational complexity (Jin 1994). Second, it provides spatial relations over objects in images, such as left, right, above, below and orientation. The similarity of objects can be measured by calculating the distance of two points in the shape space. Lastly, the features of regions, such as colour, texture, intensity moments, etc. can be extracted as indices for retrieval. An example of retrieval is shown in Figure 3.

Figure 3. Query by shape: top - query image; bottom - query results

3.2 Image retrieval using colour information

The colour and texture of the region are calculated as the identifiers of the regions. The hue modal is used as the colour descriptor. It is defined as $\max_{h} (\sum_{i,j \in \Omega} H(i,j,h))$, where Ω is the region, i and j are the coordinates, h is the hue value and H is the hue histogram. This gives the most frequent colour of the region. Hue value is independent of intensity. Its partial order is consistent with human perception of colour. Figure 4 shows query results using colour. The results are ranked based on the similarity to the query image.

3.3 Image retrieval using texture information

Texture is an important feature to distinguish regions in images (Caelli and Reye, 1993). There are many texture modeling (Elfadel and Picard, 1994). We use a set of

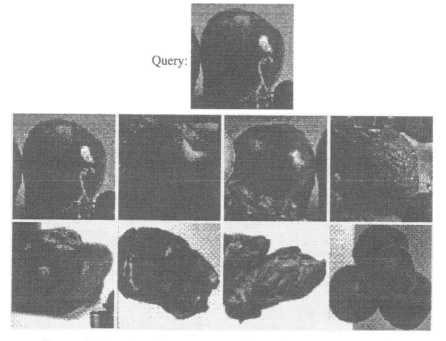

Figure 4. Query by colour: top - query image; bottom - query results

Gabor filters with five orientations and eight band-widths to calculate the texture descriptor. Gabor functions take the form:

$$g(u,v) = e^{-\frac{1}{\pi}[\frac{(u-u_0)^2}{a^2}+\frac{(v-v_0)^2}{b^2}]} e^{-2\pi i[x_0(u-u_0)+y_0(v-v_0)]}$$

where (x_0, y_0) and (u_0, v_0) are the centres of the filter in the spatial domain and the frequency domain, respectively, and a and b are the radius of the filter. Five orientations cover 180° range and eight band-widths cover 0 to 60 cyc/deg. This is consistent with the human visual system (Watson, 1983). Figure 5 gives query results using texture. The results are ranked based on the similarity to the query image.

3.4 Two-stage image retrieval

Usually the retrieval command is issued by the user with only partial information. The initial retrieval can only use this partial information and cannot utilize the system index fully. In order to use other indices and achieve an intelligent retrieval, the system should try to understand the user's retrieval request, i.e. obtain knowledge from the query. Both texture and colour spaces are clustered to form attributes for indexing. We use a two-stage retrieval method. First stage retrieval is based on the user's query. The second stage retrieval uses the knowledge obtained from first query results. The

Query: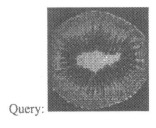

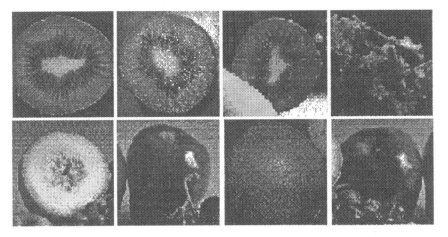

Figure 5. Query by texture: top - query image; bottom - query results

user can select a few interesting images or regions. The system extracts features automatically from these selections and retrieves again based on the combination of features.

Knowledge acquisition in the second-stage retrieval is performed by building a small feature space of the images which resulted from the first-stage retrieval. First, we perform the principal component analysis (PCA) on all features of the results to select the most significant features. Then, a clustering process is performed using these features. The clusters contain query information and the cluster centres become the indicator for further retrieval. This process can also be carried out interactively. The system asks the user to select a few images which contain similar features to those the user wants to retrieve. Then, PCA and clustering will be applied to selected images and unselected images. The significant features from selected images are used for further retrieval, whereas those from unselected images are excluded from further retrieval. The second-stage retrieval can be iterated and the sub-space of features can be expanded through iteration. In doing so, the system tries to understand the user's query and attempts to retrieve information intelligently.

The K-L transform (Murtagh, 1987) is adopted for principal component analysis. Suppose after the first-stage retrieval we obtain n images. In the texture space, we will have n 30-dimensional vectors, t_1, t_2, ..., t_n. Combining these vectors, we have a matrix $T = (t_1, t_2, ..., t_n)$, which has a dimension 30×n. Note that $T_{30 \times n}$ may not be a square matrix. The product TT' is a 30×30 matrix. Applying K-L transform over TT', 30 eigenvectors are sorted in a descending order according to their corresponding eigenvalues. The attributes topping the list will be the most significant features for retrieval. Similar transforms will be applied to shape features. Then, a multiple self-organizing memory (MSOM) clustering (Wan and Fraser, 1993) is applied over the major components of shape, texture and colour features. The number of components from each feature can be decided based on their eigenvalues and expected response time. The major computational cost in the process is the calculation of TT'. However, because the number of feature vectors in the sub-space is small, calculation of TT' will not cause significant delay. The Householder transform (Strang, 1988) is applied to calculate the K-L transform. Again, the maximum dimension of the K-L transform we have is 30. The complexity 30^3 is not of major concern here.

We have tested our scheme by choosing the major component of each feature to form a sub-space (S, T, C), where S is the major dimension in the shape space, T is the major dimension in the texture space and C is colour. The MSOM clustering is applied over all images which resulted from the first-stage retrieval. The major clusters containing the most images are the result of knowledge acquisition. Figure 6 visualizes the result by volume rendering over the sub-space of the whole index space. Testing was done over a collection of 800 images. The orange cluster in Figure 6 is the major cluster containing the largest number of images from the first-stage retrieval. The compactness of the cluster indicates a well-behaved clustering process. The centre of the cluster is the retrieval result or a new initial point for another iteration of retrieval.

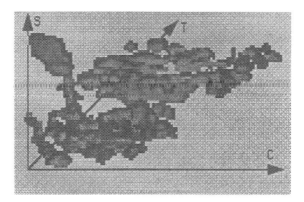

Figure 6. Visualizing the knowledge acquisition process using PCA and clustering.

We have tested the second-stage retrieval separately. Its results are consistent with human visual perception. Figure 7 shows a second-stage query. The query image shows a user selected region. The system extracts shape, texture and colour features. We perform the PCA and clustering over the entire index space. (In this case, time is

Query:

User selected region

Query output:

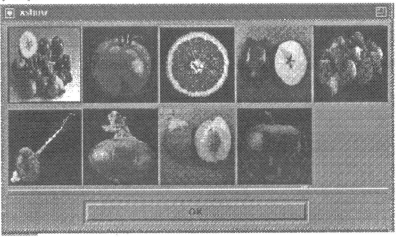

Figure 7. The second stage image retrieval in multimedia databases.

not of major concern). The cluster where the query image lies is displayed in descending order of similarity. We did not build the sub-space of features as testing was done in the second stage only without results from a first-stage retrieval.

4 Indexing high dimensional features using SS⁺-tree

Conventional access structures are not suitable for retrieving images represented by high dimensional feature vectors. In image databases, the basic and most important operation to support is similarity searches (Arya *et al.*, 1995; White and Jain, 1996b; White and Jain, 1996a), which are generalized *k*-nearest neighbor searches. A similarity search in a high-dimensional space is a difficult problem, and in general, as Minsky and Papert (1969) conjectured, will necessitate examination of a significant portion of the data. There have been a number of indexing data structures suggested to handle high-dimensional data: the Similarity Search tree (SS-tree) (White and Jain, 1996c), the Telescopic Vector tree (TV-tree) (Jagadish, 1996; Lin *et al.*, 1994), and the X-tree (Berchtold *et al.*, 1996). These new structures all perform better than the R*-tree, the best conventional multidimensional indexing structure available, for various reasons: the TV-tree actually reduces the dimension of the vectors by collapsing the first few dimensions with the same values, the SS-tree utilizes the clustering property of the data, and the X-tree tries to minimize the overlapping between nodes' bounding boxes (hyperboxes)[2].

Preliminary analytical results with R-tree-like structure (Pagel *et al.*, 1993; Kamel and Faloutsos, 1993) showed that the expected number of leaf nodes touched by a window query is proportional to the area covered by the bounding boxes, the weighted sum of the bounding boxes perimeter, and the weighted sum of the number of leaf nodes. The analytical result is in agreement with the performance enhancement techniques for the R-tree related structures. All the overlapping reduction techniques are actually an indirect way of reducing the total volume and surface area. Efforts to get high utilization will tend to minimize the number of nodes. The surface area minimizing split heuristic used by R*-tree is one of the reasons for the tree's good performance.

Some of the most often discussed properties of a R-tree based multidimensional access structure are splitting heuristics, the shape of the bounding envelope of each node, the criteria used to choose the subtree to insert the new data, and the heuristics used to reduce overlapping between the nodes and bad decisions made earlier. These properties are not independent of each other. The splitting heuristic and subtree selection criteria will determine the shape of each node and hence the goodness of the bounding envelope. The goodness of the bounding envelope will also determine the extent of the overlapping between nodes. The heuristics used to reduce overlappings and early bad decisions will also affect the shape of the nodes.

4.1 Node Split Heuristic

Almost every tree-based multidimensional access structure, e.g. the R-tree and its variants (Guttman, 1984; Beckmann *et al.*, 1990; Sellis *et al.*, 1987), SS-tree (White

---

[2]Throughout this section we will use the more familiar two-or three-dimensional term: boxes for hyperboxes, circles or spheres for hyperspheres, lines or planes for d-1 dimensional hyperplanes, and perimeters or surface areas for $(d$-1)-dimensional face volume.

and Jain, 1996c), X-tree (Berchtold *et al.*, 1996), uses a splitting plane that is perpendicular to one of the coordinate axes. Except for SS-tree, the split criteria used are mainly topological ones, e.g. the minimization of the perimeter, area, the increase of the node's area, or overlappings. Because the tree structure aims to support similarity searches, we would like nearby vectors to be collected in the same or nearby nodes. This means that we prefer a division of the data that reflects the data clustering and also means that the less variance within the nodes the better.

Dividing data into groups while optimizing a statistic has been studied extensively in the clustering area. For the SS^+-tree, we chose the widely used k-means clustering algorithm (MacQueen, 1967). The computational complexity for this clustering algorithm is $O(cni)$, where n is the number of data and c is the number of clusters, and i is the maximum number of iterations done by the algorithm. Applied as the splitting heuristic, the number of clusters c will be two, the number of data points is bounded by the maximum node's capacity plus one, and we can always set an upper boundary for the number of iterations done by the algorithm. With this splitting rule we have a greater degree of freedom and the algorithm will seek to minimize the variance in the resulting partitions. Also note that in a Euclidean space, this splitting heuristic will tend to produce spherical-shaped nodes. Related to these splitting heuristics, like the SS-tree, we use the closest centroid as the criterion for choosing the subtree into which we insert new data.

4.2 Overlap Reduction

Using k-means splitting rule has their own consequences, one node with a bigger variance might overlap a smaller node (see Figure 8a for an illustration-here we use bounding spheres for the nodes, but a similar situation will also occur even if bounding boxes are used). This situation is not desirable since it will be difficult to determine which node is better when the search is performed and also the total volume/area of the nodes is actually larger than if there is no node that "eats" another.

To alleviate the situation where a node boundary expands and heavily overlaps its siblings, the parent of the nodes which have been recently updated should check this situation (it will take $O(n)$ time, where n is the number of children within the parent node). In this case, we invalidate all the children (say k) involved and do a general k-means clustering of the grandchildren. The result of this rule can be seen in Figure 8b. The reorganization itself, if necessary, will take $O(nfki)$ time, where f is the average fan out of the child nodes and i is the number of k-means iterations performed. Measures should be taken to make this reorganization happen infrequently, like installing a guard that will decay with the insertions of new data.

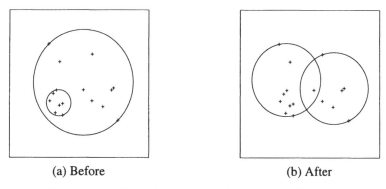

<table>
<tr><td>(a) Before</td><td>(b) After</td></tr>
</table>

Figure 8. The nodes configuration before and after the application of the local reorganization rule.

4.3 Nodes' Bounding Envelope

For the nearest neighbor queries in Euclidean space, Cleary (1979) has proved that decomposition into spherical regions is optimal in the sense that it minimizes the expected number of regions touched. Our intuition in two and three dimensional spaces leads us to expect that trees using bounding spheres for its nodes will perform worse than those using bounding boxes (see Figure 9a and Figure 9b as an example[3]). The immediately apparent problem with spheres in Euclidean space is that we cannot cover the space with spheres without overlaps; furthermore, due to the isotropic nature of the spheres, extending the spheres in one direction will extend them in every direction. Whereas with boxes, we can tile the d-dimensional space without overlapping and we can choose $2d$ direction to extend them (if we have to extend near the corners, there are fewer choices) and most of the time, the volume does not have to be expanded as much as spheres.

The formulas to calculate the volume (1) and the surface area (2) of a d-dimensional sphere radius r are:

$$V(r,d) = \frac{r^d \pi^{d/2}}{(d/2)!} \tag{1}$$

$$S(r,d) = \frac{dr^{d-1} \pi^{d/2}}{(d/2)!} \tag{2}$$

The graphs of the volume and surface area of the unit sphere ($r = 1$) are shown in Figure 10. The sphere volume will still grow exponentially with the dimension for $r > 1$, but the rate of growth is somewhat slowed down by ($d = 2$) compared to square boxes with edges of length r (see Figure 11).

---

[3] The bounding envelope of a parent node does not have to enclose all the bounding envelopes of the parent's children. We use a lazy bounding envelope enlargement scheme; we only enlarge the bounding envelope if it does not enclose the newly inserted data/reinserted node.

53

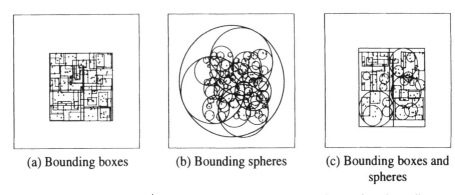

(a) Bounding boxes   (b) Bounding spheres   (c) Bounding boxes and
                                                        spheres

Figure 9. A 4-level SS⁺-tree in a 2-dimensional space using various bounding
envelopes.

Since the splitting heuristic tends to produce spherical clusters, this implies that
in a high dimensional space, spheres will be better suited as the bounding envelopes.
The amount of space wasted (Figure 12a) from using bounding boxes will increase
exponentially with respect to the dimension (see Figure 12b and Figure 12c,
respectively).

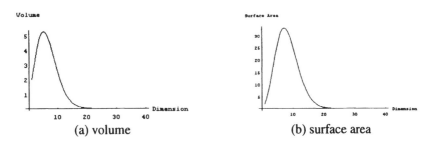

(a) volume   (b) surface area

Figure 10. The volume and surface area of the unit sphere ($r = 1$).

Because the sphere volume grows exponentially with the dimension, in a high
dimensional space a small increase in the radius of the sphere will give us a large
increase in the surface area and volume of the sphere. In accord with the analytical
results of R-tree (Pagel *et al.*, 1993; Kamel and Faloutsos, 1993), we want to
minimize the total surface area and volume of these bounding envelopes. Computing
the smallest enclosing sphere is not feasible in a high dimensional space, since the
time complexity is exponential in the number of dimensions (for approaches using
linear programming (e.g. Megiddo, 1983; Elzinga and Hearn, 1972a; Elzinga and
Hearn, 1972b)) or even super-exponential (Welzl, 1991).

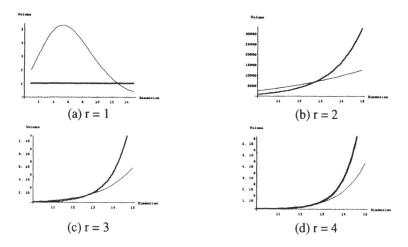

Figure 11. The volume of spheres with $r = 1; 2; 3; 4$ and the volume of square boxes with sides equal to r (the box volumes are drawn in thicker lines).

We use an approximation to the smallest enclosing sphere calculated by a spatial search utilizing the golden ratio (γ) (Schroeder, 1991) [γ is the ratio with which to divide a straight line such that the ratio of the shorter segment to the longer one equals the ratio of the longer segment to the original line ($\gamma = (\sqrt{5}-1)/2 = 0.6180339887...)$]. The use of the golden ratio in the search for the centre of the smallest enclosing sphere has been proposed (Jin *et al.*, 1994) as a way to preprocess data before feeding them to Welzl's (1991) smallest enclosing sphere algorithm. Compared to other access structures using bounding spheres, the SS-tree (White and Jain, 1996c) uses the centroid and the distance of the farthest element from the centroid as the centre and radius of the bounding sphere (which most of the time will not be the optimal one with respect to volume and surface area) and the sphere-tree (van Oosterom, 1993) uses the minimum bounding sphere computed by a variant of the method described by Elzinga and Hearn (1972b) which at best is dependent exponentially on the dimension (the sphere-tree was only tested for 2-dimensional spatial data).

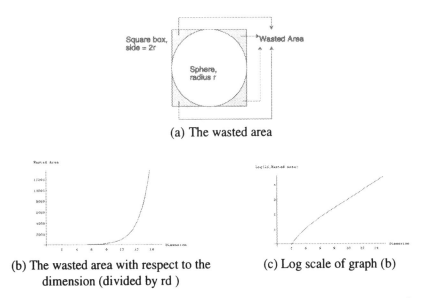

(a) The wasted area

(b) The wasted area with respect to the dimension (divided by rd)

(c) Log scale of graph (b)

Figure 12. The wasted area resulting from using boxes instead of spheres for bounding spherical shaped nodes.

An illustration of the working of the algorithm can be found in Figure 13. The algorithm starts with a guess (C1) of the initial centre of the sphere which is the midpoint of the bounding box of all the points, it then finds the farthest point from this centre (F1), and moves the centre towards this farthest point using the γ ratio (the new guess for the centre should be closer to the previous guess, hence the ratio of the distance of the new centre (C2) to the farthest point (F1) to the distance of the previous centre (C1) and F1 should be equal to $\gamma = 0.618...$). For the next iterations, we can shorten the line segment from the current centre (C2) to the farthest point (F2) using the halfspaces (A1) defined by the plane perpendicular to the previous centre-farthest point line (C1F1). These exclusion areas (A1...A3) are actually of spherical shape, planes are used to make the computation easier. Once the distance of the new centre and the previous centre is close enough (e.g. C3 and C4 are close enough), we can obtain the sphere by using the current centre point (C4) and the distance from the centre (C4) to the farthest point from it. The generalization of this algorithm to calculate the approximation to the smallest enclosing spheres of a collection of spheres and boxes is straightforward after defining a suitable farthest point for each.

4.4 Comments

Our experimental results (Kurniawati *et al.*, 1997) show that the SS⁺-tree outperformed the original SS-tree. The results also suggest that bounding spheres will perform better if we have a similar range of values for every axis. For data with unequal distribution for each axis, it might be better to use ellipsoid envelopes if we use a variance minimizing split heuristic. Compared to spheres, bounding boxes can adapt better to data with non-symmetrical distribution.

The *k*-means splitting and reorganizing heuristics result in a tree with a low variance-a low variance will also mean we have more compact nodes. The *k*-means reorganization rule helps reduce the overlappings. There are cases where overlappings are unavoidable, in which case it is better not to split the node at all but to have one big node in place of several heavily overlapping ones (similar to the supernodes in X-trees (Berchtold *et al.*, 1996)). If updates are rare, it is definitely better to use optimized static structures (White and Jain 1996b) and employ dynamization techniques (Overmars 1983).

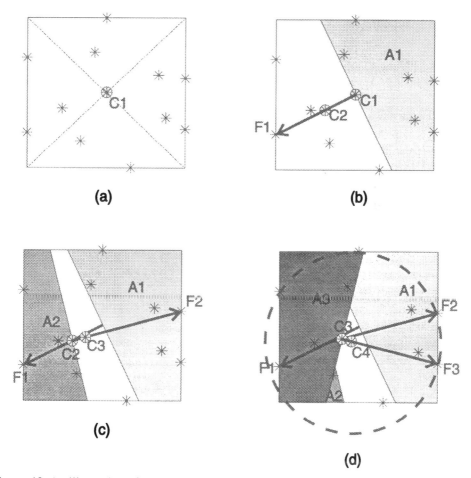

(a)

(b)

(c)

(d)

Figure 13. An illustration of the calculation of the approximation to the smallest enclosing sphere.

5 Object-oriented image processing in multimedia systems

There are many operations related to images, such as scaling, display, art-effects and high performance line-art processing, superimposing and projection, custom filtering and prescreen manipulation. Defining images as objects and grouping objects into a class make these operations easier. Large scale content-based multimedia databases have been developed by several institutions. Such systems include the QBIC (Lee *et al.*, 1994b), CANDID (Kelly *et al.*, 1995), TRADEMARK (Kato, 1992). The QBIC system supports complex multi-object and multi-feature queries of large image databases. This specific system distinguishes between the scenery of the image and the objects. In the QBIC system, the user interface has two major components, namely, the query specification windows and the query result window. The QBIC query specification window is constructed from a hierarchy of three levels. The top level is the symbolic representation of the query; the middle level controls the enabling and weighting of the feature values, and the lowest allows the feature values to be set or selected. We can apply object-oriented techniques in manipulation. We have developed an interface for image retrieval as shown in Figure 14. The shape and texture palettes give the cluster centres. Retrieval input can be selected by users or extracted from a user defined image. Figure 15 shows data flow of retrieval. Retrieval can be made on a single feature or a logical combination of multiple features.

Because images are stored in a compressed format, performing normal operations, such as scaling and transformation, without decompression is necessary. These operations can be done by convolving compressed images with a pre-designed filter. For example, scaling images can be represented as $h(i,j) = \alpha f(i,j)$, where $h(i, j)$ is a scaled image with scaling factor α. The Fourier transform of h(i, j) can be represented as:

$$H_Q(u,v) = \frac{\alpha\, q_F(u,v)}{q_H(u,v)} F_Q(u,v) = \alpha\gamma(u,v) F_Q(u,v)$$

This means that to scale an image is equivalent to filtering the image with a filter $\alpha\gamma(u, v)$. Similar results can be obtained for other operations.

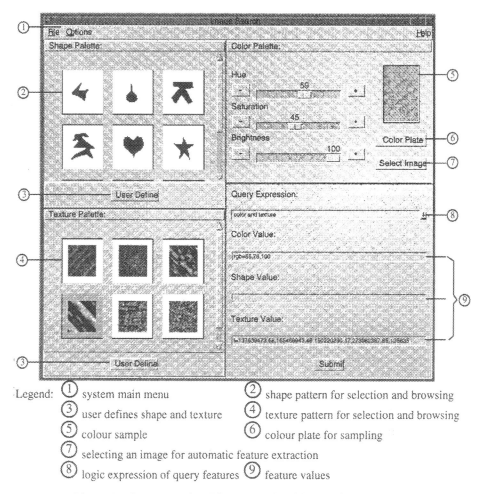

Legend: ① system main menu ② shape pattern for selection and browsing
③ user defines shape and texture ④ texture pattern for selection and browsing
⑤ colour sample ⑥ colour plate for sampling
⑦ selecting an image for automatic feature extraction
⑧ logic expression of query features ⑨ feature values

Figure 14. **Image retrieval interface for CBIR-V (or CBIR-VU).**

59

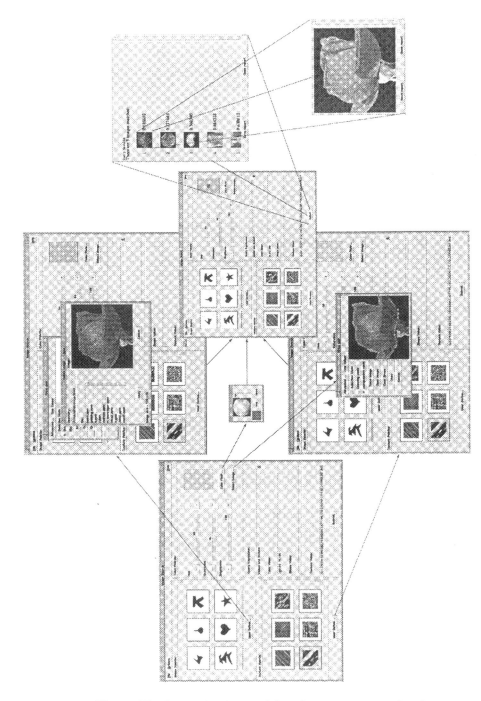

Figure 15. The mechanism and data flow of image retrieval.

6 Conclusion

We propose a consistent representation for image storage and retrieval in multimedia databases. The coding scheme preserves spatial, frequency and temporal information. The coding function has the least uncertainty over the spatial domain and the frequency domain.

This approach possesses several good properties. The coding scheme preserves the local information, which can be used to combine spatial information with statistical information. The signature proposed for describing patterns also provides geometric and temporal description for the image. The neural networks for decoding images have a simple structure suitable for parallel processing, and are easy to modify for different tasks. Multi-channel theory suggests a completely new structure for future multimedia databases. The compression scheme can be used for progressive coding, which provides a method for teleconference and other dynamic coding. It can also be used for computer graphics (Jin *et al.*, 1992).

We have developed a content-based retrieval scheme, CBIR-VU using shape, texture and colour information. The image is segmented into homogeneous regions. We propose a shape descriptor using edge features, namely zero-crossings extracted from multi-channel Laplacian of Gaussian filtering. The texture and the colour of the region are calculated as the identifiers of the regions. We use a set of Gabor filters with five orientations and six band-widths to calculate the texture descriptor. The modal of hue is used as the colour descriptor. Both texture and colour spaces are clustered to form attributes for indexing. We have shown that such a scheme can effectively retrieve images from multimedia database systems.

References

Arya, S., Mount, D. M., Netanyahu, N. S., Silverman, R., and Wu, A. Y. An optimal algorithm for approximate nearest neighbor searching. In *Proceedings of the Fifth Annual ACM-SIAM Symposium on Discrete Algorithms* (1995), 573–582. Revised version.

Asrar, G., and Dokken, J., Eds. *The EOS Reference Handbook*. Earth Science Support Office, NASA, Washington DC, 1993.

Beckmann, N., Kriegel, H.-P., Schneider, R., and Seeger, B. The R*-tree: an efficient and robust access method for points and rectangles. In *Proceedings of the ACM SIGMOD International Conference on Management of Data* (Atlantic City, NJ, May 1990), 322–331.

Berchtold, S., Keim, D. A., and Kriegel, H.-P. The X-tree: An index structure for high-dimensional data. In *Proceedings of the 22th International Conference on Very Large Data Bases* (Bombay, India, 1996), pp. 28–39.

Caelli, T., and Reye, D. On the classification of image regions by colour, texture, and shape. *Pattern Recognition* 26 (1993), 461–470.

Chang, N. S., and Fu, K. S. Picture query languages for pictorial database systems. *IEEE Computer* 14, 11 (1981), 23–33.

Chang, S. K., and Kunii, T. L. Pictorial data-base systems. *IEEE Computer* 14, 11 (1981), 13-21.

Chua, T.-S., Lim, S.-K., and Pung, H.-K. Content-based retrieval of segmented images. In *Proceedings of ACM Multimedia* (California, October 1994), pp. 211–218.

Cleary, J. G. Analysis of an algorithm for finding nearest neighbors in Euclidean space. *ACM Transactions on Mathematical Software* 5, 2 (June 1979), 183–192.

Comer, D. The ubiquitous B-Tree. *ACM Computing Surveys* 11, 2 (June 1979), 121–137.

Elfadel, I. M., and Picard, R. W. Gibbs random fields, cooccurrences, and texture modeling. *IEEE Transactions on Pattern Analysis and Machine Intelligence* 16 (1994), 24–37.

Elzinga, D., and Hearn, D. The minimum covering sphere problem. *Management Science* 19, 1 (September 1972), 96–104.

Elzinga, D. J., and Hearn, D. W. Geometrical solutions for some minimax location problems. *Transportation Science* 6, 4 (1972), 379–394.

Faloutsos, C., and Christodoulakis, S. Signature files: an access method for documents and its analytical performance evaluation. *ACM Transactions on Office Automation Systems* 2, 4 (October 1984), 267–288.

Feichtinger, H. G., and Gröchenig, K. Non-orthogonal wavelet and Gabor expansions, and group representations. In *Wavelets and their Applications*, M. B. Ruskai, G. Beylkin, R. Coifman, I. Daubechies, S. Mallat, Y. Meyer, and L. Raphael, Eds. Jones and Bartlett, Boston, MA, 1992, pp. 353-375.

Guttman, A. R-trees: A dynamic index structure for spatial searching. In *Proceedings of the 1984 ACM SIGMOD International Conference on Management of Data* (Boston, MA, June 1984), pp. 47–57.

Huffman, D. A. A method for the construction of minimum-redundancy codes. In *Proceedings of the Institute of Electronics and Radio Engineers* (September 1952), vol. **40**, pp. 1098–1101.

Jagadish, H. V. Indexing for retrieval by similarity. In *Multimedia Database Systems: Issues and Research Directions*, V. Subrahmanian and S. Jajodia, Eds. Springer-Verlag, Berlin, 1996.

Jin, J. S. A high entropy signature using optimal coding. In *International Society for Photogrammetry and Remote Sensing Commission III Symposium* (Munich, 1994), pp. 432–439.

Jin, J. S., Cao, E., and Cox, B. G. Bridging the gap: From images to graphics. In *Proceedings of the Second International Conference on Automation, Robotics, and Computer Vision* (1992), vol. **1**, pp. NW3.4.1–5.

Jin, J. S., Lowther, B. W., Robertson, D. J., and Jefferies, M. E. Shape representation and pattern matching under the multichannel theory. In *Proceedings of the Third Pacific Rim International Conference on Artificial Intelligence* (Beijing, 1994), pp. 970–975.

Jin, J. S., Tiu, L. S., and Tam, S. W. S. Partial image retrieval in multimedia databases. In *Proceedings of Image and Vision Computing New Zealand* (Christchurch, 1995), Industrial Research Ltd., pp. 179–184.

Kamel, I., and Faloutsos, C. On packing R-trees. In *Proceedings of the Second International Conference on Information and Knowledge Management* (Washington DC, November 1993), pp. 490–499.

Kato, T. *Database Architecture for Content-based Image Retrieval.* Tech. rep., Electrotechnical Laboratory, MITI, Japan, 1992.

Kelly, P. M., and Cannon, T. M. Query by image example: the CANDID approach. In *Proceedings of the SPIE: Storage and Retrieval for Image and Video Databases III* (1995), vol. **2420**, pp. 238–248.

Kurniawati, R., Jin, J. S., and Shepherd, J. A. The SS$^+$-tree: An improved index structure for similarity searches in a high-dimensional feature space. In *Proceedings of the SPIE: Storage and Retrieval for Image and Video Databases V* (San Jose, CA, February 1997), vol. **3022**. To appear.

Larish, J. Kodak's still picture exchange for print and film use. *Advanced Imaging* **10**, 4 (1995), 38-39.

Lee, D., Barber, R., Niblack, W., Flickner, M., Hafner, J., and Petkovic, D. Indexing for complex queries on a query-by-content image database. In *Proceedings of the International Conference on Pattern Recognition* (Jerusalem, October 1994), vol. **1**, pp. 142–146.

Lee, D., Barber, R., Niblack, W., Flickner, M., Hafner, J., and Petkovic, D. Query by image content using multiple object and multiple features: User interface issues. In *Proceedings of the International Conference on Image Processing*, (1994), vol. **2**, pp. 76–80.

Lewis, J., Milligan, G., and Hunt, A. *NUTTAB 95: Nutrient Data Table for Use in Australia.* Computer file. Australian Government Publishing Service, Canberra, 1995.

Lin, K.-I., Jagadish, H. V., and Faloutsos, C. The TV-tree: An index structure for high-dimensional data. *Journal of Very Large Databases (VLDB Journal)* **3**, 4 (October 1994), 517–549.

MacQueen, J. B. Some methods for classification and analysis of multivariate observations. In *Proceedings of the Berkeley Symposium on Mathematical Statistics and Probability* (1967), vol. **1**(5), pp. 281–297.

Martucci, M. Digital still marketing at PressLink. *Advanced Imaging* **10**, 4 (1995), 34-36.

Megiddo, N. Linear-time algorithms for linear programming in R^3 and related problems. *SIAM Journal on Computing* **12** (1983), 759–776.

Minsky, M., and Papert, S. *Perceptrons: An Introduction to Computational Geometry.* MIT Press, Cambridge, 1969.

Murtagh, F. *Multivariate Data Analysis.* Kluwer Academic Publishers, Boston, 1987.

Nagasaka, A., and Tanaka, Y. Automatic video indexing and full-video search for object appearances. In *IFIP: Visual Database System II* (October 1992), Elsevier Science Publishers B. V., pp. 113–127.

Niblack, W., Barber, R., Equitz, W., Flickner, M., Glasman, E., Petkovic, D., Yanker, P., Faloutsos, C., and Taubin, G. The QBIC project: Querying images by content using color, texture and shape. In *Proceedings of the SPIE: Storage and Retrieval for Image and Video Databases* (February 1993), vol. **1908**, pp. 173–187.

Overmars, M. H. *The Design of Dynamic Data Structures.* Springer-Verlag, Berlin, 1983.

Pagel, B.-U., Six, H.-W., Toben, H., and Widmayer, P. Towards an analysis of range queries performance in spatial data structures. In *Proceedings of the Twelfth ACM SIGACT-SIGMOD-SIGART Symposium on Principles of Database Systems* (Washington, DC, May 1993), pp. 214–221.

Salton, G., and McGill, M. J. *Introduction to Modern Information Retrieval*. McGraw-Hill, New York, 1983.

Schroeder, M. *Fractals, Chaos, Power Laws: Minutes From an Infinite Paradise*. W.H. Freeman and Company, New York, 1991.

Sellis, T., Roussopoulos, N., and Faloutsos, C. The R⁺-tree: A dynamic index for multi-dimensional objects. In *Proceedings of the Thirteenth Conference on Very Large Databases* (Los Altos, CA, September 1987), Morgan Kaufman, pp. 507–518.

Strang, G. Linear *Algebra and Its Applications*. Harcourt Brace Jovanovich Publishers, San Diego, 1988.

van Oosterom, P. J. M. *Reactive data structures for geographic information systems*. Oxford University Press, New York, 1993.

Wallace, G. K. The JPEG still picture compression standard. *Communications of the Association for Computing Machinery* **34**, 4 (April 1991), 30–44.

Wan, W., and Fraser, D. M2dSOMAP: Clustering and classification of remotely sensed imagery by combining multiple Kohonen self-organizing maps and associative memory. In *Proceedings of the International Joint Conference on Neural Networks* (Nagoya, Japan, 1993), vol. 3, pp. 2464–2467.

Watson, A. B. Detection and recognition of simple spatial forms. In *Physical and biological processsing of images*, O. J. Braddick and A. A. Sleigh, Eds. Springer-Verlag, New York, 1983, pp. 101–114.

Welzl, E. Smallest enclosing disks (balls and ellipsoids). In *Proceedings of the Symposium on New Results and New Trends in Computer Science* (Graz, Austria, June 1991), H. Maurer, Ed., vol. **555** of Lecture Notes in Computer Science, Springer-Verlag, pp. 359–370.

White, D. A., and Jain, R. *Algorithms and Strategies for Similarity Retrieval*. Tech. Rep. VCL-96-01, Visual Computing Laboratory, University of California, San Diego, 9500 Gilman Drive, Mail Code 0407, La Jolla, CA 92093-0407, July 1996.

White, D. A., and Jain, R. Similarity indexing: Algorithms and performance. In *Proceedings of the SPIE: Storage and Retrieval for Image and Video Databases IV* (San Jose, CA, February 1996), vol. **2670**, pp. 62–73.

White, D. A., and Jain, R. Similarity indexing with the SS-tree. In *Proceedings of the Twelfth IEEE International Conference on Data Engineering* (New Orleans, Louisiana, February 1996), pp. 516–523.

Wu, J. K., Mehtre, B. M., Gao, Y. J., Lam, P. C., and Narasimhalu, A. D. STAR - A multimedia database system for trademark registration. In *Proceedings of the First International Conference on Applications of Databases* (Vadstena, Sweden, June 1994), W. Litwin and T. Risch, Eds., vol. **819** of Lecture Notes in Computer Science, Springer-Verlag, pp. 109–122.

Design of a Distributed Planetary Image Data Archive Based on an ATM Network

Herwig Rehatschek

Institute for Computer Graphics and Vision, University of Technology, Graz
Münzgrabenstraße 11 A-8010 Graz, Austria
Voice: ++43 316 873 5018 Fax: ++43 316 873 5050
E-mail: herwig@icg.tu-graz.ac.at
WWW: http://www.icg.tu-graz.ac.at/herwig/basicinformation.html

Abstract. Ongoing and completed planetary and Earth satellite missions have spawned large image data archives distributed all over the world. The searching for specific data suffers from lack of using international query and catalogue standards, slow network connections, no graphical user interface (GUI) and no platform independent client software. The proposed GDSS (Graz Distributed Server System) project outlines the system design, the setup of a high-speed ATM (Asynchronous Transfer Mode) backbone and the prototype implementation. The GDSS prototype uses Java and JDBC (Java Data Base Connectivity) in order to access any ANSI SQL compatible relational database system with the same set of SQL statements. The client software provides remote access to search and retrieve data from a planetary meta-data set. The 500 GByte NASA Magellan data set from planet Venus was used as a first test dataset. However, the system is not restricted to the given dataset. We expect data management concepts, network technology, Java client software and database connectivity based on international standards illustrated within the GDSS project to also be applicable to Earth based remote sensing data.

1 Introduction

An increasing number of Earth observation and planetary satellite missions have spawned large image archives. The search for specific image data by means of search criteria such as acquisition, time and/or date, geographic location, surface features or the actual content of an image remains a tedious process due to the current need of either searching through low quality quicklooks of poster photo-prints or of dealing with large volumes of original image data that are usually not organized by the preferred search criteria. That is why determination of the exact image coverage is difficult. Data are often organized in a way that exceeds an area of interest by far.

These experiences are shared by a wide scientific community and are exemplified in this paper by the image data set of planet Venus which was produced by NASA's Magellan spacecraft. NASA's Planetary Data System (PDS) [1] offers access to the entire image data set from Magellan. We report on ideas and results in organizing this data set to ease the access from remote sites. In this context we also discuss issues of data-specific processing software and access to specific remote computing resources. This work results from the European Magellan Data Node [2] which is organized as a subnode to the geosciences node of the PDS under an agreement between NASA, the

Austrian Space Agency and the Institute for Computer Graphics and Vision at the University of Technology, Graz.

During the Magellan mission to Venus about 95% of the planet's surface was mapped by the spacecraft's sensors. The data set consists of SAR images (>5200 orbits) with a total volume of about 500 GByte. The raw images (polar, south to north) or FBIDRs (Full resolution Basic Image Data Records) are grouped into three "cycles" defined by the different look angles of the SAR sensor. Images from cycles 1 and 3 can be used for stereo processing because of their different same side look angles. Cycle 2 was recorded from the opposite side [3, 4].

We propose to use the Graz Distributed Server System (GDSS) not only for searching, but also for processing and retrieving of remote sensing image data. It is designed for giving easy and unified access to all planetary data, source image processing capabilities and computing tools to a geographically dispersed scientific community. This paper outlines the general design of the GDSS and introduces a first search-client prototype using JAVA and JDBC (Java Database Connectivity) connected with an Oracle relational database server. An ATM network at OC-3 speed (155 Mbit/sec) which was built up between two institutes of the University of Technology, Graz is used as a network backbone.

2 Related work

Various systems exist to spatially organize Earth observation data in image catalogs and to provide remote search and retrieval. Examples include GISIS (Graphical Intelligent Satellite Information System) [5] and VISTA (Visual Interface for Space and Terrestrial Analysis) [6] [7], which were designed to give remote access to various remote sensing data using a special purpose client software. GISIS supports the user with an intuitive GUI and a detailed zoomable 2D vector map of the Earth. VISTA additionally supports a 3D vector representation of Earth but is a special purpose solution. Eurimage [79] provides Earth Observation Products and Services in Europe, North Africa and the Middle East, offering remote sensing users the EiNet service. EiNet is an on-line subscription service that lets you access Eurimage's catalogues of Earth Observation satellite data, allowing you to browse thumbnails and meta-data of the scenes covering your geographic area and time range of interest, and download Quick Looks. The European Union's CEO (Center of Earth Observation) was initiated to develop a European wide support of multi mission data catalogues. A first spin off is the so called European Wide Service Exchange (EWSE) [8]. It has some special features that allow registered users to search, input, update and customize the information content via their WWW browsers. ImageNet from CORE Software Technology Inc. [9] supports data browsing and retrieval via WWW or a special purpose client. These free services allow easy access to both summary and detailed data product descriptions, as well as browse images and fully processed science data. The EOSDIS-IMS (Earth Observing System Data and Information System Information Management System) [10] provides search and order tools for accessing a wide variety of global Earth science data and information via a platform dependent browser program which supports a downloading facility. The image data reside at ten different data archives. Furthermore the WWW Ionia AVHRR Net Browser [11], the Arno project [12] and the Landsat/Spot browser by the Canadian Center for Remote Sensing and Earth Observation [13] should be mentioned.

In comparison, there is no proliferation of systems for planetary data retrieval. Publicly accessible applications for planetary data retrieval, provided by the member institutions of the PDS, allow searching databases for named features, or for image coverage by defining either a point or a region of interest. Two collaborative projects have recently started at NASA's Jet Propulsion Laboratory (JPL) and the US-Geological Survey (USGS): Planetary Image Access [19] and Solar System Visualization (SSV) project [20].

There are several ongoing ATM pilot projects and testbeds [18]. Most of them are currently in the USA and Canada. In Europe just one global experiment was initiated by the European Union [14]. Two of the most important pilot trials in the United states are the MagicNet [15] and the BagNet [16]. The Canarie Net [17] pilot trial network, which is currently the biggest ATM network in the world, was built in Canada. Within these networks various pilot trials are taking place including: music library, video on demand, military real-time battle applications, global internet seminar, cyber mall and guarantee of interoperability among heterogeneous ATM hardware components.

Current systems are greatly limited in their abilities such as user defined image cropping, billing for services and data, using a flexible network with high bandwidth, user management, supporting raster and vector representations, offering image processing facilities, sharing resources and dealing with distributed archives. Image data are conventionally organized by type of sensor, by satellite, by time of data acquisition and not by spatial coverage. It is the image's position or its coverage that a scientific user most likely uses in his queries. The usage of available standards should be obligatory but is usually ignored.

3 System Design

3.1 Design Goals

Raster Image Oriented Browsing Interface: On planets like Venus you cannot take advantage of many named features, so the GDSS will need a zoomable raster image oriented map browser with different levels of detail (LOD) for representing the whole planetary surface. The LOD provide an overview of the entire planet as well as a detailed representation of surface segments.

Search for Points of Interest / Regions of Interest: The system needs to handle queries for points and regions of interest via a spatial database. This is based on lossy compressed quicklooks at a reduction >1:25 of the full resolution data. At this scale the overview of all available images for a special surface point or region of interest becomes manageable.

Coverage Requests: Venus' Magellan images may be the subject of queries regarding the coverage with stereo, by a specific cycle or of a particular feature. The coverage result will be visualized at the client site by overlaying colored areas (e.g. green areas showing stereo coverage, red areas showing features and so on) on the pixel map. Clicking on these areas will retrieve all quicklooks satisfying the user's coverage criteria.

Searching for Meta Information: Besides points and regions of interest, one may want to use additional criteria to a query which can act as a filtering function on the data, one may think of multiple images covering an area in the form of an image stack. Additional criteria may address a cycle number, a date or time, type of sensor, data processing, history with a computation algorithm, processing parameters etc., the satellite itself, or the geometric resolution.

Client-Server Architecture: The underlying concept of GDSS is a distributed client-server architecture [24, 25]. As a backbone an ATM network is used for reasons explained below.

Intelligent Local Caching: An intelligent local image cache keeps response times as short as possible and reduces network traffic. The main weakness of each caching strategy is the update problem. This problem has already been efficiently solved within the Hyper-G system [26, 27, 28] using the so-called p-flood [29] procedure. We propose to use a similar algorithm for the GDSS.

Local server data prediction: There exists a Central Server which will store complete browsing maps in different levels of detail for a planet, using a special rectangular data structure denoted as „map tiles". During interactive browsing the client downloads and visualizes the tiles.

Batchjob Processing: A well-defined batchjob interface for standard procedures which can be processed in the background without supervision by the user is provided. The procedures may include retrieval of full resolution data or time consuming complex queries while the Central Server is highly utilized. This capability is especially important when the network connection is slow.

User group management: We plan that clients can be connected to one Local Server, resulting in a need for some group management facilities. These may include:

- building user groups who have access to any subset of the image data
- the definition of user rights (read, local write access permissions, authorization for full resolution data retrieval, authorization for services)
- defining priorities (e.g. students may have lower priority than scientific personnel)

Network Security and Accounting: For commercial use a system must provide accounting facilities. Hence GDSS is supposed to grant identification, authorization and charging. In such cases the system must guarantee privacy of communication.

Network management capabilities: Extensive O&M (observation and maintenance) features must be available to the system administrator. These are in detail:

- performance observation and tuning (monitoring active connections, current users in the system, ..);

- accounting;
- security management;
- fault management (diagnostic tools, trouble ticket generation, ...);
- configuration (comfortable scalability and extension).

Remote Data Processing: There may be special image processing facilities available on the distributed system. Therefore it would be useful to have a special remote processing interface for time-consuming image processing algorithms.

3.2 General Layout

The system can be thought of as consisting of five main components (illustrated in Figure 1):

- Image Archives
- Local Server
- User Retrieval Client
- Central Server
- Network

Image Archives: Image Archives are maintained by commercial vendors or public institutions but have to fulfill special requirements in order to become a participant of GDSS. Among these a global map at different LOD (Levels of Detail) and compressed quicklooks of all image data have to be created once, a database of meta info and image coverage must be built, the archive must be on-line (24 hours a day, 7 days a week) to handle requests from the Central Server, the archive must be able to handle GQP (General Query Protocol) requests, the standard query and data retrieval

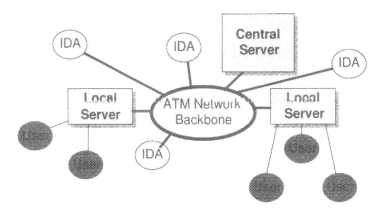

Figure 1: *General Layout of the GDSS.* The Central Server holds the browsing map and quickviews of all attached image data archives (IDA). The Central Server is accessed from clients via a Local Server at each site. The location of the various archives is invisible to clients.

protocol of GDSS, the archive must update the data on the Central Server each time new images data are added and automatic full resolution data retrieval should be possible.

Local Server: One Local Server has to be set up at every user site (see Figure 1). It will be separately described in section 3.4.

User Retrieval Client: The Retrieval Client consists of two major parts, the query definition dialog and the map browser. A set of menus and forms supports the composition of user queries.

Central Server: It is the main component of GDSS and will be separately described in section 3.3.

Network: This component is the most important of GDSS because the overall system performance and functionality depend on the efficiency of the underlying network technology. ATM [30, 31, 32, 33, 34, 35, 36] proved to meet the basic requirements of the GDSS, this will be discussed in more detail in section 4.1. To grant international worldwide scope usage of the TCP/IP protocol is recommended. TCP/IP makes the GDSS independent of the underlying physical components. Because IP over ATM still suffers from lack of performance, there are several ongoing research projects investigating TCP/IP over ATM [37, 38, 39, 40] for performance improvements

3.3 Design of the Central Server

Figure 2 outlines the main modules and communication paths of the CS.

General Query Protocol (GQP): Since the usage of standards is crucial in a global system like the GDSS, we propose GQP to be an extension of the existing following two standards: by the ANSI Z39.50 [22, 23] standard and the CEOS extension CIP (Catalogue Interchange Protocol) [41]. GQP must be able to handle spatial queries, administrative queries, service requests and update commands.

Request distribution module: The Request distribution module has two main functions, (1) it is responsible for security tasks (identification, authorization) (2) it has to manage the distribution of incoming requests.

Database Search Module: The Database Search Module should be a massively parallel RDBMS handling multiple spatial requests at the same time. This module of the CS is responsible for coverage and quickview requests.

Map Browsing Module: The purpose of the Map Browsing Module is to provide the user with fast delivery of requested map tiles that should be currently displayed on the screen. This process should be interactive and is time critical.

Archive Request Module: This module holds as many waiting queues as archives are attached to GDSS. The GQP queries are sent from there to the archives. The archives respond with the requested full resolution data and optionally with the billable costs. If the price has a non zero value, the account server will be started and accounting with the Local Server takes place. This transaction is subject to high security because

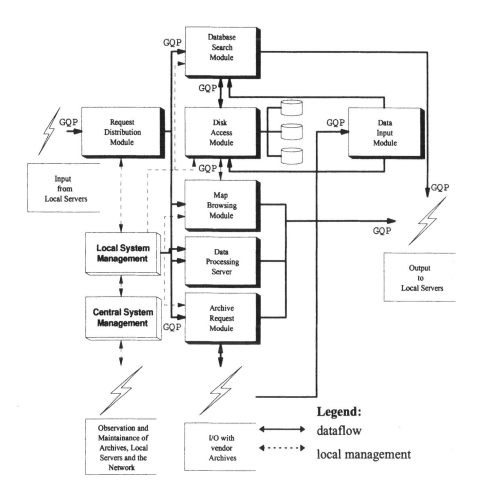

Figure 2: The main modules of the Central Server, with the internal dataflow and the links to external components such as vendor archives or Local Servers.

someone could manipulate the price sent to the Local Server for confirmation. Privacy will be accomplished with a common key system [41]. The result, usually an image stack, is sent to the user.

Disk Access Module: The browsing maps of the whole planetary surface are stored here at different levels of detail forming a resolution pyramid. Furthermore 1:4 reduced JPEG compressed quicklooks will be kept within this module. Advantages of a central Disk Access Module are the easy update facility, and the highly optimized fast image delivery.

Data Input Module: The Data Input Module is responsible for bringing in data as well as updating existing data. These processes affect the image data, the coverage and the meta info databases of the Database Search Module.

Local and Central System Management: The local management module addresses tasks like local fault management, local configurations, performance tuning and local security issues. The global management tool manages the entire GDSS network down to the Local Servers, which have their own local management.

3.4 Design of the Local Server

The basic layout of the Local Server (LS) and the information flow grouped by internal dataflow, local management and internal communication is illustrated in Figure 3. We propose to use a relational DBMS to maintain and exchange all the information stored within the LS.

Local Traffic Management Module: This is the layer where users of the local site can connect and therefore must provide a proper interface. The module has to perform several user management tasks including notification at the identification module, user authorization, storage of the traffic parameters of each user, making new connections and getting data from the local cache management module.

Identification module: This module holds all relevant user data which are allowed to access the GDSS. Parameters like name, login, password, address, office, etc. are stored in a database table.

Authorization Module: Authorization rights include local read/write permissions as well as maximum amount of money a user can spend on images ordered from archives and network costs. These rights can be set and edited only by the local system administrator, who is responsible for costs caused by his local users being paid in time.

Accounting Module: This module archives the current network access costs and the data ordered by the individual users. Its tables are used by the authorization module in order to check if a user is authorized to order data with costs.

Security Module: The security module acts like a firewall. The traffic of the entire LS has to go through here and will be filtered and analyzed. Actions like hack trials, failed logins, tries to change system database tables etc. will be logged in a special table.

Local Cache Management Module: The main purpose of this module is to cache browsed map data and quicklooks, which are currently accessed by users in order to keep network traffic and costs low.

Local system management: This module should be the central application of the system administrator to control and maintain all modules introduced so far.

4 Implementation

We have implemented a functional prototype of the proposed GDSS. This implementation initially focuses on the Magellan data set and the needs of PDS scientists. The work done so far is addressed in the following subsections.

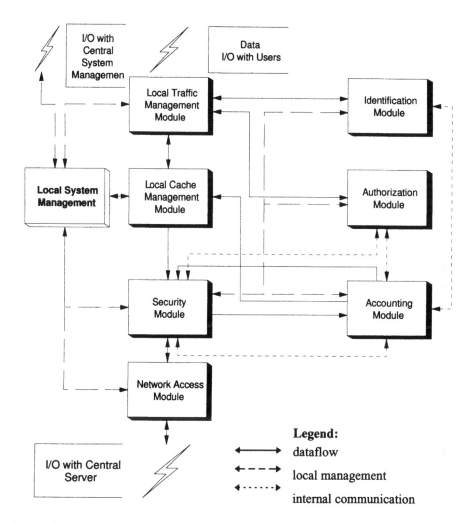

Figure 3: The modules of the Local Server. Information flow within the server is grouped by internal communication, internal management flow and dataflow.

4.1 Building the Network

The first step of the GDSS implementation was finding an appropriate network backbone technology having several alternatives in mind. The next section discusses the migration of the institute network and building up the OC-3 cluster between two institutes of the University of Technology, Graz.

4.1.1 Choosing ATM Network Technology

For a global system a network backbone must meet several requirements as follows: international standard, high transfer speed, global scope, scalability, support of asynchronous synchronous and isochronous traffic types, proper quality of service definition, support of video, voice and data transfer service

The only currently known technology which fairly fulfills the above requirements is ATM (Asynchronous Transfer Mode), which was introduced and standardized in 1991 by the ITU-T [42] to be the standard for B-ISDN [31]. ATM was chosen because of the following advantages:

- High bandwidth available even for WANs with a large geographical scope.
- Currently the only known architecture which effectively integrates three completely different kinds of traffic: data, voice and video.
- ATM allows a quality of service definition at setup time, which will be guaranteed throughout the communication session.
- ATM has been standardized for various existing physical layers, including STM-1[1] (155.520 Mbit/sec), STM-4[2] (622.08 Mbit/sec), DS1 (1.544 Mbit/sec), DS2 (6.312 Mbit/sec), DS3 (44.736 Mbit/sec), FDDI , DQDB, 155.52 Mbit/sec Multi-mode Fiber Interface, E3 (34.368 Mbit/sec), E4 (139.264 Mbit/sec) [32, 50]. Hence ATM is defined at OSI Layer 2. ATM can be regarded as a physical layer independent protocol.
- Interface to existing LANs (Ethernet, Token Ring and FDDI) is provided via the ATM LAN - Emulation (LANE). V1.0, specified in Feb.1995 by the ATM Forum, provides Permanent Virtual Circuits (PVCs) and Switched Virtual Circuits (SVCs) for: Ethernet-Ethernet, Ethernet-ATM, Token Ring - Token Ring, Token Ring - ATM, ATM-ATM. Transmission of FDDI frames is also supported.

Since UNI (User Network Interface) Version 3.1 [43] ATM supports a quality of service definition consisting of 7 traffic parameters including peak cell rate, sustained cell rate, cell loss ratio, cell transfer delay, cell delay variation, burst tolerance and minimum cell rate. Optionally you can define an unspecified service contract on a best effort base where not all mentioned traffic parameters are specified mandatory [44].

Several alternatives were taken into consideration. A summary of the evaluation process and a comparison to ATM can be found in Table 1. As a conclusion ATM is in all aspects except transfer speed - where currently Fibre Channel supports a higher throughput - at least equal to its competitors, in most even better. So ATM was chosen to be the backbone technology of the GDSS because it optimally meets the requirements.

---

[1] This corresponds exactly to SONET OC-3 (STS-3c)

[2] This corresponds exactly to SONET OC-12 (STS-12c)

	ISDN	FDDI	FDDI II	DQDB
max. transfer speed	64 kb*	100 Mb	100 Mb	155 Mb
QoS definition	—	—	—	—
scalability	⊗	⊗	⊗	☺
services	O / D	V / D	O / V / D	O / V / D
traffic mode	VO	VL	VL	VO / VL
scope	global	100 km	100 km	50 km
supported traffic types	S / I	A / S	A / S / I	A / S / I
physical protocols	SDH, PDH, SONET	-	-	SDH, PDH, SONET

(a)

	Frame Relay	SMDS	Fibre Channel	ATM
max. transfer speed	1,544 Mb	45 Mb	1,062 Gb	622,08 Mb
QoS definition	—	—	✓	✓
scalability	☺	☺	☻	☻
services	V / D	O / V / D	V / D	O / V / D
traffic mode	VL	VL	VL / VO	VO
scope	global**	global	10 km	global
supported traffic types	A / S	A / S / I	A / S	A / S / I
physical protocols	SDH, PDH	SDH, PDH	SCSI, IPI, HIPPI, AAL-5, FC-LE, SBCCS, IEEE 802.2	SONET, SDH, PDH, FDDI, DQDB, MM Fiber Interface

(b)

✓ .... supported	.... unsupported	
⊗ .... bad	☺ .... fair	☻ ... . excellent
A ..... asynchronous	I ...... isochronous	S .... synchronous
O ..... voice	V .... video	D .... data

* 128 kb/sec when combining both B-channels
** is limited to about 1000 nodes because of its addressing mode [32]

Table 1: (a) and (b) give a summary of the evaluation of alternative technologies in comparison to ATM. Nearly in all relevant requirements ATM is better than its competitors.

4.1.2 Migration from FDDI and Ethernet to ATM and Switched Ethernet

In 1994 we started at our institute with research on ATM technology. At this time there was a second institute, the Institute for Applied Information Processing and

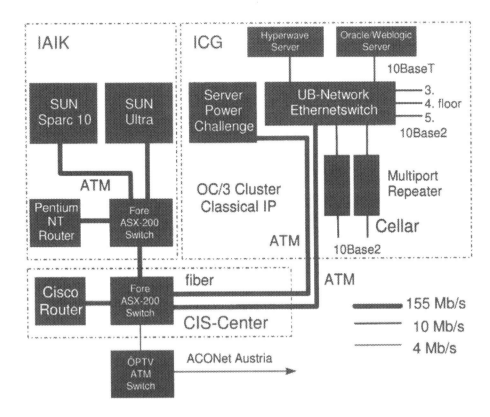

Figure 4: Final layout of the OC-3 cluster. The standard Ethernet of the ICG was upgraded to a switched Ethernet. All attached subnetworks now have their own collision domain, network traffic was reduced significantly. The server of the institute was attached via an ATM interface and the existing ATM connection to the CISC at OC-3 directly to the Ethernet switch.

Communications (IAIK), which had already built up a local ATM network using a FORE Systems ASX-100 switch and several SUN workstations connected to it.

The ICG was equipped so far with a standard IEEE 802.3 Ethernet working at 10 Mbit/sec. Performance got significantly low due to the connection of 38 SGI and 5 SUN workstations, 16 PCs and 8 Macs which all shared just one collision domain. To increase performance an upgrade to a switched Ethernet which additionally should take advantage of the available ATM backbone was proposed. The final layout of the network can be seen in Figure 4.

With this upgrade the performance was increased rather than the bandwidth, which stayed the same. The advantage of the switch is the separation of the one big collision domain which results in a performance increase, since the other domains are just loaded when a packet has to go there. The server of the institute is connected via ATM to the Ethernet switch, the global routing is done via the router in the CISC. This solution dramatically increases the availability of the server, because all 7 attached domains can access the server in parallel at their full bandwidth of 10 Mbit/sec.

4.2 Choosing a data Model

Generally five data models can be distinguished: deductive data model, network data model, hyper-media data model, object-oriented data model, relational data model.

The *deductive data model* is based on facts and rules, which are stored in the DBMS. Using the rules, new facts can be derived [69]. These database model is often used in artificial intelligence systems which take advantage of knowledge bases. For the GDSS such a database system is not required, because (1) there is no need for storing knowledge (2) the meta data is static and does not need changes.

The *network data model* or CODASYL (COnference on DAta SYstems Language) was introduced in 1971 by the DBTG (Data Base Task Group) of the Programming Language Committee [70]. Similarly to the relational model it defines a schema data description language (DDL), a subschema data description language and a data manipulation language (DML). The network data model suffers from the manual search process (navigation through records) and problems with deleting records. Implementations of the network data model do not have a significant market presence. These are the main reasons why it does not meet the requirements for the GDSS.

The *hyper-media model* is specially suited for structuring all kinds of data including images, data, audio, video, postscript, etc. [71] Basically this data model consists of multi-media objects, which contain any kind of information, links between them and anchors. Links are just stored within the database and are invisible to the user, anchors are visualized on the screen and give the user the possibility to navigate through multi-media documents. A MM-document is a semantic unit consisting of different MM-objects. Each of them has a particular procedure attached to it which visualizes the object on the screen [64]. There is no standard available for the hyper-media model, thus a lot of implementations supporting different features exist. The hyper-media model is perfect for storing and visualizing different kind of data - this model would be an overkill for the Magellan meta dataset, since it consists just of text information. In addition there are no special data structures supporting spatial search.

The *object oriented model* [72, 73] is perfectly suitable for modeling complex data structures, which cannot be done easily with conventional relational databases. For the GDSS spatial search can be increased tremendously by implementing a R-tree spatial data structure within the database. The object oriented model would be a perfect solution for the GDSS, however, it currently suffers from two disadvantages: (1) there is no international standard for data querying and retrieval, (2) the market presence is very low and available products are very expensive in comparison to RDBMS. Development is currently underway to enhance the ANSI SQL-92 standard into a computationally complete language called SQL3 for the definition and management of persistent, complex objects. In the USA, the entirety of SQL3 is being processed as both an ANSI Domestic project and as an ISO project. The expected time frame for completion of SQL3 is currently 1999 [74]. Because of the outlined restrictions the object oriented model failed to meet the requirements for the GDSS.

The *relational data model*, [75] which is a subset of the network data model, is currently the most popular and wide spread data model in the world. There exist powerful tools for design and application development as well as very stable server software, due to experience collected over many years. However, modeling of complex data structures like R-trees, which are required for searching spatial data cannot be implemented in relational data models without significant performance loss. Recently relational database vendors started to provide their products with object-oriented extension kits (e.g. Oracle, Illustra, Sybase). These so called ORDBMS (Object Relational Data Base Management Systems) suffer from lack of performance because they still have a RDBMS and all queries have to be converted to SQL statements and all results to objects. The main advantage of the relational data model is the existence of an international ANSI standard (X3.135-1992, "Database Language SQL"), which is supported by the big database vendors (e.g. Oracle, Informix, Sybase, Microsoft, etc.). This and because of the high availability in the world market was the main reason why the relational data model was chosen for implementing the GDSS prototype.

4.3 The Magellan FBIDR Meta-Data set

The ICG received the 110.897 MB Magellan FBIDR meta-data from the Washington University in St. Louis, Missouri which runs a geosciences subnode of the NASA PDS. According to the chosen data model, a relational data schema was designed, which is illustrated as an entity-relationship diagram in Figure 5. The arrows in the diagram indicate 1:n relations between the tables.

The *uplink table* contains comments associated with each command upload. Each upload number can have n lines text. An upload is a set of commands which was sent to the spacecraft. One upload command affected a group of orbits. Each FBIDR or orbit (polar, north to south) consists of about 700 by the satellite recorded points. The number of points is stored in the upload table.

The *upload info table* stores information about the orbits affected by the upload command (start and stop orbit) and the number of orbit points, which were recorded for these orbits.

The *downlink table* contains comments about the actual results of a command upload. Each upload number can have n lines of text.

The *point info table* holds the predicted orbital parameters such as boresight latitude, look angle, etc., for each point in a group of orbits belonging to one command upload. For example, suppose one upload command covers the orbits 400 through 450. The points are numbered from north to south, starting with number 1. So the expected latitude at point 1 might be 89 degrees, at point 2 it might be 88.75, at point 3 it might be 88.50, etc. The values would be the same for all the orbits in the group (400-450).

The *orbit points table* stores the few parameters that would have different values for each point within each orbit. Those are the boresight longitude, the subspacecraft longitude, and the event time. So this table has one record for each point, in each orbit, in each upload. This table separates the points and orbits. Consider for example the uplink info table has stored 699 points to record for orbits 400 to 450. The orbit points table contains now for each orbit from 400 to 450 699 points in the table. That is why it has 1796466 records which need 98.1 MB storage volume.

The *orbit info* table contains predicted orbital parameters such as start and stop times, look direction, inclination, eccentricity, etc., for each recorded orbit. It has 9455 entries, which refer to the number of existing FBIDRs.

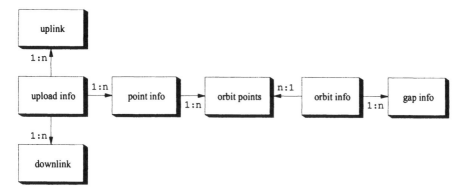

Figure 5: Database schema of the Magellan FBIDR (orbit) meta-data. 1:n relations are indicated by arrows. For a detailed explanation of the tables see text.

The *gap info table* stores the starting and ending latitude and longitude of data gaps in each orbit. Due to interferences the data sent by the satellite was corrupted and caused gaps in the resulting image data. Exact locations and lengths of these gaps can be found within this table. A more detailed description of the data and the tables can be found in [45].

4.4 JAVA-JDBC GDSS Prototype

In 1995 Java was announced at SunWorld95 by Sun Microsystems. Even before the first release of the Java compiler in January 1996, Java was considered to become an industry standard for internet development [46]. In the first six months of 1996 Java was licensed by leading software and hardware companies including Adobe, Asymetrix, Borland, IBM, Microsoft, Novell, Oracle and Symantec. Java is fully object oriented and an open language which can be easily extended by additional APIs. The main advantages of JAVA are platform independence, network orientation, flexibility and security [47, 48, 49]. Applets are precompiled software pieces of Java source code, which are downloaded from a server and are executed locally with any Java compatible browser (e.g. Netscape, MS Explorer, Hot Java,...). Because of the above mentioned reasons a Java applet client optimally meets the requirements of GDSS.

It was up to us to find an optimal transparent database connectivity for such user clients, since transparent database and archive access is also a main component in the GDSS. Here the Java JDBC (Java Data Base Connectivity) API was the best solution available. JDBC is a relational API class for Java applets and applications. It is part of the Java 1.1 release and is platform and database independent. JDBC supports the ANSI SQL-92 (ISO/IEC 9075:1992 and ANSI X3.135-1992) standard. To access a specific ANSI SQL compatible database a native JDBC driver is needed. Leading database vendors including Borland, IBM, Informix, Microsoft, Oracle, and Sybase have already endorsed the JDBC API and are developing products using JDBC [51]. For the first GDSS prototype developed at the ICG the world leader in relational databases Oracle was chosen. After setting up an Oracle database server on an SGI Indy the database schema as discussed in section 4.3 and the Magellan meta-data set were brought into the system. The last hurdle to take was to build a connection between the Java applet and the Oracle database. Because the Oracle developers did not have their native JDBC driver ready we chose a three tier solution provided by a third party, Weblogic Inc. [52]. Since the first RDBMS was introduced in the 80s [53] three different architectures have developed, called the 1,2 and 3-tier architecture.

The multitier architecture (also called three-tier) extends the standard 2-tier client-server by placing a multithreaded application server between the client and the DBMS. Clients communicate with the DBMS through the application server, using high-level, vendor-independent requests and replies. The application server is responsible for executing those requests, and makes calls as needed into each DBMS vendor's client library to communicate with DBMSes. Properly applied, multitier architecture can solve each of the problems of the traditional two-tier client-server.

The chosen Weblogic product, which consists of the jdbcKona/Oracle native JDBC driver and the jdbcKona/T3 application server, is a three-tier solution. It breaks the common two-tier architecture by introducing an application server, which actually handles the database specific communication part and can use any native JDBC driver. The advantage of the chosen three-tier architecture is that through this application server every JDBC and ANSI capable relational DBMS can be accessed without having any vendor specific libraries at the client site. These libraries reside at the application server and are executed on incoming high-level, vendor-independent queries of the client. Finally a scenario as illustrated in Figure 6 was built up. The

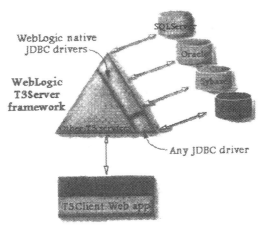

Figure 6: The Weblogic jdbcKona/T3 three-tier architecture. The platform independent client can pass high-level, vendor independent queries to the Weblogic T3 server. From there the queries are passed to the specific relational DBMS using a native library, which resides at the server side. (Graphic taken from Weblogic. Inc. <URL: http://www.weblogic.com>)

Weblogic application server itself is completely written in Java and hence platform independent. Currently Weblogic delivers native JDBC drivers for Oracle[3], Sybase and MS SQL Server.

Based on this installed software a user client was created which is able to connect to any JDBC capable DBMS. The basic design goals of the client include standardized access to any ANSI SQL relational DBMS, access to Magellan FBIDR meta-data, download of quicklooks which should be stored as BLOBs (Binary Large OBjects) within the database, platform independence and object oriented approach. According to these design goals a fully Java written client was designed and programmed. The Magellan meta-data and one exemplary quicklook were stored in the Oracle database. Using JDBC and the Weblogic T3 product it can access any ANSI compatible RDBMS including the Oracle server. Furthermore the client supports a comfortable platform independent GUI illustrated in Figure 7. It can be executed with each Java capable browser, e.g. Netscape, MS Explorer or Hot Java [77].

The main buttons of the GUI are responsible for connecting/disconnecting from the database, querying the Magellan database and downloading a test quicklook stored in the Oracle database. An additional test query button demonstrates some JDBC facilities by showing how to insert, update and delete records in a test table. For querying the Magellan database an additional input window is raised (shown in the upper left corner), where the user can specify his query by the coordinates of the point of interest, the input of the search area and the desired cycles he wants to retrieve. The results themselves are displayed in three result windows shown at the left border of Figure 7 separated by cycles. The test quicklook which can be downloaded is shown in a separate window as well as in the display area of the applet, where currently the prototype logo is displayed.

4.5 Data Experiments

Three kinds of data experiments took place at our institute. The first kind of trials were performance measurements taken between our institute and the IAIK using the HP netperf tool. In the second and third pilot trial the Vienna Center for Parallel Computing (VCPC) took part. The second experiment demonstrated a video conferencing tool over the new ATM backbone and in the last trial we tested an application sharing tool between the two sites Graz and Vienna. In the following subsections these experiments are described in more detail.

4.5.1 Performance Measurements

Performance measurements were taken using the testbed shown in Figure 4 and the HP Network Performance Tool Version 2.1 [54]. Using two types of protocols, FORE IP (FIP) and Classical IP (CIP), the throughput of UDP and TCP/IP over ATM was tested. The platforms and hardware used for the experiments is given in Table 2.

---

[3] the Oracle JDBC driver is also contained on the Oracle Web Server CD

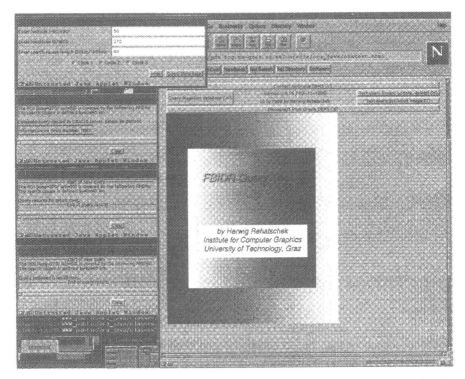

Figure 7: GUI of the first GDSS prototype. The Java applet GUI supports querying for FBIDR meta-data within a region of interest using JDBC and an Oracle database. The results are displayed according to the chosen cycles in three different result windows referring to cycle 1 to 3. In addition a test quicklook can be downloaded, which is stored as a BLOB in the database.

Platform	Operating system	ATM HW	Supp. Protocols	Max. transf. speed
SUN Sparc-10/512	Sun OS 4.1.3	SBA-200	CIP, FIP, LANE	155 Mbit/sec
SUN ULTRA-1	Solaris 2.5	SBA-200	CIP, FIP, LANE	155 Mbit/sec
PC Pentium-100	Windows NT 3.51	PCA-200PC	FIP, LANE	155 Mbit/sec
SGI Power Chall. L	IRIX 6.2	VMA-200	CIP, FIP, LANE	155 Mbit/sec

Table 2: Overview of the hardware used in the performance data experiments. All adapter cards are from FORE systems.

In order to interpret the results a theoretically available bandwidth was calculated. The overhead of the protocol data units (PDU) were taken into consideration rather than the overhead caused by the OS and inter-process communication. For physical transmission SONET STS-3c/OC-3c framing was used. In general the overhead for OC-Nc is given by N * section overhead + 1 * path overhead + N * line overhead. The section and the path overhead is 9 bytes[4], the line overhead is 18 bytes [35]. The entire overhead for N=3 is 90 bytes. The available bandwidth for the physical layer is given in equation (1) [31].

$$BWphy = \frac{FramePayload}{FrameLength} * Bitrate = \frac{2430-90}{2430} * 155.520 = 149.760 \, Mbit \, / \, \sec \quad (1)$$

The next layer is the ATM layer, which maps incoming cells into the for ATM typical 48 bytes payload and 5 bytes header cell format [31]. The overhead caused by the ATM layer is given in (2).

$$BWatm = \frac{CellPayload}{CellLength} * BWphy = \frac{48}{53} * 149.760 = 135.632 \, Mbit \, / \, \sec \quad (2)$$

The VMA-200 and the SBA-200 adapter card allow transmission of two implementations of IP over ATM's Adaptation Layer 5 (AAL5) using the same physical interface as follows: Classical IP (CIP) using Q.2931 signaling [55] and FORE IP using Fore's Simple Protocol for ATM Network Signaling (SPAN). CIP uses IEEE 802.2 LLC/SNAP (Logical Link Control/SubNetwork Attachment Point) encapsulation and the default IP MTU (Maximum Transmission Unit) of 9180 bytes with 9140 bytes payload. FORE IP uses a broadcast ARP (Address Resolution Protocol) and no encapsulation which results in a MTU of 9188 bytes and a maximum payload of 9148 bytes [56]. According to [57] and a TCP and IP header á 20 bytes an available bandwidth for TCP/IP over ATM using CIP and FIP can be calculated as given in equations (3-6). The CPCS (Common Part Convergence Sublayer) is used in the AAL5 to encapsulate the data coming from BSD socket API interface and has a variable length between 1 and 65535. The implementation of the AAL5 adds 36 (CIP) or 28 (FIP) bytes overhead which results for both, CIP and FIP in a packet length of 9216 bytes (MTU + overhead).

$$BWip(CIP) = \frac{CIP\_MTU}{CPCS\_PDU} * BWatm = \frac{9180}{9216} * 135.632 = 135.102 \, Mbit \, / \, \sec \quad (3)$$

$$BWtcp(CIP) = \frac{CIP\_MTU - TCPhdr - IPhdr}{CIP\_MTU} * BWip = \frac{9180-20-20}{9180} * 135.102 = 134.513 \, Mbit \, / \, \sec \quad (4)$$

$$BWip(FIP) = \frac{FIP\_MTU}{CPCS\_PDU} * BWatm = \frac{9188}{9216} * 135.632 = 135.220 \, Mbit \, / \, \sec \quad (5)$$

$$BWtcp(FIP) = \frac{FIP\_MTU - TChdr - IPhdr}{FIP\_MTU} * BWip = \frac{9188-20-20}{9188} * 135.220 = 134.631 \, Mbit \, / \, \sec \quad (6)$$

---

[4] The OC-Nc framing differs from OC-N framing in the way that in OC-Nc framing just one synchronous payload envelope is sent and therefore just one path overhead. Using OC-N framing the path overhead would be N x 9.

Measurements were taken using point to point connections on an unloaded network from the SGI Power Challenge to the SUNs, and the PC. Four kinds of tests were taken as follows: UDP using FIP and CIP, TCP using FIP and CIP. The TCP tests were executed with the following parameters: for UDP the send/receive socket size was varied from 9000 to 9896 bytes with an increment of 128 bytes. For TCP the send/receive socket was constant 53248 byte (maximum buffer socket size for SUNs), the message size was varied between 512 and 65535 bytes with an increment of 12 bytes. The summary of the measurements is shown in Table 3.

	Maximum throughput in Mbit/sec			
Platform	TCP/FIP	TCP/CIP	UDP/FIP	UDP/CIP
SGI⇔SUN Sparc 10	52.75	46.83	55.37	62.34
SGI⇔SUN Ultra-1	54.43	73.26	78.18	91.25
SGI⇔PC Pentium 100	48.24	N/A	30.65	N/A

Table 3: Summary of TCP and UDP over ATM performance results using the HP performance measurement tool. For details concerning parameters and test environment see text.

4.5.2 Video Conferencing

In order to test ATM's capability of carrying data traffic as well as video and voice we used a public domain video conferencing tool (VIC) [58] in combination with a Video Audio Tool (VAT) [59] and a white board [60]. To coordinate the video sessions the public domain Session Directory (SD) [61] tool was used. All tools are designed for

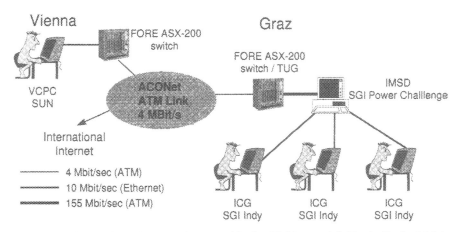

Figure 8: Video conferencing scenario as used in the GDSS test trial. Physically the ICG in Graz was connected via the 155 Mbit/sec ATM backbone of the University of Technology, Graz. From there a 4 Mbit/sec ATM link was set up to Vienna. The VCPC was connected via an ASX-200 switch located at the University of Technology, Vienna.

using the Internet M-Bone (Multicasting Backbone) [62] and still work with low bandwidth environments usually provided by the Internet. For the pilot trial the scenario illustrated in Figure 8 was used.
This pilot trial was carried out for the DIANE [63] EU project, which evaluates distributed annotation of scientific work and multimedia services on heterogeneous platforms connected via an ATM network backbone. The trial was used to annotate and explain program code of the VCPC via the white board tool.

In conclusion the tools turned out to be very useful for setting up a geographically dispersed conference, especially when the available bandwidth is low. The maximum video transmission bandwidth was limited in the tested version to 1 Mbit/sec, hence the full available bandwidth of 4 Mbit/sec could not be utilized by one session. This caused problems for the smooth transmission of the video, because for smooth transmission e.g. with MPEG a minimum bandwidth of 1.5 Mbit/sec is required [64]. Another disadvantage was the limitation of the white board for postscript file import up to a size of 32.768 bytes.

4.5.3 Application Sharing

This pilot trial was performed to test the capabilities of an ATM backbone for usage of shared X-Windows applications with GUIs. Because of their immersive graphical interfaces these applications consume very high bandwidth, which can be provided by an ATM network. For this trial a public domain tool called X-wedge was used [65, 66, 67, 68]. X-wedge allows X-Windows applications to be shared among heterogeneous UNIX platforms, currently including SUN, SGI and soon Windows NT[5]. X-wedge does not just simply distribute the visualization among the other users but allows the setting of access rights. The owner of an application can allow the participants to access his local running program as if they were sitting at a local workstation. Remote processing becomes available. This pilot was also carried out within the DIANE project (see section 4.5.2). So the same scenario as illustrated in Figure 8 was used. In the trial two applications - one from the VCPC, one from the ICG - were shared in order to (1) explain how to work with the SW to the other party (2) to demonstrate the functionality of the SW package.

The first version of X-wedge for SGIs suffered from many problems including incorrect color representation and several crashes. The current distribution (Version 5.1) proves to be stable and nearly got rid of the problems mentioned before. Just the colors still look strange, but this problem is caused by the different color tables of SGIs and SUNs and does not occur among homogenous platforms. Version 5.1 was tested with Netscape and a running applet - which used to cause big problems to the X-wedge tool - within the scenario shown in Figure 8. All in all the test was a success, the ATM backbone proved to meet the bandwidth requirements.

---

[5] The portion depends on the availability of a Windows-X server, since X-wedge can just share X-applications

5 Conclusions and Future work

The initial steps of the GDSS project resulted in three deliveries including the design of a global system architecture, the set up of a proper network backbone and the implementation of a prototype [77]. The system architecture is an open one, main design goals are usage of international standards, high-speed network backbone, graphical user interface, platform independent client software and usage of the same query interface for all connected archives.

The current GDSS prototype can be extended by using all available Magellan FBIDR meta-data including the feature table and the FMIDR information. Furthermore the gap information could be used for intelligent querying image coverage in a region of interest or to visualize the complete coverage of the Magellan image data set on the planet's surface. In addition the FMIDR and the image table could be used to display quicklooks of the current search area.

Future steps include further investigations in ATM technology, extending existing client SW by new features like remote data processing, cost management and migration to an object oriented DBMS as soon as an appropriate standard is available. This project will be started in the first quarter of 1997. A digital Venus atlas is being developed in a parallel project [76].

The stimulus for the GDSS project drives from the planetary image processing requirements, as reflected in NASA's PDS. However, we are optimistic that ideas, concepts and software of the GDSS can also be applied to international Earth-observation projects such as the European Union's Center for Earth Observation (CEO) or NASA's Mission to Planet Earth (MTPE), and national programs such as Austria's project MISSION (Multi-Image Synergistic Satellite Information for the Observation of Nature) [78]. And we hope that the ideas, software and experiences of the GDSS can provide benefits to fields other than remote sensing.

6 Acknowledgments

Parts of this work are funded by Project 1/task 4 (Parallel Processing Strategies For Large Image Data Sets) of the Austrian "Fond zur Förderung wissenschaftlicher Forschung" (FWF) research program "Theory and applications of digital image processing and pattern recognition" and by the Space Research Programme of the Austrian Academy of Sciences. A warm thank you to my girlfriend Vanessa Keitel, who generously helped me to proofread this paper.

7 References

[1] NASA PDS (Planetary Data System), Central Node, Nov. 1995, <URL: http://stardust.jpl.nasa.gov>

[2] EMDN (European Magellan Data Node) at the ICG (Institute for Computergraphics) Technical University Graz, Resources on Magellan Mission to planet Venus, Dec. 95, <URL: //www.icg.tu-graz.ac.at/PDS/emdn.html>

[3] P. Poehler, Digital Workstation for Venus Topographic Mapping. SPIE Vol. 1943, State-Of-The-Art Mapping 1993, pp 45-56.

[4] W. Walcher, H. Rehatschek, Design of a Distributed Database for the Magellan Data Set from Planet Venus. IGARSS 95, IEEE Proceedings catalog number 95CH35770, Vol. II, 1610-1612

[5] H.J. Lotz-Iwen, Earth Observation User Information Services in Germany. EEOS Workshop on European data networks and earth observation user information services; proceedings; Document refs: CEO/130/1994; March 1995, pp 359-363, <URL: http://pid.da.ap.dlr.de/de/ISIS/index.html>

[6] W. Snyder, Meta-data management and the VISTA System. HICSS-27 Conference of System Sciences, DSS/Knowledge-Based Systems, Vol.III, 418-427, Jan.1994

[7] W. Snyder, Visual Interface for Space and Terrestrial Analysis. NASA book publication of the AGU Special Session on Visualization, May 1993

[8] EWSE (European Wide Service Exchange), testbed of the European Commission's "Center for Earth Observation" (CEO), Nov. 96, <URL :http://ewse.ceo.org>

[9] CORE Software Technology, Inc.,"ImageNet" - testsite and information page, Nov.96, <URL: http://coresw.com>

[10] EOSDIS-IMS (Earth Observing System Data and Information System Information Management System), Homepage, Nov. 96, <URL: http://harp.gsfc.nasa.gov:1729/eosdis_documents/eosdis_home.html>

[11] F. Mungo, O. Arino, AVHRR CD-Browser Ionia 1km net browser. Proc. of the 6th international symposium on physical measurements and signatures in remote sensing, ISPRS, Val d'Isere, 17-21 January, 1994

[12] S. Nativi, D. Giuli, P.F. Pellegrini, A distributed multimedia information system designed for the Arno Project. ISPRS Journal, Vol. 50 Nr.1 1995, pp. 12-22

[13] Canada Center of Remote Sensing and Earth Observation, Landsat/spot browser, Nov. 96, <URL: http://www.ccrs.nrcan.gc.ca/ccrs/imgprod/imgprode.html>

[14] European ATM Trial, Homepage, Nov. 96, <URL: http://www.com21.com/pages/eap.html>

[15] Magic (Multidimensional Applications and Gigabit Internetwork Consortium), Homepage, Nov. 96, <URL: http://www.magic.net>

[16] BAGNet, Bay Area Gigabit Netwok at San Francisco Bay, Homepage and papers, Nov. 96, <URL: http://george.lbl.gov/BAGNet.html>

[17] Canarie, Canadian Network for the Advancement of Research, Industry and Education, Homepage, Nov. 96, <URL: http://www.canarie.ca/eng/main.html>

[18] ATM page - collection of ATM related topics by Herwig Rehatschek, homepage, Nov. 96, <URL: http://www.icg.tu-graz.ac.at/herwig/research/ATM/ATM.html>

[19] PIA (Planetary Image Access), NASA service to provide users easy with publicly released images from various Solar System exploration progrms, Nov. 95, http://acheron.jpl.nasa.gov/PIA/PIA.html

[20] SSV (Solar System Visualization), NASA/JPL homepage, Nov. 96, <URL: http://www-ssv.jpl.nasa.gov/~srl/SSV7SSV_home.html>

[21] CEOS IDN (The Committee on Earth Observation Satellites International Directory Network), Homepage, <URL: http://gcmd.gsfc.nasa.gov/ceosidn/>

[22]ANSI/NISO Z39.50-1992, American National Standard, Information Retrieval Application Service Definition and Protocol Specification for Open Systems Interconnection, 1992. ftp://ftp.cni.org/pub/NISO/docs/Z39.501-992/www/Z39.50.toc.html, hardcopy from NISO Press Fulfillment, P.O. Box 338, Oxon Hill, Maryland 20750-0338; phone 800-282-6476 or 301-567-9522; Fax: 301-567-9533.

[23] ANSI/NISO Z39.50-1995, Information Retrieval Service and Protocol, homepage, Nov. 96., <URL: http://lcweb.loc.gov/Z3950/agency>

[24] L. Vaughn, Client/Server System Design & Implementation. ISBN: 0-07-067375-6, McGraw Hill, 1994

[25] S. Mullender, Distributed Systems. Addison Wesley, ISBN: 0-201-62427-3, 1994

[26] F. Kappe, G. Pani, F. Schnabel, The Architecture of a Massively Distributed Hypermedia System. Internet Research: Electronic Networking Applications and Policy, 3(1):10-24, Spring 1993

[27] F. Kappe, Hyper-G: A Distributed Hypermedia System. Proc. INET'93, San Francisco, California, pages DCC-1 - DCC-9, Internet Society, August 1993

[28] Hyper-G/HyperWave, Homepage, Nov. 96, <URL: http://www.iicm.tu-graz.ac.at>

[29] F. Kappe, A Scaleable Architecture for maintaining Referential Integrity in Distributed Information Systems. JUCS, Vol.1 No.2, Feb. 28, 1995

[30] R. Händel, M. Huber, S. Schröder, ATM Networks - Concepts, Protocols, Applications. ISBN: 0-201-42274-3, Addison Wesley, 1994

[31] M. de Prycker, Asynchronous Transfer Mode. ISBN: 3-930436-03-5 Prentice Hall, 1994

[32] D. McDysan, D. Spohn, ATM - Theory and Application. ISBN: 0-07-060362-6, McGraw-Hill, 1994

[33] H. Saito, Teletraffic Technologies in ATM Networks. ISBN: 0-89006-622-1, Artech House, 1994

[34] ESA/ESRIN EEOS Workshop on European Data Networks and Earth Observation User Information Services. Marino (Rome), 13-15 December 1994, CEO/130/1994 ESRIN EEOS-WS1-001-FP-1.0

[35] M. Sadiku, Metropolitan Area Networks. ISBN: 0-8493-2474-2, CRC-Press, 1995

[36] Hedrick C., 1987. „Introduction to the Internet Protocols". Rutgers State University of New Jersey,
<URL: http://NIC.MERIT.EDU/introducing.the.internet/intro.to.ip>

[37] IETF (Internet Engineering Task Force), Working group for internet standards, Nov. 96, <URL: http://www.ietf.cnri.reston.va.us/home.html>

[38] M. Perloff, K. Reiss, Improvements to TCP performance in High Speed ATM Networks. Communications of the ACM, Vol. 38 No. 2, Feb. 1995

[39] L. Hongqing, S. Kai-Yeung, T. Hong-Yi, Chinatsu I., Hiroshi S., TCP Performance over ABR and UBR Services in ATM. Proc. of International Phoenix Conference on Computers and Communications, Sept. 1995

[40] D. Sisalem, H.Schulzrinne, Congestion Control in TCP: Performance of Binary Congestion Notification Enhanced TCP Compared to Reno and Tahoe TCP. Proc. of International Conference on Networks and Protocols (ICNP), Columbia Ohio 1996, <URL:http://www.fokus.gmd.de/step/employees/sisalem.signature.html>
oder <URL: http://www.icg.tu-graz.ac.at/herwig/Research/ATM/ATM.html>

[41] CIP (Catalogue Interchange Standard), CEOS Working Group on Data Protocol Task Team, CIP Release A specification document (Version 1.2) from march 1996, <URL: ftp://styx.esrin.esa.it/pub/od/CIP/>

[41] D. Stevenson, N. Hillery, G. Byrd, Secure Communications in ATM networks. Communications of the ACM, Vol. 38 No 2, February 1995, 46-53

[42] ITU-T, International Telecommunication Union, Homepage, Nov. 96, <URL: http://www.itu.ch/>

[43] ATM Forum, User Network Specification Version 3.1. ISBN 0-13-393828-X, Prentice Hall, 1996

[44] Siu K., Jain R., A Brief Overview of ATM: Protocol Layers, LAN Emulation, and Traffic Management. unpublished, 1995, download: <URL: http://www.icg.tu-graz.ac.at/herwig/Research/ATM/ATM.html>

[45] Magellan Meta-data description, European Magellan Data Node (EMDN) homepage, Nov. 96
<URL: http://www.icg.tu-graz.ac.at/PDS/Magellan_Meta.html>

[46] Vanhelsuwé L., Phillips I., Hsu G., Sankar K., Ries E., Rohaly T., Zukowski J., Mastering Java. Sybex, ISBN: 0-7821-1935-2, 1996

[47] Java Soft, Homepage, Nov. 1996, <URL: http://java.sun.com/>

[48] Arnold K., Gasling J., Java die Programmiersprache. Addsion Wesley, ISBN: 3-8273-1034-2, 1996

[49] Back S., Beier S., Bergius K., Majorczyk P., Professionelle Java Programmierung - Leitfaden für Entwickler. Thomson Verlag, ISBN: 3-8266-0249-8, 1996

[50] R. Onvural, Asynchronous Transfer Networks: Performance Issues. ISBN 0-89006-662-0, Artech House 1994

[51] JDBC (Java Data Base Connectivity) from Sun Microsystems, Homepage, Nov. 1996, <URL: http://splash.javasoft.com/jdbc/>

[52] Weblogic Inc., JDBC driver provider for Oracle, Sybase and MS SQL Server, Nov. 96, homepage,
<URL: http://www.weblogic.com>

[53] Codd E.F., A relational model of data for large shared data bases. Comm. ACM, 13, 377-387, 1970

[54] Hewlett-Packard Company, Netperf: A Network Performance Benchmark, Revision 2.1, <URL: http://ww.oup.hp.com/netperf/Netperfl'age.html>

[55] Laubach M., Classical IP and ARP over ATM. Hewlett-Packard Laboratories, IETF RFC 1577, January 1994, <URL: http://www.es.net/pub/rfcs/rfc1577.txt>

[56] Fore Systems Inc., ForeRunner SBA-100/200 ATM Sbus Adapter User's Manual. May 1995

[57] I. Andrikopolous, T. Örs, M. Matijasevic, H. Leitold, S. Jones, R. Posch, TCP/IP Throughput Performance Evaluation for ATM Local Area Networks. Proc. of the IFIP TC6 „Fourth workshop on Performance Modeling and Evaluation of ATM Networks", Illkey/Great Britain, July 1996, pp. 72/1 - 72/11

[58] Video Conferencing Tool (VIC) Version 2.7a29, Public domain tool implemented by the Network Research Group at the Lawrence Berkeley National Laboratory,
<URL: http://www-nrg.ee.lbl.gov/vic/>

[59] Video Audio Tool (VAT) Version 4.0a2, Public domain tool implemented by the Network Research Group at the Lawrence Berkeley National Laboratory, <URL: http://www-nrg.ee.lbl.gov/vat/>

[60] White Board Tool (WB) Version 1.60, Public domain tool implemented by the Network Research Group at the Lawrence Berkeley National Laboratory, <URL: http://www-nrg.ee.lbl.gov/wb/>

[61] Session Directory (SD) Version 1.18, Public domain white board tool developed by University College London (UCL), <URL: ftp://ftp.ee.lbl.gov/conferencing/sd/>

[62] M. Macedonia, D. Brutzman, M-Bone - An Overview. Unpublished, Nov. 96, <URL: http://www-mice.cs.ucl.ac.uk/mice/mbone_review.html>

[63] DIANE (DIstributed ANnotation Environment), EU project description VCPC, Dec. 96, <URL: http://www.vcpc.univie.ac.at:80/activities/projects/DIANE.html >

[64] H. Rehatschek, N. Sharda, A Classification of Networked Multimedia Systems and Applications of ATM Technology to Networked Multimedia Systems. Submitted to Multimedia Tools and Applications, Kluwer Academic Publishers, Aug. 1996

[65] Broadband Exchange for Trans-European Usage (BETEUS), ETH-Zürich, project description, Dec. 96, <URL: http://www.tik.ee.ethz.ch/Projects/projects.html >

[66] T. Walter, M. Brunner, B. Plattner, BETEUS - Broadband Exchange for Trans-European Usage. Proceedings of the IEEE Symposium on Data Highways, Bern, Switzerland, October 1995

[67] S. Znaty, T. Walter, M. Brunner, J. Hubaux, B. Plattner, Multimedia Multipoint Teleteaching over the European ATM Pilot. Proc. of the 1996 Int. Zürich Seminar on Digital Comm.: Broadband Comm., Lecture Notes Computer Science 1044, February 1996

[68] T. Gutekunst, D. Bauer, G. Caronni, B. Plattner, A Distributed and Policy-Free General-Purpose Shared Window System. IEEE/ACM Transactions on Networking, Vol. 3, No. 1, February 1995.

[69] S. Das, Deductive databases and logic programming. ISBN 0-201-56897-7, Addison-Wesley, 1992

[70] T. Olle, The CODASYL approach to Data Base Management. John Willey Sons Publ. Company, 1980

[71] H. Maurer, Hyperwave - The Next Generation Web Solution. ISBN 0-201-40346-3, Addison Wesley, 1996

[72] W. Kim, Introduction to object-oriented databases. ISBN 0-262-11124-1, MIT Pr., 1990

[73] C. Delobel, Databases : from relational to object-oriented systems. ISBN 1-850-32124-8, International Thomson Publ., 1995

[74] SQL Standards, homepage, Dec. 1996, <URL: http://www.jcc.com/sql_stnd.html>

[75] H, Mannila, The design of relational databases. ISBN 0-201-56523-4, Addison-Wesley, 1992

[76] W. Walcher, Design Aspects of Information Systems for Planetary Image Data. PhD thesis, Institute for Computer Graphics, University of Technology, Graz-Austria, Jan. 1997

[77] FBIDR Query Tool Applet, Dec. 1996, Applet access page, <URL: http://pds.icg.tu-graz.ac.at/~oracle/ora_java/oratest.html>

[78] MISSION (Multi-Image Synergistic Satellite Information for the Observation of Nature), Dec. 96, Homepage, <URL: http://www.icg.tu-graz.ac.at/mission>

[79] Eurimage, homepage, Jan. 1997, <URL: http://www.eurimage.it/>

An Object-Oriented Model for a Visual Information System of Patient Folders

Fernando Ferri, Patrizia Grifoni, Fabrizio L. Ricci

ISRDS - CNR, Via C. De Lollis, 00185 Roma, Italy.

Keywords: Patient Folder, Object-Oriented Modelling, Data Modelling

Abstract

In this paper we present an information model – the MIC/MIE model – able to represent the heterogeneous data composing a patient folder related to clinical activities.

The management of clinical data is a complex task. In fact, patient related information reported in patient folders is a set of heterogeneous documents accessed by different user having different goals (e.g. choice of a therapeutic strategy, quality assessment) and may be rendered by means of different modalities.

Data can originate from direct observations made by physicians like in the case of objective examination. In other cases physiologic phenomena are captured by means of the involved electrical activity (like in the case of heart or brain activity), whereas anatomical structure details are obtained by means of radiologic techniques.

The proposed model adopts an object-oriented approach. It is able to represent multimedia nature of patient folder data. This model has an adequate flexibility for adapting the most different clinical environment. It allows the physician to structure the information needed for his patient folder without employing a programming language.

Finally we show some features of the CADMIO system, a tool for designing patient folder management systems, based on this model.

1 Introduction

In a clinical information systems, the patient folder is the main source of clinical information. Its main purpose is to document the medical activity performed in relation to each admission. Several heterogeneous categories of users of patient folders can be identified, for example: physicians, nurses, administrators, political authorities, researchers and patients themselves.

The concept of patient folders has now been effectively extended to include documents theoretically beyond their original scope. They range from documents referring to operations and actions performed on the patient during or after his stay to admission documents, discharge reports, records of information transmitted by the medical and nursing staff to the patient (including duplicates of X-ray examinations).

The literature has suggested various models for the organisation of information contained in the patient folder. Each one of them stresses some aspects of the patient or of clinical activity to the detriment of others. Wide-ranging analysis of the literature has allowed us to classify patient folders as basically: person-oriented, organised according to the classic systematic approach to the patient; problem-oriented, according to Weed's original formulation [1, 2] or to one of the subsequent modifications thereof [3, 4]; symptom-oriented, in which information is organised according to diagnostic records based on a symptom or specific syndromic pattern; or finally, decision-oriented [5].

In the real practice, a patient folder is more than just a structured set of documentary information. It is also a professional tool made up of a collection of miscellaneous documents which are used in different ways for different purposes [6-8].

It is possible to identify five different ways in which the information contained in a patient folder is used, and they, in turn, correspond to five different classes of processes: the clinical process, the ward activities, the epidemiological context, the tutorial activities, the legal aspects.

This means that the same piece of information may be used and analysed by different perspectives and may be rendered by means of different modalities [8]. Let us consider a X-ray examination, for example:

- in the context of a clinical process, an X-ray is used for diagnosis, prognosis and therapy. It must therefore be represented in its complete multimedia dimension as an image associated with a text (the report) and, if necessary, with the informal exchange of information between the clinician and the radiologist. In [9-12] it is possible to see the prominence of the patient folder on the clinical process.

- in the context of ward activity, an X-ray is essentially an action to which other actions are connected, prior thereto (request, booking, patient preparation) or as a consequence thereof (exchanges of information between ward physicians and radiologists, forwarding of the report, reading of the report). The dominant aspect is thus action management through controlled language: therefore the X-ray will be represented by an identifier and by a state which allow us to determine the phase of the management process in which it is located. In [13-15] it is possible to see the prominence of the patient folder on the ward activity.

- in an epidemiological context, an X-ray represents a procedure which has a certain value in terms of its effects on health or of resource consumption. It requires aggregations of a statistical type; hence data codified according to systems that are standard for different users and stable in the course of time. The X-ray will thus be represented by a code. In [16-18] it is possible to see the prominence of the patient folder on the epidemiological aspects.

The goal of this work is to define an object-oriented model of a multimedia patient folder. In the last years, object-oriented data models (and consequently analysis and design methodologies) have appeared and several applications have been implemented in clinical domain [19-22]. Also public bodies like NHS in the United Kingdom are gradually introducing these methodologies in their modelling activity [23]. The proposed model has been employed for implementing an environment for the design of patient folders: the CADMIO system. CADMIO has been used in two departments of the University Hospital of Rome, one department of the "Careggi" Hospital of Florence and one department of the Hospital of Ancona. It allowed the realisation of different patient folder management systems. The systems were configured by the users themselves (physicians of the hospital) and can share data thanks to the common base functionalities.

In the next paragraph we define the Local Entity Dictionary (LED) as the set of information and concepts used by physicians of the same unit. In the third paragraph we introduce an object-oriented model which represents information in the medical domain, whereas in the fourth one we show how to employ it in populating a particular Local Entity Dictionary. In the fifth paragraph we define the Generalised Scheme of a Patient Folder, the Scheme of a Patient Folder and the Instance of Patient Folder. Finally we illustrate some features of the prototype developed.

2 Local Entity Dictionary

In order to represent the complexity of the information of the patient folder, here we shall no longer speak of data (representations of single pieces of information), but of more complex *entities* (the medical concepts represented and the sets of their properties, irrespective of memorisation and representation) which, according to their use, may assume different aspects and roles.

When describing the patient status in the patient folder all physicians of a ward use a set of common entities. We define such a set: Local Entity Dictionary (LED).

In order to define an entity, it is essential to identify the context in which the entity is used, the properties which describe it and finally the management of its properties.

The purpose of constructing the LED is not only to provide a simple classification of the entities that have to be managed, but also to provide a tool to describe their logical organisation.

The relations designed to represent the logical organisation of these entities are the classic ones of generalisation (IS_A) and aggregation (PART_OF). Entities are organised by levels of abstraction which returns each of them to more general entities which specify increasingly general properties and application-oriented contexts.

Moreover, each entity may be broken down into more elementary entities and, vice versa, various entities may be aggregated in more complex entities. It is possible to attribute different properties and characteristics to these aggregations depending on whether they are the consequence of the temporal, spatial or semantic composition of information.

3 The Model

The MIC/MIE (Medical Information Category / Medical Information Elements) model allows a physician to define the Local Entity Dictionary (LED), i.e. the local entities constituting the patient folder and their logical organisation. The awareness of the existence of a natural hierarchical system among the entities which express the various medical concepts is at the basis of the definition of the MIC/MIE model. For example, if we consider a part of the patient folder such as case history or anamnesis in order to model it, we may define a hierarchy of entities, each identifying a set of data about the patient, but also consider this hierarchy a tool for organising data pertaining to the patient's case history. The hierarchy shown in Figure 1 may be regarded as representative of both aspects.

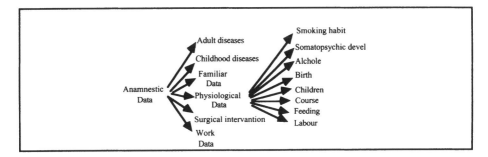

Fig. 1. A fragment of a possible hierarchy of entities

Depending on his own particular specialisation, a physician might want this part of the patient folder to be organised differently (for example, with greater or less detail given to the entities which may be part of case history or anamnesis) in such a way as to highlight the aspects which interest him most. And these concepts might of course be extended naturally to each and every other part of the patient folder.

The aim of enabling the physician to define the set of entities which he wishes to fit into the patient folder together with definition of how they must be organised was achieved by defining a prototypical class which combines every common feature of the entities contained in the patient folder. Starting from this root prototypical class, it is possible to define a hierarchy of classes. Such a hierarchy has to match the entity hierarchy represented in the patient folder.

The properties of the prototypical class are described by variables and metavariables. A metavariable [24] is a variable which can only assume types as a value. It is possible to model class hierarchies by assigning types to metavariables.

3.1 The Medical Concept Prototype

The central aspect of the MIC/MIE model is the root prototypical class defined Medical Concept Prototype (MCP). This class represents the conceptualisation of medical entities through primitive terms designed to represent their static and dynamic properties. The Medical Concept Prototype represents the general aspects common to all entities. Itemising these aspects, it is possible to reproduce any entity of the LED designed to represent a set of patient folder data. It thus stressed information about the organisation of reality and serves to interpret the semantics of abstractions.

Through its metavariables and variables, the Medical Concept Prototype (MCP) encompasses all the relevant aspects capable of classifying the entity itself semantically, temporally and functionally.

Medical Concept Prototype Metavariables

Metavariables represent all the properties of entities to which a value cannot be directly assigned. For example "media" (text, image, sound) is assigned to the type "type" in the MCP.

Such properties differ from entity to entity according to the set of values they assume. As the entity hierarchy develops, they must , therefore, be defined with the greater accuracy. It is necessary , in fact, to define first a type: only later is it possible to assign a value to it. In the case of a tool for the execution of a diagnostic examination, it is necessary first to define the types of suitable tool, then it is possible to specify a model of that type of tool available on the market. The different Prototype metavariables are described below.

The *Type* is used to characterise the original nature of the entity, just the way the performing operator registers it in the conventional medium (patient folder etc.). Entities are heterogeneous and hard to organise in a detailed pre-established way. Depending on their nature, they may be classified, as structured data, free texts, images or biosignals, or as a combination thereof. According to Type, the methods applied to the graphical management of entities change. For example, if the entity can be visualised by a text, it is necessary to associate text management methods (writing, editing etc.) with the information. Likewise, if the entity can be visualised by an image, it is necessary to manage that entity by means of other methods which enable the user to read, memorise and process the image.

By *Format* we mean entity registration procedures. Once each entity has been defined for a computerised patient folder, it should be memorised in a format which will retain the informative content of the initial information. A certain number of registration formats have been identified for each Type. It is of course important to use the most efficient format in terms of memory occupation and processing.

By *Representation*, we mean all the various entity presentation procedures. Besides, "data entry", "data retrieve" and the possible processing of the entity are also worthy of note. Since the same entity may be presented in different ways according to the aspect to be displayed, the development of different presentation procedures highlights the different peculiarities of the entity (or of a certain set of entities). The system customises the presentation of entities according to their characteristics, semantics, and importance and to the role of the user requesting the information.

The *Performing Operator* must be a person (a physician or a nurse). Even when the entity is produced directly by a piece of equipment (as, for example, in the case of the spectrophotometer for blood tests), the performing operator may be identified as the subject who, under his own responsibility, certifies the acquisition and validity of the entity. The performing operator always has a name to identify him and unambiguously qualify him/her, and he is authorised to write in the patient folder. The metavariable "Performing Operator" permits management of the medico-legal aspects of the entity, allowing us to specify the person who certifies the veracity of the entity in the patient folder. On the basis of the professional position held by the person inside the facility defined, the system can authorise or prevent his writing on any given entity in the patient folder.

The *User* may be a physician or a nurse or another health care professional This metavariable allows us to identify the professional category or categories allowed to access the entity. Once the professional category or categories of persons who are allowed access to a certain entity have been defined, all the individuals belonging to such categories may have access to it, unless the entity has been specifically forbidden to some of the possible users.

By *Tool* we mean the physical means we use to record the entity. In a physical examination using the classic method of inspection, palpation, percussion and auscultation, the tool used is the sensory system of the physician himself. The tool is also described with a name which identifies it. For each class of tools a set of interface is identified to acquire information for the patient folder directly from the tool which generates it.

Life Cycle. Any entity has its own life cycle and may pass through different states which identify it and characterise it. Let us consider the following example: the chest X-ray to be executed for a given patient. It must be requested, then agreed upon [25]. The exam is then performed and a report must be written about it. The entity evolves through various states before it is completely defined. The definition of the type of evolution provides a solution to the management aspects of the entity itself. By means of the metavariable "Life Cycle", it is possible to synchronise activities among the various professional categories inside a single department and among different departments. For example, it is possible to establish the time and means in which an entity may be transferred from the person who has produced it (e.g. the radiologists) to the person who uses it (e.g. the clinician).

Medical Concept Prototype Variables

The variables describe constant characteristics common to all the entities which make up the patient folder. Values may thus be assigned to them directly without passing through the intermediate phase of definition necessary in the case of metavariables.
Medical Concept Prototype Variables are:

The *Unit of Measurement*, which identifies the system of measurement used.
The *Legal Values*, which define the range of validity of the entity according to the system of measurement. The variable "Legal Values" allows the validation of the data introduced by the user.
The *Coding System*, which specifies which of the internationally defined coding systems is used to codify a given entity.
The *Code*, which indicates the code assigned to the entity in the coding system used. Through the coding system and the code, it is possible to check whether different terms have been used to indicate the same entity.

By means of these two variables it is possible to have a terminology support integrated with CADMIO for synchronisation of the various terms used in different department.

3.2 Metaclasses

Modelling the entities of the patient folder is a complex activity. It is not enough to define all the entities from the Medical Concept Prototype to highlight relations between such entities adequately. This is why intermediate levels have been introduced between the Medical Concept Prototype and the entities instanceable with the facts which form part of a patient folder. These intermediate levels offer pointers about the organisation of information in the patient folder. On the other hand, they modulate the applicability of properties to more or less vast entities. To characterise these levels, it was necessary to introduce the concept of the metaclass. In fact, forcing the principle that an object is an instance of a class, but that a class may also be seen as an object, it is possible to introduce the concept of the metaclass as a class of classes. In our case, metaclasses are entities which refer to more general medical concepts and hence may identify more than one entity referring to more specific medical concepts.
As in many object-oriented database [24, 26], the notion of metaclass used here is not limited. Besides, as a class of other classes, the metaclass is also seen as the root of a

hierarchy of classes and, as such, it acts as a superclass. This is why we use the link IS_A to represent the relationship existing between the metaclass and its classes.

To model the entities which are part of a clinical folder, having only one level of metaclasses is not enough. A hierarchy of metaclasses is necessary. Entities are, in fact, naturally organised by levels of generalisation and, in this scale, the prototype represents the most generic entity.

By specifying the characteristics of the prototype (that is, by assigning types to metavariables) the physician can define a hierarchy of metaclasses.

The process of definition of metaclasses starting from the medical concept prototype does not occur through extension of variables and methods to the variables and methods of ancestors, but rather by assigning types to metavariables and/or limiting the types that can be assigned to them. The metaclasses on the lower levels of the hierarchy thus posses a lower number of metavariables and/or a lower number of types is assigned to each metavariable. Finally, the metavariables cannot be instanced by the physician who compiles the patient folder.

This process also forces a process of method overriding. By imposing one type rather than another to metavariables, we can specialise the method to process the type assigned to the metavariable .

For example, if we assign the type "tomograph" to the metavariable "tool", the metaclass will inherit the methods for data acquisition of such an instrument.

Metaclasses are referred to as Medical Information Categories (MIC). They generally constitute the description of fragments of medical knowledge shared by different medical specialists. Examples of Medical Information Categories are: Anamnestic Data, Diagnosis, Diagnostic Examination, Histological Examination, X-ray Examination, X-ray Image and Report.

3.3 Classes

Classes are instances/subclasses of metaclasses. They identify groups of objects with similar (variable) properties, identical behaviour (methods) and the same semantics. For these objects the same relations are valid as for other objects, whether they are part of the patient folder of John Smith or Tom Brown, and whether the object is the first or the nth in the class in John Smith's (J.S.) patient folder.

For classes too, the process of definition starting from metaclasses does not occur through an extension of variables and methods to the variables and methods of ancestors, but rather by assigning types to metavariables and/or limiting the types that can be assigned to them.

Classes are referred to as Medical Information Elements (MIEs). MIEs describe the medical information common to the users of a department. Medical Information Elements are directly instanceable with data about the patient. There are some constraints on the assignation of types to metavariables. In fact, only some of the types defined can be assigned to each metavariable. For example, to the metavariable "Type" it is possible to assign the types "Integer", "String", "Image Class", "Text Class", "Hypertext Class", "Multimedia Class" and "Hypermedia Class". The entity in question has to be managed according to the type assigned to the metavariable. Hence, if the type is "Integer", it is possible to verify whether the value assigned (eg.,40) to the concept (eg, the "Serum Bilirubin Level") fits into a certain domain (eg, 30-70). Examples of Medical Information Elements are: "Thyroid Nodule", "Serum Bilirubin Level Test", "Chest X-ray", "Abdominal Pain", "Hydrosalin Infusion".

3.4 Instances

Instances are the facts which describe the patient's clinical condition and history and constitute patient folder. Whereas metaclasses and classes are defined as part of the description of the organisation of the patient folder, instances are defined as part of its instantiation. Instances are high-level MIEs which assume a spatial identity (the patient) and a temporal identity (the time in which the information is produced). Values compatible with the types defined in MICs and MIEs are assigned to the variables generated directly or through the metavariables. Examples of facts are: "Total Serum Bilirubin Level of J.S. on 20/11/93", "Serum of Indirect Bilirubin of J.S. on 20/11/93", "Chest X-ray of J.S. on 22/11/93", "Hydrosalin Infusion of J.S. on 21/11/93".

3.5 Formal Definition of MCP, MIC, MIE

In the following we give a formal definition of MCP, MIC and MIE.
A MCP defines a conceptualisation of medical entities through primitives terms. It represents aspects common with all entities. In particular it contains relevant aspects for classifying the entity semantically, temporally and functionally. It can be formally defined as follows:

Definition: MCP is a 5-pla

$$MCP = <Id_p,\ M_p,\ V_p,\ Typ_p,\ Val_p>$$

where Id_p is the identifier of MCP, M_p is a set of metavariables defined by MCP, V_p is a set of variables defined by MCP, Typ_p is a set of functions that associates all possible types to each metavariable, Val_p is a set of functions that associates all possible values to each variable.

The MIC is defined on: a set of metavariables, each formally defined on a values domain that points out the MIE variables and a set of variables, each formally defined on a value domain, that is, a set of allowed values for that variable. The MIC is structured on a hierarchy of classes (organised according to generalisation-specialisation links). It can not exist an instance of a MIC at level of clinical folder.

Definition: A MIC is a 5-pla

$$MIC = <Id_C,\ M_C,\ V_C,\ Typ_C,\ Val_C>$$

where Id_C is the identifier of MIC, M_C is a set of metavariables defined by MIC, V_C is a set of variables defined in MIC, Typ_C is a set of functions that assign to each metavariable type or set of types. Such types must belong to the set of allowable types to the metavariable.

Val$_C$ is a set of functions that assigns to each variable a value that belongs to the set of allowable values.

The MIE represents the instance of the highest specialisation level of MIC. A MIC has to be defined preliminary of the definition of each MIE. The MIE for each variable of MIC assumes one and only one value and for each metavariable assumes one and only one variable.

Definition: A MIE is a 3-pla

$$MIE = <Id_E, \ V, \ Val >$$

where: Id_E is the identifier of MIE, V is the set of MIE variables, *Val* is the set of functions that selects a sub-set of the set of allowable values.

The following paragraph shows how the definition of a local dictionary of entities uses MIC and MIE.

4 Definition of the LED

The description of the organisation of the local entities which constitute the application definition universe results from identification of the properties of information and the contexts in which it is used. It involves an accurate definition both of properties and of the procedures of presentation and manipulation of these entities.
Let us consider an example of how it is possible to define the LED using the MIC/MIE model. The Medical Concept Prototype is the class which provides the basis for the construction of the whole hierarchy and is the class supplied by the developed prototype described in the following paragraph.
If we consider the entity hierarchy represented in Figure 2 it is possible to define the entity "Chest X-ray" through the following steps:

Definition of the MIC Diagnostic Examination beginning from the MCP.
Definition of the MIC X-ray examination beginning from the MIC Diagnostic Examination.
Definition of the MIE Chest X-ray beginning from the MIC X-ray examination.

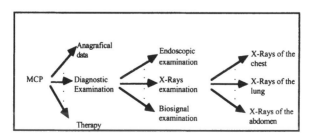

Fig. 2. An example of LED definition using the MIC/MIE model

The number of levels between the MCP and MIE depends only on the degree of property detail which the user wishes to obtain in his definition of entities according to his vision of reality. It is also necessary to consider the costs of a very detailed hierarchy in relation to possible advantages in functional terms. Through the steps set out above it is possible to define the following entities: Diagnostic Examination, X-ray Examination and Chest X-ray and a hierarchical relationship among them.

Figure 3 shows how it is possible to specify the entity "Diagnostic Examination" starting from the MCP (the metavariables are shown in bold type, while the MEdical Concept Prototype variables are underlined). The figure does not include the operations defined from time to time for the MICs and MIEs.

```
MIC Diagnostic examination OF MCP
   life cycle={time in which the need for a datum arose,
         time of request,
         expected time for the execution,
         time of real execution,
         time of first "on line" gross evaluation,
         foreseen time for the reporting of the results,
         time of report writing, time of report sending,
         time of reading of the report by the physician,
         time in which datum looses clinical interest};
   type;
   format;
   rendering;
   tool;
   performing operator = {physician};
   user;
   coding system;
   code;
   measure unit;
   admissible values;
END;
```

Fig. 3. A simple formalism specifying the entity "Diagnostic Examination" starting from the MCP

According to the formal definition of MIC for "Diagnostic examination" we have:

Id_C = Diagnostic examination

M_C = {life cycle, type, format, rendering, tool, performing operator, user}

V_C = {coding system, code, measure unit, admissible values}

Typ_C = {T1, T2, T3, T4, T5, T6, T7} where:

   T1: life cycle → {time in which the need for a datum arose, time of request, expected time for the execution, time of real execution, time of first "on line" gross evaluation, foreseen time for the reporting of the results, time of report writing, time of report sending, time of reading of the report by the physician, time in which datum looses clinical interest}

T2 : type → Φ
T3 : format → Φ
T4 : rendering → Φ
T5 : tool → Φ
T6 : performing operator → {physician}
T7 : user → Φ

Val_C = {V1, V2, V3, V4} where:

V1: coding system→ Φ
V2 : code→ Φ
V3 : measure unit→ Φ
V4 : admissible values→ Φ

In the definition of the Medical Information Category it is possible to note how not all metavariables have been assigned. In the subsequent definition, "X-ray Examination" is still a MIC defined starting from "Diagnostic Examination" (the types assigned to the metavariables "Life Cycle" and "Performing Operator" remain defined), for which it is also possible to define the metavariables "Tool" (teleradiograph) and "User" (physician), to limit the metavariable "Performing Operator" (Radiologist), the variable "Coding System" (ACR), and which has not "units of measurement" or constraints on "Admissible Values" (see Figure 4).

MIC X-ray examination **OF** Diagnostic examination
   life cycle = {time in which the need for a datum arose,
          time of request,
          expected time for the execution,
          time of real execution,
          time of first "on line" gross evaluation,
          foreseen time for the reporting of the results,
          time of report writing, time of report sending,
          time of reading of the report by the physician,
          time in which datum looses clinical interest};
   type;
   format;
   rendering;
   tool = {teleradiograph};
   performing operator = {radiologist};
   user = {physician};
   coding system = ACR;
   code;
   measure unit = {no};
   admissible values = {no};
END;

Fig. 4. The definition of a MIC

The formal definition of X-ray examination MIC of fig. 4 identifies:

Id_C = X-ray examination

M_C = {life cycle, type, format, rendering, tool, performing operator, user}

V_C = {coding system, code, measure unit, admissible values}

Typ_C = {T1, T2, T3, T4, T5, T6, T7}   where:

    T1: life cycle → {time in which the need for a datum arose, time of request, expected time for the execution, time of real execution, time of first "on line" gross evaluation, foreseen time for the reporting of the results, time of report writing, time of report sending, time of reading of the report by the physician, time in which datum looses clinical interest}

    T2 : type → Φ

    T3 : format → Φ

    T4 : rendering → Φ

    T5 : tool → {teleradiograph}

    T6 : performing operator →{physician->radiologist}

    T7 : user → {physician}

Val_C = {V1, V2, V3, V4}   where:

    V1: coding system→ ACR

    V2 : code→ Φ

    V3 : measure unit→ {no}

    V4 : admissible values→ {no}

Figure 5 shows how it is possible to specify the concept Chest X-ray Examination beginning from X-ray Examination.

MIE X-ray examination of the chest **OF** X-ray examination
  life cycle = {time in which the need for a datum arose,
      time of request,
      expected time for the execution,
      time of real execution,
      time of first "on line" gross evaluation,
      foreseen time for the reporting of the results,
      time of report writing, time of report sending,
      time of reading of the report by the physician,
      time in which datum looses clinical interest};
  type = {hypermedia class};
  format = {typeFormat9};
  rendering = {typeRendering16};
  tool = {teleradiograph};
  performing operator = {radiologist};
  user = {physician};
  coding system = ACR;
  code = 125.56.32;
  measure unit = {no};
  admissible values = {no};
END;

Fig. 5. The definition of a MIE

A Standard Chest X-ray must be considered as an entity - a sequence of images and an attached report describing them. It must be certified by a specialist radiologist, but may be used by a variety of specialists (surgeons, clinicians etc) or General Practitioners, though not by nurses. The type of tool which produces this entity is the teleradiograph.

Chronologically speaking, it is possible to define various states (from the moment of the request) through which the entity passes prior to begin definitively stored in a historical archive.

According to the formal definition of MIE, X-ray examination of the chest is defined as follows:

d_E = X-ray examination of the chest

V = {time in which the need for a datum arose, time of request, expected time for the execution, time of real execution, time of first "on line" gross evaluation, foreseen time for the reporting of the results, time of report writing, time of report sending, time of reading of the report by the physician, time in which datum looses clinical interest, hypermedia class, typeFormat9, typeRendering16, teleradiograph, radiologist, physician, coding system, code, measure unit, admissible values}

Val = {V1, ..., V20} where:

  V1: time in which the need for a datum arose $\rightarrow \Phi$
  V2: time of request $\rightarrow \Phi$
  V3: expected time for the execution $\rightarrow \Phi$
  V4: time of real execution $\rightarrow \Phi$
  V5: time of first "on line" gross evaluation $\rightarrow \Phi$
  V6: foreseen time for the reporting of the results $\rightarrow \Phi$
  V7: time of report writing $\rightarrow \Phi$
  V8: time of report sending $\rightarrow \Phi$
  V9: time of reading of the report by the physician $\rightarrow \Phi$
  V10:   time in which datum looses clinical interest $\rightarrow \Phi$
  V11:   hypermedia class $\rightarrow \Phi$
  V12:   typeFormat9 $\rightarrow \Phi$
  V13:   typeRendering16 $\rightarrow \Phi$
  V14:   teleradiograph $\rightarrow \Phi$
  V15:   radiologist $\rightarrow \Phi$
  V16.   physician $\rightarrow \Phi$
  V17:   coding system $\rightarrow$ ACR
  V18:   code $\rightarrow$ 125.56.32
  V19:   measure unit $\rightarrow$ {no}
  V20:   admissible values $\rightarrow$ {no}

TypeFormat9 and typeRendering16 are also types for, respectively, memorising and rendering information. The example also shows how all the metavariables are instanced in the MIE.

```
FACT X-ray examination of the chest of J.S. of 22/11/93 OF X-ray examination of
the chest
  time in which the need for a datum arose =12/11/93;
  time of request =14/11/93;
  expected time for the execution =22/11/93;
  time of real execution =22/11/93;
  time of first "on line" gross evaluation =22/11/93;
  foreseen time for the reporting of the results =24/11/93;
  time of report writing, time of report sending =24/11/93;
  time of reading of the report by the physician =24/11/93;
  time in which datum looses clinical interest =22/1/94;
  hypermedia class = instance n. 4356 (object identity);
  typeFormat9 = coordinates in memory;
  typeRendering16 = coordinates on video;
  teleradiograph= Siemens AS1, GE X23;
  radiologist = Drudi Mario;
  physician = Consorti Fabrizio;
  coding system = ACR;
  code = 125.56.32;
END;
```

Fig. 6. The definition of a fact (instance)

Once he has constructed the entity hierarchy, the physician has defined the pattern of his patient folder. The process of entity specification represented in the patient folder allows us to specify metavariables completely and hence to represent classes exclusively with variables and no longer with metavariables. The subsequent phase is represented by the instancing of the medical folders of patients, specifying the single facts about each one of them.

The facts are the objects which constitute the patient's medical folder.

Figure 6 shows how it is possible to instance the concept "Chest X-ray Examination".

5 Formal Definition of a Generalised Scheme of a Patient Folder, Scheme of a Patient Folder, Instance of Patient Folder

In the following we give a formal definition of generalised scheme of patient folder, scheme of patient folder and instance of patient folder.

Several generalised scheme of patient folder can be defined in the database.

Such schemes can be updated versions of the same folder, or they can be different patient folders used for different objectives. For example, it is possible to have a generalised scheme of a patient folder for admittance to the hospital, another scheme for the follow-up, another scheme for the drug testing.

Definition: A *generalised scheme S of patient folder* is a set of MIE associated to a hierarchy of MIC univocally indicated by an identifier. Formally, a generalised scheme of patient folder is a 4-pla.

$$S = <Id_D,\ IC,\ IE,\ IA>$$

IC is a set of identifiers of MIC belonging to the hierarchy, *IE* is a set of identifiers of MIE belonging to the hierarchy. *IA* is a set of specialisation links that define the hierarchy of MIC and the links between MIC and MIE.

Definition: A specialisation link is formally defined as a 3-pla

$$ia= <Id_1,\ Id_2,\ L>$$

where Id_1 is the identifier of a MIC, Id_2 is the identifier of a MIC that represents a specialisation of MIC identified by Id_1, or is the identifier of MIE that instanties the MIC identified by Id_1, L is the function that maps each metavariable of MIC in a subset of the set of allowable types for a metavariable.

On each generalised scheme of a patient folder we can create an instance of the scheme and adjust it to the characteristics of the folder of each patient. In fact, every patient follows a clinical path completely different from all others with different clinical information data.

Definition: A *scheme Sc of patient folder* is a 5-pla

$$S c = <Id_S,\ Id_D,\ IC_c,\ IE_c,\ IA>$$

the identifier (Id_S) of the patient folder scheme Sc, the identifier (Id_D) of the general scheme of a patient folder S on which it is defined. The subset IC_c of a set of MIC (IC) assigned to the hierarchy that define the general scheme of a patient folder S, the subset IE_c of a set of MIE (IE) identified by the general scheme of a patient folder S (with identifier Id_D). *IA* is the set of specialisation links that define the hierarchy of MIC and the links between MIC and MIE.

Now we give the definition of instance of patient folder

Definition: An *instance of patient folder* defined by a scheme $S\ c$ for a single patient is a 3-pla

$$Cc = <Id_{CC},\ S c,\ D>$$

where Id_{CC} is the identifier of the instance of patient folder, Sc represents the scheme on which the instance is defined and D is the function which assigns a value to each variable defined in MIE that make up the patient folder.

5.1 Graphical representation

To show the concepts of generalised scheme of a patient folder and of scheme of a patient folder previously defined we give a simple graphical representation. The suggested model consists in representing a database of patient folders through a direct and acyclic graph containing three types of nodes:
a) node MCP;
b) node MIC;
c) node MIE.

In the following are showed the connecting rules of the G graph representing a database of patient folders.

1) R1   MCP node is the root node of the graph;
2) R2   A MIC node can be connected to MCP node , to one or more MIC nodes
3) R3   At least one MIC node must be connected to MCP node
4) R4   A MIE node must be connected at least to a MIC node

The minimum graph G assigned to a database of patient folders is represented in Figure 7.

Following (Figure 8) we give an example of a database of patient folders represented through a graph. Therefore, we indicate the MCP node, the hierarchy of MIC nodes, MIE nodes, the general scheme of a patient folder and the scheme of a patient folder. The graph of Figure 8 identifies the *generalised scheme S of patient folder*.
MCP is explicitly denoted in Figure 8. MIE are represented by nodes with italic character. MIC are represented by the remaining nodes of the graph.

Fig. 7. The minimum graph for a set of patient folder

The *scheme Sc of the patient folder* defined on the *general scheme S* is represented by the graph in Figure 9. Note that the graph of Figure 9 is a sub-graph of Figure 8.

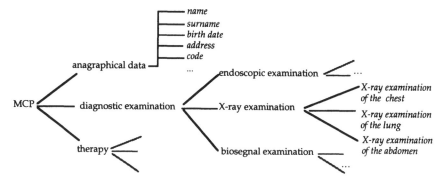

Fig. 8. The graph of the general scheme S of patient folder

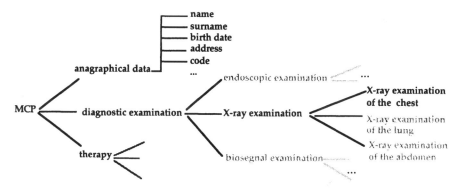

Fig. 9. The graph of the scheme Sc of the patient folder

6 The implementation of the system

Starting from the abstract categorisation of the clinical data, a prototype has been implemented. Such a prototype allows the physicians to describe the clinical data which form his patient folder model.

This description is used by the system in order to build a patient folder according to the user requirements. The name of this prototype is CADMIO (Computer Aided Design of Medical Information Objects) and it has two main features. It gives the user the capability of defining his own patient folder model, by specifying which information belong to the patient folder and how they have to be structured. This feature is useful to the user in organising those clinical data view he mostly needs.

The second feature is the dynamic management of the interface that, in the consulting phase and at user's request, makes him able to escape from the rigid structure given to the information in the physician's patient folder model definition.

In fact, during the data input/output, it is possible that the user doesn't want to use the clinical data views defined in the patient folder model. If that is the case, the system sets up dynamically the new clinical data views required from the information selected by the user and the recognition of the user's needs.

6.1 The Architecture

Physicians do not always share the same concepts in managing information on their patients. Whereas some parts of a patient folder are more constant (sections like "personal data" and "present history"), other parts strongly depend on the physicians' specific interest and specialty.

The tool that we describe in this paragraph allows medical users to choose the concepts to be present in their target application starting from a default configuration. It generates a customised patient folder management system by means of a friendly interface and without the need of a programming language. The system automatically created can be effectively employed for reporting and storing clinical cases. It will be always possible to modify its structure according to subsequent needs.

The tool supports multimediality, managing texts and images in an integrated way. The impact that such an integration may achieve on the users is not to be stressed here. We plan to incorporate bio-signals and voice annotation in future releases.

Object-oriented design allows to encapsulate behavioural features into classes of objects and propagating them by means of the inheritance mechanism (e.g.: from "endoscopic exam" to "duodenoscopy"). This capability is exploited in the interface management, with respect to data presentation and manipulation requirements.

The overall architecture of the CADMIO system is composed by the following five modules:

A) patient folder designer;
B) multimedia patient folder manager;
C) presentation manager;
D) user interface;
E) user-models manager.

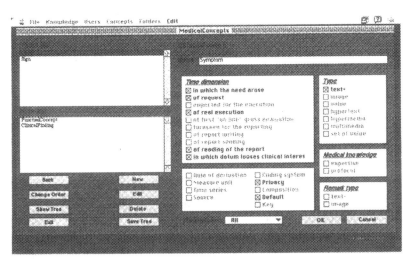

Fig. 10. The patient folder designer interface

Three of these modules (A, C, D) are relevant in order to show how the system allows the physician to model his view on clinical data and how he set up his patient folder.

The *patient folder designer* allows the definition of the patient folder information's organisation, according to the requirements specified by one or more physician; moreover it allows to describe each of the informational contents of a patient folder.

This definition process starts from the MCP (the only class initially available). During the definition process, the user uses the window displayed in Figure 10 in order to specify the hierarchy and the characteristics of the concepts of the patient folder.

Hence, the user can define his own patient folder model without being constrained nor to a certain kind of pre-defined interaction, nor to a pre-defined interface, nor to an interface modifiable only just before an interaction session is to be started.

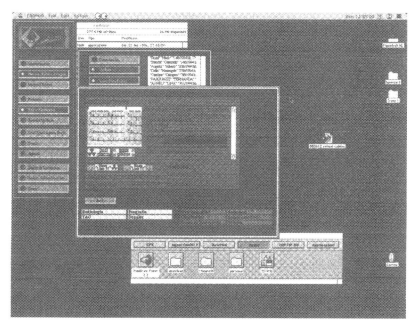

Fig. 11. A sample window created dynamically by the system during consultation

Being that medical data can be of different kinds, that they can be used to achieve different goals and, finally, they can be organised to constitute more than one patient folder model, depending on the context (i.e. department, ambulatory, administration...), the patient folder designer was designed to provide the physician with a tool capable of describing every significant characteristic of the medical data together with the organisation of the patient folder information.

The interface of the patient folder designer is extremely user-friendly. Only few days of training were required for the physicians who experimented the tool.

The *presentation manager* is the heart of the system. In fact, it determines the access to the patient folder contents having as inputs the output that originates from the user's queries through the interface module, and possibly the information originated from the user-modelling module (a module which capture objectives of the user in order to adapt the interaction of the system).

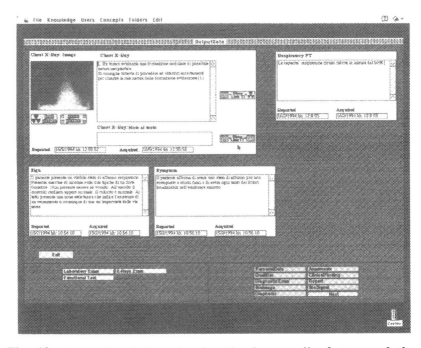

Fig. 12. A sample window showing the hypermedia features of the system

Accordingly to the user's requirements and to the information acquired through the user-modelling module, the dialogue management module decides the information the interface has to show to the user.

The *user interface* defines, starting with the specifications provided by the dialogue management module, the human-computer interface that will be likely used by the physician to acquire and visualise the contents of a patient folder.

This definition is made up dynamically, i.e. the system creates run-timc thc windows needed to show the user's required information.

In Figure 11 and in Figure 12 two windows are shown created by the system during a session. These windows present a part in which the patient data are shown and a part which allows to the user to browse other information contained in the patient folder.

The design and the development of a system capable of dynamically defining the human-computer interface, have required the analysis of the different possible data formats of a patient folder (i.e. text, images...), and the individuation of those objects involved in the constructive process.

As a result it was found that data in a patient folder can be represented either by means of text, or images , or values (numeric and / or alpha-numeric values); timely, those different data formats can be joined together into a more complex structure, e.g. the same data could be stored into a patient folder either as a text or image.

The current prototype allows the management of six different object-classes (i.e. alpha-numeric String; Image; Text; Value; Hypermedia; Hypertext; and Multimedia), each one associated to the corresponding data format. Each of these objects is created run-time by the system whenever it is necessary to manage the data related to the involved object-class.

7 The Clinical Testing of Cadmio

The system has been tested at the 4th Clinical Surgery Department of teaching hospital of the University of Rome "La Sapienza" ("Policlinico Umberto I"). The hospital is a 2500 beds structure, whereas the department is structured into three wards of 24 beds each, 8 different diagnostic services, a day hospital and an outpatient service for minor surgery.

In particular, we acknowledge the contribution of Fabrizio Consorti and Alessandra Piermattei.

The department has a laboratory for Medical Informatics as operative structure supporting research activities and the management of the clinical information system of the department itself. For these it was considered a good testing environment for a prototype application. Some of the physicians joining the project were skilled users of information technology, while others could be considered naïve users. This was particularly valuable in our opinion, since having the application tested only by expert users would have result in missing a critical evaluation of the real impact in everyday practice of the system.

Different models of folders were developed by five physicians who had not been involved in the design phase of CADMIO. Before these implementations took place, the selected physicians had some meetings with the technical partners of the project, during which the philosophy of CADMIO system was presented and discussed and a preliminary analysis of the relevant clinical information for each of the three testing environments was done.

No formal models of clinical information was produced and the physicians were left free to interact with the system to define the database of MICs and MIEs and to design the forms of their folder.

After the implementation of the folders, testing went on for two months, during which the applications were used to insert and access clinical information. At the beginning the system was used "off line", then the evaluating physicians started using CADMIO during clinical practice to store and retrieve clinical information. During this second phase some more changes were made both to the database scheme and to the folders structure, reflecting an evolution in the capability of the users to take advantage from the features of CADMIO system.

7.1 Evaluation of the basic concepts

After some initial difficulties in understanding terms and methods to which they are not used, the involved physicians agreed that the proposed way to represent medical information was expressive and useful, mainly because it let them free to define the structure of their own database in a rather simple way. As already mentioned, apart from a short period of training in the use of CADMIO system, neither guidelines nor methodology was given to design clinical databases.

Differences emerged between the more experienced and the more naive users with respect to the structure of the database.

While the expert ones proposed multi-level hierarchies, the naïve users defined simpler trees, in which Categories coupled the conventional sections of a medical record. After the first implementation, all the users made some changes to the structure of their clinical databases, making a more sophisticated use of the possibility of the hierarchy.

7.2 Evaluation of the patient folder definition module

The users had not difficulties in using the module to define their own scheme of MICs/MIEs.

A common request after the first period of testing was a more powerful tool to browse along the tree while designing it, especially if they were designing a complex hierarchy with more levels.

A window to show the position of an element in the tree was then added, together with "Previous level" and "Next level" buttons.

7.3 Evaluation of the dialogue management module

All the users started the experimentation using a rather "standard" format of folder, based on the usual sections of a traditional medical record.

Two users considered this approach satisfactory, while the others designed some customised forms and tested the direct browsing modality of access to data.

The problem of access to data was strongly stressed during the final discussion, especially by considering the medical added value aspects: an electronic patient folder should not be just the electronic copy of a paper-based medical record.

The highest value was assigned to the possibility of a very flexible, goal driven access to data, even if in our experimentation this awareness was related to the expertise of the user: more naive users tended to use a more traditional environment and one of the two physicians who at the beginning preferred the "default" mode of access to data, after two months of use of CADMIO system expressed the interest for a more advanced use of the system itself.

The possibility of establishing hypermedia link between MIEs was considered another very important functionality. From a clinical point of view this is relevant both for clinicians and for specialists dealing with imaging and biosignals.

In the first case, for example, it is interesting to have sentences of a report pointing to region of interest of an image, or vice versa. It helps in getting more of the clinical information content of an X-rays exam.

In the second case it may be useful to establish a connection across several exams by linking hypermedially regions of interest representing the same findings. These links can be powerful tools of browsing through the database.

8 Conclusions

In this work we started by analysing the clinical data and by the individualisation of the different uses of the clinical data in order to define a model which allows a physician to describe the structure of the information and the concepts which appear in the patient folder.

By means of this work we defined a modality to design and to construct a patient folder, implemented in the CADMIO system. The tool runs on Macintosh platform and has been developed using the Prograph® programming environment.

CADMIO system has been used in order to implement four different patient folders; the first one at the IV Semeiotica Chirurgica, the second one at the IV Clinica Chirurgica of the Policlinico 'Umberto I' of Rome, the third patient folder has been implemented and used at the Psychiatric Department of the Ancona Hospital and the fourth has been used at the Cardiologic Department of the "Careggi" Hospital of Florence. After the necessary training period, the involved physicians agreed that the proposed way to represent medical information was expressive and useful, mainly because it let them free to define the structure of their own database in a rather simple way. Differences emerged between the more experienced and the more naive users. While the first ones tended to implement more abstract hierarchies, with more levels, the latter ones tended to build simpler trees, in which Categories coupled the conventional sections of a medical record.

After having modelled the clinical data we are modelling the clinical organisation, the patient administration and the clinical processes in order to manage the synchronisation of the various activities of the different departments.

References

[1] Weed LL. Medical records that guide and teach. *New England Journal of Medicine.* 1968;12:593-600, 652-657.

[2] Weed LL. The Problem-Oriented Record as a basic tool in medical eductions, patient care and clinical research. *Ann Clin Res*, 1971:131- 134.

[3] Aranda JM. The problem-oriented medical records: Experiences in a community hospital. *Journal of the American Medical Association* 1974;229:549-551.

[4] Assimacopoulos A, Revillard C, Hermann H, et al. , An electronic notebook for problem oriented patient progress notes: testing a concept. In: Barber B, Qin D, Wagner G ed. *Proc MEDINFO 89*. Amsterdam: North-Holland, 1989:813-817.

[5] Acheson HWK. The Clinical Record as an Aid to Continuing Education in General Practice. *A Medical Self-Audit British Journal of Medical Education*, 1972;7:6-26.

[6] Stead WW, Borden R, McNulty P, Sitting DF. Building an Information Management Infrastructure in the 90s: The Vanderbilt Experiment. In: Safran C, ed. *Proc Seventeenth Annual Symposium on Computer Applications in Medical Care.* New York: MacGraw-Hill, 1993:534-538

[7] Heathfield HA, Kirby J, PEN&PAD (Elderly Care): Designing a Patient Record System for Elderly Care. In: Safran C, ed. *Proceedings Seventeenth Symposium on Computer Applications in Medical Care,* New York: McGraw-Hill, 1993: 129-133.

[8] Ricci FL, Pisanelli DM, Ferri F, Consorti F. Modeling the Structural and Behavioural Features of Medical Concepts: A Tool for Generating Multimedia

Patient Folders, In Barahona P, Veloso M and Brayant J ed. *Proc. of Medical Informatics Europe 94*, Berlin, Springer Verlag, 1994:470-474.

[9] Van der Lej J, van der Does E, Manintveld AJ. Critiquing Physicians Decision making using Data from automated Medical records. In *Proc Fourth Annual Symposium on Computer Applications in Medical Care*. New York: MacGraw-Hill, 1979:559-563.

[10] Evans RS, Classen DC, Stevens LE et al. Hospital Information System To Assess The Effects Of Adverse Drug Events. In Clayton PD ed. *Proc Seventeenth Annual Symposium on Computer Applications in Medical Care*. New York: MacGraw-Hill. 1993:161-165

[11] Rector AL , Helping with a humanly impossible task: integrating knowledge based system into clinical care. In: Hanmu J, Seppo L ed. Proc. *SCAI'89*. Tampere: Research Institute for Information Tecnlogy. 1989:560-572.

[12] Rector AL, Nowlan WA, Kay S, Goble CA, Howkins TJ , The Foundations of Computerized of the Medical Folders. *Methods of Information in Medicine*, 1992;30:179-186.

[13] Scherrer JR, Baud RH, Hochstrasser D, Osman R. An integrated hospital information system in general. *MD Computing*, 1990;7:253-61.

[14] Scherrer JR. , Nouvelles architectures destinées à des réseaux d'ordinateurs hospitaliers ouvrant le monde médical à plus de facilités de communications de tous ordres. *Schweizerische medizinische Wochenschrift*. 1991;49:204-216.

[15] Roger France FH, Santucci G ed. *Perspectives of Information Processing in Medical Application*, Berlin, Springer-Verlag, 1991.

[16] de Bliek R, Friedman CP, Wildemuth BM et al. Database Access and Problem Solving in the Basic Sciences. In Clayton PD ed. Proc. *Seventeenth Annual Symposium on Computer Applications in Medical Care*. New York: MacGraw-Hill. 1993:678-682

[17] Barnet GO, Winickoff R, Dorsey JL, Morgan MM and Lurie RS.Quality assurance through automated monitoring and concurrent feedback using a computer-based medical monitoring system. *Medical care* 1978;16:962-970.

[18] Whiting-O'Keefe QE, Simborg DW, Epstein WV, Warger A. A computerized summary medical record can provide more information than the standard medical record. *JAMA* 1985;254:1185-1192.

[19] Jean FC, Thelliez T, Mascart JJ, Degoulet P, "Object-oriented information system in the HELIOS medical software engineering environment", *Proceedings 16th Symposium on Computer Applications in Medical Care*, New York, McGraw-Hill, 1992.

[20] Dolin RH, "A High-Level Object-Oriented Model for Representing Relationships in an Electronic Medical Record", *Proceedings 18th Symposium on Computer Applications in Medical Care,* Philadelphia, Hanley & Belfus, 1994.

[21] Kuma H, Tsuchiya Y, "Database Access Method for Autonomous Distributed Total Hospital Information System and Its Object-Oriented Design", *Proceedings MEDINFO 95,* Amsterdam, North-Holland, 1995.

[22] Graeber S,"Object-Oriented Modeling Of Hospital Information Systems", *Proceedings MEDINFO 95,* Amsterdam, North-Holland, 1995.

[23] National Health Service Information Management Centre, *The Common Basic Specification,* London, Her Majesty Stationery Office, 1990.

[24] Lou Y, Ozsoyoglu M. LLO: An Object-Oriented Deductive Language with Methods and Method Inheritance. *SIGMOD Record,* 1991;20:198-207.

[25] Consorti F., Ferri F., Gargiulo A., Di Paola M., Passariello R., Pisanelli D.M., Ricci F.L., Zobel B., "Specification of the Medical Requirements", *Project Report MILORD A.2,* 1992.

[26] Kim W. Object-Oriented Databases: Definition and Research Directions. *IEEE Transaction on Knowledge and Data Engineering* 1990;2:327-341.

"Filmification" of Methods and Film Databases

Nikolay Mirenkov and Tatiana Mirenkova

The University of Aizu, Aizu-Wakamatsu City, Fukushima, 965-80, Japan
E-mail: nikmir@u-aizu.ac.jp

Abstract. A concept of a new type of information systems is proposed for consideration. This concept views film databases as a core of a problem-solving environment. Items of such databases are special-purpose animation or video films. These films are considered as units for data/knowledge acquisition and as communication units for computer-human dialog. Operations with data/knowledge units as well as retrieval operations on databases are specified by films, too. This paper presents briefly a basis of the VIM system project related to the development of a problem-solving environment (a special data warehouse) which integrates multimedia units for the specification of application algorithms (including data mining), experiment control strategies, and visualization of data generated during an experiment. Some details of a few films as well as the film management are also discussed.

1 Introduction

Visualization technology is becoming very important both for just computer-human interface and for data/knowledge analysis in many research fields and business. The source information for visualization is usually related to large amounts of various type data. Visualization at information retrieval processes and visualization of data content are two main topics being considered in this technology ([27, 20, 35, 25, 28, 3]).

Efficiency in processing large collections of data by providing sufficient and suitable reduction of the data search space and respecting performance characteristics of the available store system is obtained, in general, through indexing [17]. Storage structures for processing attribute-based data have been developed for many years, so a large spectrum of efficient techniques is now available. Now a substantial extension of the current indexing technology is expected for new types of queries, based on some notion of similarity. The similarity retrieval is a content-based technique. In general, it is related to the feature of color, shape, texture, location of the objects in image, as well as to image statistics, histograms, etc ([8, 21, 22, 39]). However, in spite of essential progress in developing this technique in particular and visual information systems as a whole, a lot of very difficult problems still remain. One of the reasons for the lack of essential successes for content-based retrieval is that during query, systems emulate a similar indiscriminate statistical pixel-to-pixel distance evaluation giving equal importance to all the pixels in the sample image [23]. Another reason is that some of systems retrieve images based on simple image features. Obviously, it is difficult to use only such features to represent the content of complex images. In order to develop efficient image information retrieval systems, it is necessary to use a knowledge-based approach. To perform sophisticated tasks, the knowledge base should be domain specific [37].

There are a variety of means for indexing imagery and the form of indexing which is most useful will depend on the application. No one index will satisfy all needs and in fact multiple indexes may be useful. To allow more flexible querying of the database, visual information systems will need to support queries on image metadata derived from image processing and computer vision algorithms, as well as more traditional metadata such as associated text and geographical locations [18]. Other problems are related to the following. Due to advances in data acquisition and computer technologies, many new applications involving video information retrieval systems are emerging. Video can provide more information than text, graphic, and image. The information related to the position, timing, distance, temporal and spatial relationships are included in the video data implicitly. Related change of objects between different frames provides much information about the behavior of these objects in the video. This frame-by-frame time series data is essential to many areas. A formal definition, content-based retrieval of video data is a retrieval process based on the understanding of the semantics of the objects in a collection [6]. It is also worth mentioning the following opinion [7]. To successfully apply the formal approach in visual information systems, the application domains must be very specific to yield interesting results. We must pay very close attention to the application domain.

We have only considered a part of visual information system problems. There are many other problems related to generality, complexity, performance, and semantic content. To summarize them, it may be possible to say that for the management of the problems we should use special types of computer-human dialog, knowledge-based approaches, domain specific techniques, multiple indexes, the semantics of the objects in a collection, etc.

Nobody doubts that step by step these serious problems will be more or less successfully resolved. However, it is important to note, that information retrieval even in a multi media database is only a part of a more general procedure in computer-human dialog. A multi-media database is only a part of a more general environment. Well-known visualization systems such as AVS, Explorers, apE, Khoros, etc. ([1], [11], [12], [26], [34], [38]) provide only simple data management support. So a number of projects are being developed to change them from pure visualization systems into data exploration systems. Built on top of AVS and other commercial packages, as well as on database management system technology, these project systems support essential interactive capabilities for data visualization (see, for example [24], [36]). Meanwhile, there is growing interest today in the development of problem solving environments which integrate both visualization and the computation process which generates the data [4]. In addition, the value of storing volumes of data depends on our ability to extract useful reports, spot interesting events and trends, support decisions and policy based on statistical analysis and inference, and exploit the data to achieve business, operational, or scientific goals [13]. Machines are still far from approaching human abilities in the areas of synthesis of new knowledge, hypothesis formation, and creative modeling [14].

In fact, we need a new type of information systems for designing information models of source systems, implementing these models on computer systems, and combining these within the system of the actual world, maintenance and management. We should also be able to verify the consistency of the actual world system and system product and constructing a total system in which both are a single unit. Therefore, a new base of algorithmic entities for the presentation of methods (method is a plan of action for solving a problem) should be developed.

As a rule, visual programming interfaces and visual languages allow the user to create visual programs by connecting modules written in a conventional programming language. The modules are depicted on the screen as nodes of a directed graph. Unfortunately, this popular approach is not always convenient for support of other application paradigms. It does not consider various features of algorithms, reality, and human abilities. We know often a lot of information about some events, phenomena, etc., however, we do not provide it because of the existing tools or because we do not consider the possible use of this information. Though it can be difficult to know, in advance, details of the use, as a rule there is no problem to making a scheme.

In other words, we should think about new possible paradigms and about new strategies to resolve or go round these problems. The idea behind our approach is a new type of information systems based on film machines where both data items and operations on data are represented by special-purpose animation or video films. In this approach a database is a set of films. Films are also used to specify application algorithms as well as data retrieval. Each film is a "shape" of computation. It based on a rather big piece of information about a class of algorithms. The basis of these films is close to ideas of algorithmic skeletons (higher order functions) ([9], [2], [5], [10], [15]). However, algorithmic skeletons leave a big gap between the reality and a human (a multi-channel being). So, we use algorithmic multimedia skeletons based on both mathematical and physical abstractions. To specify a problem and corresponding program for a computer, the user employs modifications of the system films, compositions of these films, and examinations of a film being created. A few click operations are enough to perform these transformations. The approach is being implemented within the VIM (VIsualization of Methods) project [29] - [32]. It is based on developing a filmbase, a subsystem of the filmbase management, and a library of scalable parallel procedures/templates supporting automatic programming and data visualization.

In this paper, we consider briefly the basis of our approach and describe a film database being developed for specification (programming) application algorithms. Some details of a few films as well as the film management are also discussed. We consider this as the first step in creating the film machines, that is a special type of data warehouses [19].

2 Animation films

We live in 4-dimensional space-time. Moving objects, color scenes, and various sounds as well as different kinds of hierarchies are elements of this reality. These should be the notions of new programming technologies; via these elements we should model the phenomena of reality. In the past, computer technologies did not allow us to use this approach. Natural objects and phenomena were split into very artificial components: images were separated from movement, sound from colors, data storage from data retrieval, etc. In addition, multimedia information were modeled by single-medium information, and multi-disciplinary models by single-disciplinary models, etc. This made normal people "blind or deaf" because they could use only their ears or eyes. It is important to note, that, as a rule, after the algorithmic partition all components are reduced to formulas (functions). But, what is a function? A relation, nothing more. The symbolic mentality builds long chains of inferences and abstracts them. Users must sit for hours and days pursuing a chain of logic. The majority of people, even mathematicians, don't use symbolism in their problem solving. They use images or other figurative means. So, we need a new type of abstraction combining mathematical and physical concepts. Physical abstractions should be used to represent relations based on space, time, and color/sound. A great part of the possible relations are represented by these natural means. Of course, conventional functions are also used. However, their role is drastically decreased. Some people like formal reasoning about system behavior on the basis of the formulas. In our case, we often prefer to watch or listen to system behavior, rather than to reason about it. So, in the VIM technology, the above-mentioned notions are represented by sets of animation films of special purpose types. The films are used as units for computer-human dialog and as units for knowledge/data acquisition. Each film is a series of frames (computational steps) displaying one or more parameterized sets of nodes and/or moving objects in multi-dimensional space-time. Each frame highlights a subset of these nodes/objects or rules of specifying this subset.

Each film defines a partial order of scanning of nodes or objects (and possibly, colors and sounds). Partial orders of scanning are defined via:

- positions of nodes and objects,
- trajectories of movement,
- external configurations of surrounding nodes and/or
- internal configurations (variable values) of nodes.

Partial orders can also be represented by movements of control structures, by changing the colors and sounds, as well as by sound durations. For example, "light" or "shadow" of scanning control structures can trigger or terminate computations on respective points or moving objects. As a rule, computation specified on different nodes (objects) of a frame is considered to be performed in parallel. Computation specified in different frames is performed sequentially. So, it is possible to say: *the shorter film the better*. Our approach assumes that color, sound, text, and movement join to create a total effect richer than that of any component alone, that the four parts are commensurate and reinforcing.

In this way we are trying to mobilize additional dimensions of human capacity. (Frankly speaking, we would also like to consider tactile, olfactory, and even gustatory information if corresponding sensors or synthesizers can be attached to computers.) As an example, let us consider a role of color and sound.

Of course, **colors** are used to have decorative effects. However, the most important aspects to point out are: different coloring of nodes (objects) to specify different operations, conditional type of computation on multi-colored nodes (objects), indication of the different hierarchical levels of computation related to composition of different animation films.

Sounds are used to provide "musical tags" for films and to enhance emotional effects. However, the most important aspects are to sound out: certain events (transitions between levels of hierarchy, passing some points in computational structures, reaching boundaries, etc.), homogeneous or heterogeneous types of computation, speed of moving objects and control structures, imitations of physical objects in terms of sound, relations between real-time and time of data processing, voice supports of frames, etc.

The user can transform the system frame series and the subsets of nodes/objects into a new series being more suitable for his plan of action. Then his task is to specify computations (to attach some arithmetic or logical expressions, sound or time) on the subsets or on the subset elements. For this purpose it may be necessary to use other films. So, the hierarchy of films are allowed.

Computers supporting such technology may be considered as film machines, where operations, data and knowledge are specified by films. Each film machine has an access to a set of databases. There should be system databases and application databases. From the very beginning each item of a database is a film, that is a unit of a multi-media format. You can watch and/or hear this film (you can even smell it if corresponding synthesizers are attached to the computer). Such a film is a large-grained unit of data/knowledge. **It is a dual object.** On the one hand, it is an abstract data type, on the other, it is a skeleton of an operation. To perform a search the user calls a film or creates a new film. To create a film the user may employ modifications of system films, compositions of these films, and examinations of a film being created. A few click operations are enough to perform these transformations. Films may be used to specify an algorithm/program. The program execution may also provide a film as a result. Watching and listening are main "operations" for data retrieval inside a film. If a film is very large, a content-based retrieval approach to select frames is used. To search a film the user may watch films about films and then employ a navigator on cover frames of films.

As the first step of our project, we are developing a system film database. In fact, it is a film database for visualization and sonification of application methods. As the second step, we will use this system film database for developing application film databases.

3 Algorithm classification

The important basis of our technology is a classification of application algorithms. As a rule, existent classifications of algorithms are just some enumeration of special cases. Often, they do not differentiate essential algorithms, and do not forecast new algorithms [16]. So we are developing our own classification. Though there are literally thousands of algorithms, there are very few design techniques. To extract these techniques and build a new classification, we exploit the fact of our living in 4-D space-time and our internalization of some features of the environment. Some details of this classification can be find in [32].

We guess that any method can be reduced to computational schemes on grids, trees, multi-stage and neural networks, pyramids, moving particles/objects and a few other structures. So, for coordinates of the classification space we use forms of multi-dimensional structures, types of partial scanning of nodes/objects in structures and types of possible parallel implementations. Our approach is a combination of mathematical and physical abstractions. It is a user-oriented approach. This classification is a basis for systematic selection and creation of the system notions and constructions. One film usually provides the information/knowledge for specifying a lot of application algorithms. For example, the divide-and-conquer model can be presented by one or a few animation films. Meanwhile, a great variety of the best and most widely used computer algorithms are reduced to this model. Nevertheless, this model is a partial case of more common computation on trees. Another example is the branch-and-bound model. It is a general-purpose enumerative technique for solving a wide range of problems in combinatorial optimizations, operation research and artificial intelligence. This model can also be presented by a few computational schemes on trees.

A similar situation obtains for algorithms on other structures. Film sections of our current classification are depicted by Fig. 1. It is worth mentioning that this classification supports multi-paradigm techniques that can cover both algorithms for computation and algorithms for control of computer experiments and/or visualization of results, data retrieval, etc. We believe that less than 100 films will be enough to have a general-purpose programming system of the next generation. Of course, the developing system will be open. In the next section we mention examples of the films and consider the basis of the film management.

4 Film management

We are developing five modes to manipulate films: watching, editing, composing, specifying and audio editing, as well as one mode to help users.

The watching mode allows the user to select some animation films from the filmbase and to see them. To select the films s/he can look through not only the list of titles in the dialog box of the corresponding section (Fig. 1), but also look at the first frames and hear musical (sound) patterns. After the selection, the user can choose the speed of the animation, switch on/off the sound, jump forward or backward, etc. S/he can also use non-stop or step-wise types of watching.

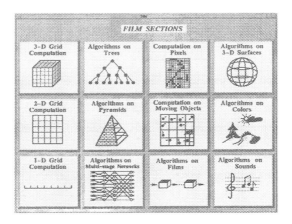

Fig. 1. Film sections of the system database

Fig. 2 depicts a frame of a film for computation on moving objects. This film shows that object positions are used to create a tree. After that, the computation is related to a partial order of scanning the tree nodes. It means that different frames highlight different subsets of the tree nodes.

Fig. 3 depicts a frame of a film for computation on 3-D grids. This film shows the movement of a 2-D grid of nodes along three dimensions: left-right, bottom-top, and front-back. Each frame highlights a position of this 2-D grid.

Each film provides some stable information/knowledge about data processing and predefines a skeleton of computation. The user should embed his algorithmic ideas into accessible skeletons or perform operations of "gene engineering", that is to change frame chains or compose them. The watching mode allows users to study existent computational schemes and immediately to use them. This is a manual-less technology.

The editing mode permits the user to edit the selected film as a whole or its separate frames. **Global** editing is performed by changing the speed (step size) of control structures, their initial positions, and the direction of their movement. This is easily done with a few clicks. Fig. 4 depicts the cover frame of a film for 2-D algorithms with a striped control structure. This control structure moves along the ↗ diagonal. So, different frames of the film are related to different positions of the structure. During the movement this structure provides a "special light" and a "special shadow" on grid nodes. The nodes under this "light" are pointed out to specify a computation. The nodes under this "shadow" are skipped for a step. For a global transformation of this film, the user can open an additional window of the editing mode. This window is used for watching and selecting other control structures. In this example, we can see a chessboard control structure.

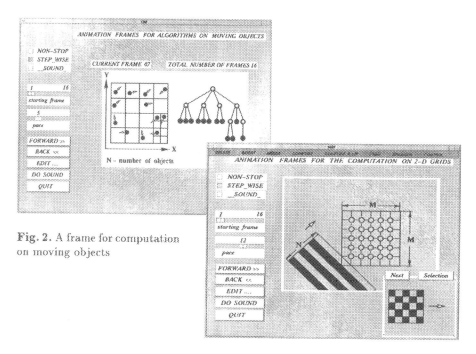

Fig. 2. A frame for computation
on moving objects

Fig. 4. A frame for 2-D algorithms

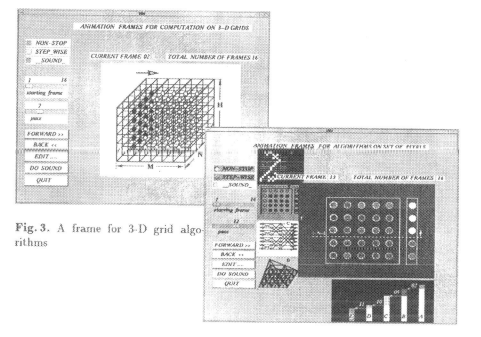

Fig. 3. A frame for 3-D grid algorithms

Fig. 5. A sample of the film hierarchy

One click operation is enough to replace one control structure by another. The **local** editing is also performed by a few click operations to delete a frame, to insert a frame from a special editing film, etc. This editing film is also displayed in the additional window of the editing mode. The user can watch it in a step-wise mode and select frames to insert into the film being created.

The composing mode allows the user to combine different films for creation a new film. In a sense, top-down and bottom-up compositions can be used. The top-down composition supports calls of other films to disclose computation in a node (or on a set of nodes) in detail. The user can watch frames of different levels of the hierarchy in different windows. The bottom-up composition provides a unification of a few films within the framework of one of the following models: parallel, pipelined, master/workers, and a few others. Fig. 5 depicts a sample of the film hierarchy. On the screen we can see 1 large-sized window, 1 medium-sized window, and four small-sized windows. The large-sized window is used for frames of a current film, that is for a film of the lowest (fifth, or E) level of the hierarchy. The small-size windows (from top to bottom) are used for films of the first (A), second (B), third (C), and fourth (D) levels. The medium-size window is used to present the hierarchy as a whole. In this window, five vertical strips (from right to left) correspond to five hierarchical films, respectively. In the first film (titled "Algorithms on set of pixels"), to specify computation for the second frame, the second film ("Algorithms on matrixes") was called. In the second film, to define computation for the fifth frame, the third film ("Algorithms on multi-stage networks") was taken. In the third film, to specify computation for the tenth frame, the fourth film ("Algorithms on pyramids") was called. Finally, in the fourth film, to define computation for the eleventh frame, the fifth film was taken. Number 13 is the current frame number in the composite film, and number 16 is the total number of frames involved by the present stage of the composition. It is worth mentioning that each hierarchical level has its own colors. In existent implementation of the VIM system, for cases where number of levels is greater than five, the windows are used for films of the five lowest level of the hierarchy. The corresponding shift of films across the windows is employed if the number of hierarchical levels is changed.

The specifying mode is related to the description of local and global computation on nodes (objects) brightened by each frame. This mode is also used to specify input/output operations, the initialization of data, sizes of parameterized structures, and data transformations, etc. In fact, the user should attach some arithmetic or logical expressions to the user's film frames. Fig. 6 depicts a snapshot of the specifying mode. In the white window the user's film related to computation on pixels can be watched in step-wise manner. In the main window we can see a template prepared by the system on the basis of the user's film. This template consists of "an introduction" and "frame fields." In the introduction the system informs the user that it employs $A[i][j]$ as an element of the node array and i, j are the correspondent indexes. The user should insert the values of the array sizes and a name of the initial data file instead of question marks. In addition, the user can declare some new variables (for example $B[M][N]$). In the frame fields the user can replace question marks by some formulas or delete them. For example, a line

$$B[i][j] = (A[i-1][j] + A[i][j-1] + A[i+1][j] + A[i][j+1])/4$$

means that this local formula is employed for each node (i, j) brightened by the corresponding frame. The user can also employ some global expressions. For example, a line

$$B[1][1] = SUM(A[i][j])$$

means that this global function (the sum of elements) is evaluated on all nodes (i, j) brightened by the corresponding frame. At the end the user should provide variables to be stored and a name of the corresponding file. In addition to this "individual" (frame by frame) provision of expressions for film frames, a "collective" attachment can be used. The collective technique supports providing the same expressions to a group of frames. To point out the group, the user should click to buttons with the corresponding frame numbers.

The audio editing mode allows the user to "attach" or replace voice, music or other sounds for the accompaniment of film frames. Time events can also be attached to frames. Fig. 7 depicts a snapshot related to this mode. There are three main regions on the screen. The first region is a window where frames of a film prepared by the user can be watched. The second and third regions consist of buttons related to numbers of the film frames and different types of sounds, respectively. Like for the specifying mode, "individual" and "collective" attachments can also be used. After pushing a button from the third region, the user can hear some sounds and decide: are they suitable for corresponding frames or not? For the "individual" attachment, the sounds will accompany a current frame in the window of the first region. For the "collective" attachment, the sounds will accompany a group of frames which numbers are highlighted by buttons of the second region.

The help mode. A manual-less technology is an important component of the VIM system implementation. So, each film, mode and the system as a whole will be supported by a help subsystem. Fig. 8 depicts a snapshot related to this mode. The user can read some explanation in English or hear the interpretation in Japanese, Chinese, and Russian. Special films to explain the system use will be developed. To illustrate our technology, in the next section we will consider a few other films from our database. These films are related to image processing and cellular automation-like algorithms. They can also be used to specify content-based retrieval operations.

5   A description of some other films

Film sections of our system database are depicted by Fig. 1. Films considered are from section "Computation on pixels". However, they can be used for specifying computation on 2-D grids, sets and tuples, etc. In fact, 2-D structure of colored nodes is considered, so, nodes can have different surrounders. The partial

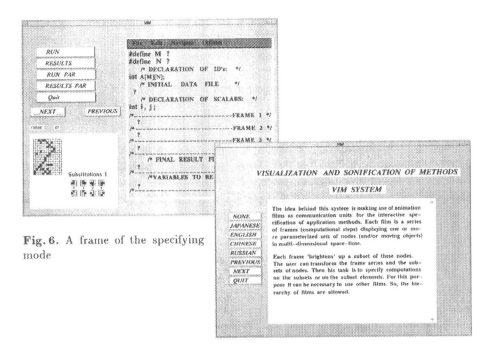

Fig. 6. A frame of the specifying mode

Fig. 8. A frame of the help mode

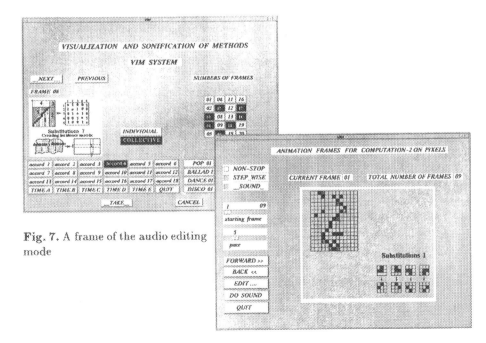

Fig. 7. A frame of the audio editing mode

Fig. 9. A local substitution frame

order of the node scanning is not defined by addresses (positions) of nodes but by external configurations (stencils, masks) around nodes or internal configurations (some variable values) of nodes. This means that in a frame all nodes with the corresponding configuration are selected for the specification of computation. In other words, the visually spatial relations between nodes are used for computation steps. Some frames employ a few configurations; if at least one of them is applicable then the corresponding node is selected. This is the first group of frames.

The second group employs a set of substitutions. Each substitution consists of two configurations. The first defines the selection of nodes or a mask for each node. The second configuration replays the first one or introduces an internal configuration into a node. Fig. 9 depicts a frame sample related to four local substitutions and seven grey nodes presenting the result of these substitutions. In this way we implicitly point out nodes where computation should be specified and a rule for changing "the image" of the node array. In addition, a number of frames use global configurations and substitutions to extract some features of the node array as a whole. Fig. 10 depicts a frame sample related to a global substitution. The first configuration of the substitution is a stripe cross, the second is an internal configuration for a node. For each node (i,j) this substitution provides a data structure including numbers of crossing strokes from (i,j) to the corresponding boundaries. Fig. 11 shows another frame sample of a global substitution. This substitution creates an incidence matrix for an existing set of domains. In fact, it performs the date structure transformation and prepares input data for computation on matrices (2-D grids). To specify this computation the user can call another animation film, for example, from sections "Algorithms on Pyramid" or "2-D Grid Computation". Fig. 12 depicts also an example of data structure transformation. Nodes specified by the substitutions are extracted from 2-D structure for a new 1-D structure.

The third group of frames employs conditional configurations and substitutions. Fig. 13 depicts a frame sample related to unifying two neighboring nodes (domains) under the condition that the internal configurations of nodes are coincident.

The fourth group of frames is related to other sets of stencils and internal structures. A set of stencils/masks is used to visualize patterns of nodes where data are taken for computation on nodes highlighted. A set of internal structures is used to specify possible schemes of this node computation. In the central big window, Fig. 14 shows three configurations to specify nodes where the computation should be performed. In the right small window it depicts a stencil pointing the neighboring nodes where some data will be taken for the computation. Finally, in the bottom small window, Fig. 14 shows a browser for selecting an internal scheme of the node computation. This film is a basic series of frames. It gives a piece of advice to the user. To develop his own film the user can delete any frames from this series and insert others from the database. In fact, this section of the database includes a few films.

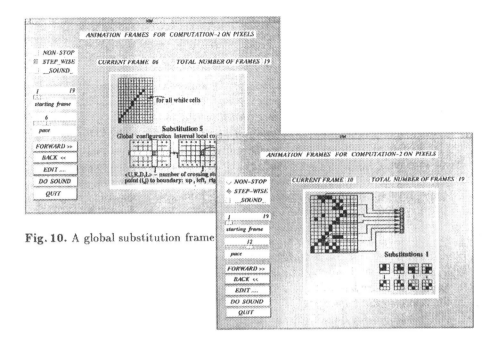

Fig. 10. A global substitution frame

Fig. 12. Another example of the date structure transformation

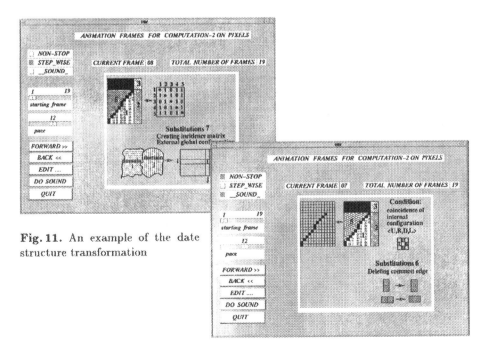

Fig. 11. An example of the date structure transformation

Fig. 13. An example of a conditional substitution frame

Each film can be considered as a complementary film supporting the basic series of frames. In addition, frames can be merged. The merging operations can be used for configurations, substitutions and conditions. The negation of conditions is also provided by this type of operation. Fig. 15 depicts a frame of 4 local substitutions in the main window and a frame of another local substitution in an additional window of the editing mode. This additional window is used for watching and selecting the complementary film frames.

If several substitutions of a frame are applicable on a node then only one of them is used. Which one depends on the user's choice. The user can select a non-deterministic approach or some priority. In the case of the overlapping of substitutions being used for different nodes there are two choices, too. A film developed by the user is also a series of frames, that is, a series of configurations and substitutions. The computation based on this film is an iterative procedure. Two types of iteration can be used:

- the cyclic execution of the frames where frame $i+1$ follows frame i and frame N is followed by frame 1; the computation is stopped if no substitutions in any frame is applicable,
- the lesser-number priority execution of the frames where frame $i+1$ can follow frame i if no substitutions in the frame i are applicable; otherwise the computation related to frame 1 is performed; the computation is stopped if no substitution in any frame is applicable.

Two special animations are used to explain these types of iteration.

The user can select the frame of Fig. 14 instead of the frame of Fig. 9. Then for the specifying mode the system will provide the frame of Fig. 16 instead of the frame of Fig. 6.

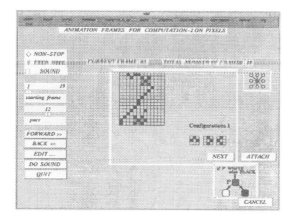

Fig. 14. A frame with an internal structure and a stencil for nodes

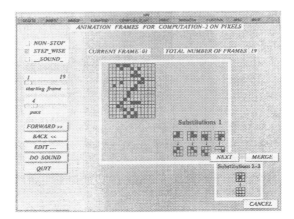

Fig. 15. A frame of the editing mode

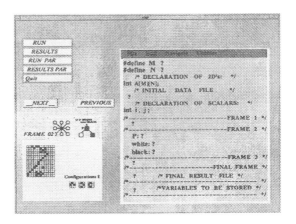

Fig. 16. A modification of the Fig.6 frame

6   Conclusion

We consider future information systems as an environment that supports creating models of a large variety of target systems in society and the natural world and mapping these by data into the artificial world of computers. To develop such environment, we have presented a concept of a new computer technology based on film databases. In this technology special-purpose films are used as units for computer-human dialog and as units for data/knowledge acquisition. From the very beginning each item of a database is a film, that is a unit of a multi-media format. You can watch and/or hear this film. To find a film in a database the user may browse some films about films. Then s/he may call a corresponding film to perform the search. A new film may be created to specify an original retrieval method or some data mining. To manipulate films, a film machine supports watching, editing, composing, specifying, and audio editing modes. This technology provides an integrated environment for creating new items of film databases, specifying content-based retrieval or knowledge discovery algorithms in the film format and performing these algorithms. This environment supports not only above-mentioned algorithms but also other types of data processing.

The film hierarchy allows us to consider application methods in the small and in the large as well as in the framework of any reasonable number of hierarchical levels. In addition, multi-dimensional structures are depicted by parameterized sets of nodes and partial orders of node scanning are naturally presented by different frames. These features of our approach will not only provide good support for effective use of screen real estate but will also allow making use of "the filmification of methods" as an advanced large-scale programming technology. Some attention to sounds and colors will also increase the credibility of this technology. The filmification of methods is not only a new visual technique for the interactive specification of application algorithms and very-high-level programming but also a new type of data/knowledge acquisition. The technology supports "a complement principle". It means that the user can return to the conventional style of programming at any stage of the algorithm filmification.

Implementation of this technology is performed as a two-stage project. The first stage is related to system film databases, the second - to application film databases. Now we are developing a system film database related to visualization and sonification of application methods. In fact, this film database will include the best data/knowledge of algorithm design techniques. Though the VIM system is an integrated meta-tool, each animation film is developed as a special-purpose toolkit. This allows us to employ a film-by-film approach for the implementation of the system. The X window system, Motif, and Xfig are used as a basis for this implementation. Now we are developing films related to computations on trees, pyramids, grids, sets of pixels and moving objects. A demo version of the system is ready to be used for the presentation of basic ideas of the VIM technology. Our future work is to improve all components of the system.

References

1. Advanced Visual Systems, Inc., AVS Developer's Guide, 1992.
2. Bailey, P., Newey, M., Sitsky, D., and Stanton, R.: Supporting Coarse and Fine Grain Parallelism in an Extension of ML. in: Lecture Notes in Computer Science (854), Parallel Processing: CONPAR'94-VAPP'VI, Springer-Verlag (1994) 593-604
3. Becker, R.A., Eick, S.G., and Wilks, A.R.: Visualizing Network Data, IEEE Trans. on Visualization and Computer Graphics, Vol.1, No.1 (1995).
4. Brodlie, K., Poon, A., Wright, H., Brankin, L., Banecki, G., Gay, A.: GRASPARC - A Problem Solving Environment Integrating Computation and Visualization, Visualization'93, IEEE Computer Society Press (1993) 102-109
5. Burkhart, H., Gutzwiller, S.: Parallel Software Reuse and Portability of Parallel Programs, in: Proc. of the 28th Annual Hawaii Int. Conference on System Sciences, IEEE Press (1995) 289-298

6. Chang C.-W. and Lee S.-Y.: Indexing and Approximate Matching for Content-based Time-series Data in Video Databases, in: Proc. of The First International Conference on Visual Information Systems, Victoria University, Australia (1996) 567-576

7. Chang, S.-K.: Towards Multidimensional Languages, in: Proc. of The First International Conference on Visual Information Systems, Victoria University, Australia (1996) 9-19

8. Ciaccia, P., Rabitti, F., Zezula, P.: Similarity Search in Multimedia Database Systems, in: Proc. of The First International Conference on Visual Information Systems, Victoria University, Australia (1996) 107-115

9. Cole, M.: Algorithmic Skeletons: Structured Management of Parallel Computation, The MIT Press (1989)

10. Darlington, J., Field, A., Harrison, P., Kelly, P., Sharp, D., and Wu, Q.: Parallel Programming Using Skeleton Functions, in: Proc. 5th Int. Conf. PARLE, Springer (1993) 146-160

11. Dyer, D.S.: A dataflow toolkit for visualization, IEEE Computer Graphics and Applications, 10(4) (1990) 60-69

12. Edwards, G.: Visualization - the second generation, Image Processing (1987) 48-53

13. Fayyad, U., Piatetsky-Shapiro, G., and Smyth, P.: The KDD Process for Extracting Useful Knowledge from Volumes of Data, Communications of the ACM, Vol. 39, 11 (1996) 27-34

14. Fayyad, U., Haussler, D., and Stolorz, P.: Mining Scientific Data, Communications of the ACM, November, Vol. 39, 11 (1996) 51-57

15. Geerling, A. Max: Program Transformations and Skeletons: Formal Derivation of Parallel Programs, in: Proc. of The First Aizu International Symposium on Parallel Algorithms/ Architecture Synthesis, Japan, IEEE Press (1995) 250-256

16. Händler, W.: Innovative computer architecture - how to increase parallelism but not complexity, in: Parallel Processing System, Cambridge University Press, Cambridge (1982) 1-41

17. Hildebrant J. et al: An implementation of image database systems using differing indexing methods, SPIE Proc., Vol.2606, Digital Image Storage and Archiving Systems (1995).

18. Hildebrant J. and Tang, K.: Integration of an image processing and database system, in: Proc. of The First International Conference on Visual Information Systems, Victoria University, Australia (1996) 226-234

19. Inmon, W.H.: The Data Warehouse and Data Mining, Communications of the ACM, November, Vol. 39, 11 1996 49-50

20. Jacobson, A.S., Berkin A.L., and Orton, M.N.: Linkwinds: Interactive Scientific Data Analysis and Visualization, Communications of the ACM, Vol.37, 4 (1994)

21. Jagadish, H.V., Mendelzon, A.O., and Milo, T.: Similarity-based queries, in: Proc. of the 14th ACM SIGACT-SIGMOD-SIGART Symposium on Principles of Database Systems, San Jose, CA, (1995) 36-45

22. Jain, R. (Ed.): NSF Workshop on Visual Information Management Systems, SIGMOD RECORD, Vol.22, 3 (1993) 57-75

23. Khan, J.I. and Yun, D.Y.Y.: Object-oriented associative learning and retrieval with complex dynamics, in: Proc. of The First International Conference on Visual Information Systems, Victoria University, Australia (1996) 116-125

24. Kochevar, P., Ahmed, Z., Shade, J., Sharp, C.: Bridging the Gap Between Visualization and Data Management: A Simple Visualization Management System, Visualization'93. ISBN:0-8186-3940-7. IEEE Computer Society Press (1993) 94-101

25. Kurokawa, K., Isobe S., and Shiohara, H.: Information Visualization Environment for Character-based Database Systems, in: Proc. of The First International Conference on Visual Information Systems, Victoria University, Australia (1996) 38-47

26. Lucas, B., Abram, G.D., Collins, N.S., Epstein, D.A., Gresh, D.L., and McAuliffe K.P.: An architecture for a scientific visualization system, Visualization'92. IEEE Computer Society Press (1992) 107-114

27. MacCormik, B.H., DeFanti T.A., and Brown, M.D. eds.: Visualization in Scientific Computing, Computer Graphics, Vol.21, **6**, ACM Siggraph, Nov. (1987)

28. Masuda, Y., Ishitobi Y., and Ueda, M.: Frame-Axis Model for Automatic Information Organizing and Spatial Navigation, ACM ECHT'94, Sep. (1994) 146-157

29. Mirenkov, N.: VIM Language Paradigm, in: Lecture Notes in Computer Science (**854**): CONPAR'94-VAPP'VI, Springer-Verlag (1994) 569-580

30. Mirenkov, N.: Visualization and Sonification of Methods, in: Proc. of The First Aizu International Symposium on Parallel Algorithms/ Architecture Synthesis, Japan, IEEE Press (1995) 63-72

31. Mirenkov, N, Mirenkova, T.: VIM Film System, in: Proc. of 7th IEEE Int. Conference on Tools with Artificial Intelligence, November 5-8, Washington, D.C. (1995) 49-54

32. Mirenkov, N.: "Filmification" of Methods: Programming Technology for the 21-st Century, in: Proceedings of the Second World Congress of Nonlinear Analysts, Elsvier Science (1997)

33. Mirenkov, N, Mirenkova, T.: Multimedia Skeletons and "Filmification" of Methods, in: Proc. of The First International Conference on Visual Information Systems, Victoria University, Australia (1996) 58-67

34. Rasure, J., Argiro, D., Sauer, T., and Williams, C.: A visual language and software development environment for image processing, International Journal of Imaging Systems and Technology (1991)

35. Ster, J. and Estes, J.: Geographical Information Systems: An Introduction, Prentice Hall, Englewood Cliffs, N.J. (1990)

36. Stonebraker, M., Chen, J., Nathan, N., Paxson, C., Su, A., Wu, J.: Tioga: A Database-Oriented Visual Tool, Visualization'93. ISBN:0-8186-3940-7. IEEE Computer Society Press (1993) 86-93

37. Sun, J.P., Liu, Z.-Q., and Sacks-Davist, R.: Knowledge-Based and Content-Driven Image Retrieval System, in: Proc. of The First International Conference on Visual Information Systems, Victoria University, Australia (1996) 142-151

38. Upson, C., Faulhaber, T., Kamins, D., Laidlaw, D., Schegel, D., Vroom, J., Gurwitz, R., and van Dam A.: The application visualization system: A computational environment for scientific visualization, IEEE Computer Graphics and Applications, **9(4)** (1989) 30-42

39. Zheng Z.J. and Leung, C.H.C.: Quantitative Measurements of Feature Indexing for 2D Binary Images of Hexagonal Grid for Image Retrieval, in: Proc. of ISO T/SPIE Symposium on Electronic Imaging, Vol.2420 (1995) 116-124

Chain Code-Based Shape Representation and Similarity Measure

Guojun Lu

Gippsland School of Computing and Information Technology
Monash University, Gippsland Campus
Churchill, Victoria 3842
Australia

Abstract

Object shape is an important feature of images and is used in content-based image retrieval. Two important issues of shape based image retrieval are how to find a shape representation which is invariant to translation, scale and rotation, and a similarity measure which conforms with human perception. The purpose of this paper is to present a shape representation and similarity measure which meet these requirements.

We first describe a normalization process to obtain the unique chain code for each shape which is invariant to translation, scale and rotation. The unique chain code is suitable for shape representation but it is difficult to calculate shape similarity based shape chain codes. We then derive an alternative shape representation based on which shape similarity can be computed easily. Experiments show that the proposed shape representation and similarity measure compare favourable with the Fourier descriptor-based method in both retrieval effectiveness and efficiency.

Keywords: chain code, shape representation and similarity measure, image retrieval

1. Introduction

In an image retrieval system or visual information management system, two of the most important issues are how to describe image content (indexing) and how to measure the similarity between two images [1, 2, 3].

Earlier image retrieval systems are text-based: indexing and retrieval of images are based on text description of images. Because of incompleteness and subjectiveness of the text description, the retrieval performance is limited. To improve the retrieval performance, relevance feedback and domain knowledge are introduced into the image retrieval systems [4]. The new trend of image retrieval is towards content based image retrieval. Since automatic high-level image and object recognition techniques are not mature enough for general domain applications, current content-based retrieval techniques are based on low level features, such as colour, texture and shape [5, 6, 7, 8].

It is believed that no single method will be suitable for all applications and in most applications, an integrated method combining a number of techniques is required. In this paper, we concentrate on shape representation and similarity measure.

A suitable shape representation and similarity measure for content-based image retrieval should meet the following criteria:

- The representation of a shape should be invariant to scale, translation and rotation.

- The similarity measure based on the shape representation should conform to human perception, i.e., perceptually similar shapes should have high similarity measure.

- The shape representation should be compact and easy to derive, and the calculation of similarity measure should be efficient.

There are many types of shape representations. Section 2 provides a brief review of main shape representation techniques, with the focus on their applications to image retrieval.

Chain codes have been used for shape boundary representation. There are a number of advantages of chain code representation. First of all, it is compact. Secondly, The chain code is translation invariant. Thirdly, the chain code can be used to compute many shape features, such as the perimeter and area. However, chain codes are variant to boundary size and orientation. In Section 3, we derive the normalized chain code which is invariant to translation, scale and rotation.

The normalized chain codes are good for shape representation, but it is difficult to use them for computing shape similarity. In Section 4, we derive an alternative shape representation from the normalization process described in Section 3. The representation is region-based instead of boundary-based, and is invariant to translation, scale and rotation. The shape distance based on this representation is easy to calculate.

In Section 5, we briefly describe experimental results of shape based image retrieval using the region based shape representation and similarity measure. Section 6 concludes the paper with a brief discussion.

2. Review of Shape-Based Image Retrieval Techniques

Shape description or representation is an important issue both in image analysis for object recognition and classification and in image synthesis for graphics applications. Many techniques, including chain code, polygonal approximations, curvature, Fourier descriptors and moment descriptors, have been proposed and used in various applications [9, 10].

Recently, content-based image retrieval became important. As object shape is one of the important features of images, a number of shape representations have been used in content based image retrieval systems. Note that in almost all work, techniques integrating a number of features, such as colour, shape and texture, are used. But in this paper, we are only interested in shape representation and similarity measure. In QBIC [5], moment invariants are used for shape representation and similarity measure.

Mohamad et al also used moment invariants for trademark matching [11]. But it is found that similar moment invariants do not guarantee perceptually similar shapes. Cortelazzo et al described a trademark shape description based on chain coding and string matching technique [12]. Chain codes are not normalized and shape distance is measured using string matching , so it is not invariant to shape scale. In STAR [6, 7], both contour Fourier descriptors and moment invariants are used for shape representation and similarity measure. Jain and Vailaya proposed a shape representation based on a histogram of the edge directions [8]. But the scale normalisation with respect to the number of edge points in the image is questionable as the number of edge points is not directly proportional to scale. Also, the similarity measure is computationally expensive as it requires to calculate all possible histogram shifts in order to achieve rotation normalisation. Mehrotra and Gary used coordinates of significant points on the boundary as shape representation [13]. The representation is not compact and similarity measure is computationally expensive as these coordinates must be rotated to achieve rotation normalisation. In the retrieval techniques proposed by Jagadish [14], shapes are decomposed into a number of rectangles and two pairs of coordinates for each rectangle are used as the representation of the shape. The representation is not invariant to rotation. Recently, Kauppinen compared autoregressive and Fourier descriptors for 2D shape classification and found the later is better [15]. Sajjanhar et al compared moment invariants and Fourier descriptors for image retrieval and found their performance is not significantly different [16]. Scassellati et al studied image retrieval by 2D shape representations, including algebraic moments, spline curve distances, cumulative turning angle, sign of curvature and Hausdorff-distance [17]. Their study results are not conclusive and performance based on these measures is generally poor judged by human perception.

The above review indicates that there is a need for a better shape representation and similarity measure. This paper proposes an alternative shape representation and similarity measure, and compare its performance with one of the most popular methods, namely the FD-based method.

3. Chain Code Based Shape Representation

3.1 Basic Concepts of Chain Codes

Chain code representation approximates a boundary using directed straight line segments. Chain code of a boundary is obtained as follows (Figure 1). A plane with grids is overlaid on top of the boundary (Figure 1(a)). We traverse the boundary in a fixed direction (normally clockwise) and assign each boundary pixel to a node of the grid, depending on the proximity of the original boundary to that node, as shown in Figure 1(b). The spatially resampled boundary obtained in this way can then be represented by straight line segments. Typically, this representation is based on the 4- or 8-directional segments, where the direction of each segment is coded using a numbering scheme such as ones shown in Figure 2. The lengths of the segments are determined by grid spacing used to sample the boundary. In 4-directional chain codes, all segments have the same length, equal to the grid spacing. In 8-directional chain codes, horizontal and vertical segments have the length of grid spacing, while the diagonal segments have the length of 1.414 times grid spacing. If we select the node marked by letter S as the starting point and traverse the resampled boundaries clockwise, the 4- and 8-directional chain codes for the boundary shown in Figure 1(a) are 0303332221211010 (Figure 1(c)) and 776644424120 (Figure 1(d)), respectively.

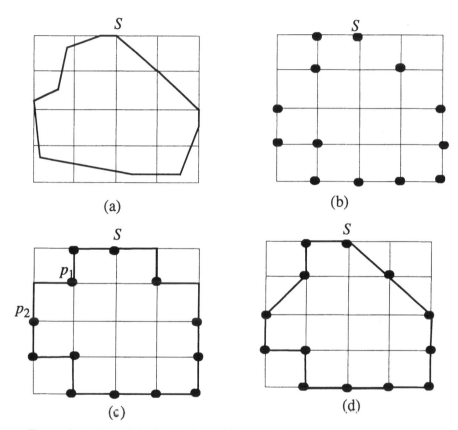

Figure 1 (a) The original boundary with resampling grid superimposed;
(b) Result of resampling; (c) 4-directional chain code;
(d) 8-directional chain code.

Note that for 4-directional code, the path between two points is sometimes not unique. For example, there are two possible paths to connect the two nodes $p1$ and $p2$ in Figure 1(c). In this case, the *shortest allowable external path* should be used.

We can see that the smaller the grid spacing, the more accurate the resampled boundary. When the grid spacing and the original pixel spacing are the same, the resampled boundary is the same as the original boundary. However, a too-small grid spacing (grid cell size)results in very long chain codes. An 8-directional chain code is more accurate to describe a boundary than a 4-directional chain code, and the code length (order) may be smaller as well. But for simplicity, we use 4-directional codes as examples in the following discussion.

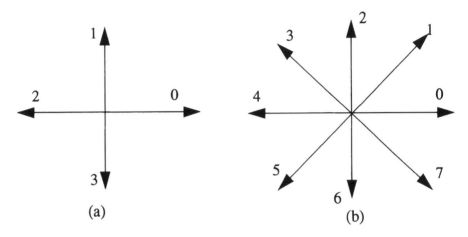

Figure 2 Directions and their corresponding values for (a) 4-directional
chain code and (b) 8-directional chain code.

The chain codes obtained using the above methods are dependent on the starting point, a different starting point will result in different chain code. The chain code also depends on rotation, grid size, and boundary size. A normalization process is required to obtain a unique chain code for each shape.

3.2 Starting Point Normalization

Given a chain code generated by an arbitrary starting point, we treat it as a circular sequence of direction numbers and redefine the starting point so that the resulting sequence of numbers forms an integer of *minimum magnitude*. For example, the chain code of Figure 1(c) becomes 00303332221211O1 after normalizing. In this case, a boundary under given orientation, scale and grid size has a unique chain code.

3.3 Rotation Normalization - Shape Number

A boundary after rotation has a different chain code. This is because rotation changes the spatial relationships between the grid space and the boundary. This problem can be solved using the *first difference* of the chain code, instead of the code itself. The difference reflects the spatial relationships between boundary segments, which are independent of rotation. The difference is computed simply by counting in a counterclockwise manner the number of directions that separate two adjacent elements of the code. For instance, the first difference of the 4-directional chain code 00332211 is

0303030. If we treat the code as a circular sequence, then the first element of the difference is computed using the transition between the last and the first components of the chain. In this example the result is 30303030.

A chain-coded boundary has several first differences, depending on the starting point. The *shape number* of a boundary is defined as the first difference of the smallest magnitude. The *order n* of a shape number is defined as the number of digits in its representation. For example, a first difference of the chain code in Figure 1(c) is 0313003003130313 and the shape number of boundary is 0030031303130313 with order of 16. It is clear that order *n* is even for a closed boundary, and that this value limits the number of possible different shapes. For example, for order *n* equal to 4, there is only one possible shape—a square.

3.4 Scale Normalization

Both boundary size and grid size affect the chain code of a boundary. One way to solve this problem is to alter grid spacing for boundaries of different scale. This will be clear after the discussion of the next section.

3.5 Unique Shape Number

After going through the above normalization, it seems that we can obtain the unique shape number for each boundary. It is not true, however, because the above normalization is exact only if the resampled boundaries themselves are invariant to rotation and scale change. In practice, this is seldom the case. For example, Figures 3(a) and 3(c) show a triangle and its chain code, which is 01103300322221. The triangle in Figure 3(b) is obtained by rotating the triangle in Figure 3 (a) by a certain angle around point P. Figure 3(d) shows the chain code of the rotated triangle. It is 0110330303221221, obviously different from the chain code in Figure 3(c). Their corresponding shape numbers are also different. The cause of this problem is that the spatial relationship between the grid space and boundary is not fixed. One solution to this problem is to orient the resampling grid along the principal (major) axis of the object to be coded. In this case, the grid space and the boundary have fixed spatial relationships; thus obtaining the unique shape number.

The major axis of a boundary is the straight line segment joining the two points on the boundary furthest away from each other. The minor axis is perpendicular to the major axis and of such length that a rectangle that just encloses the boundary could be formed using the lengths of the major and minor axes. The ratio of the major to the minor axes is called *eccentricity* of the boundary, and the rectangle just described is called the *basic rectangle*.

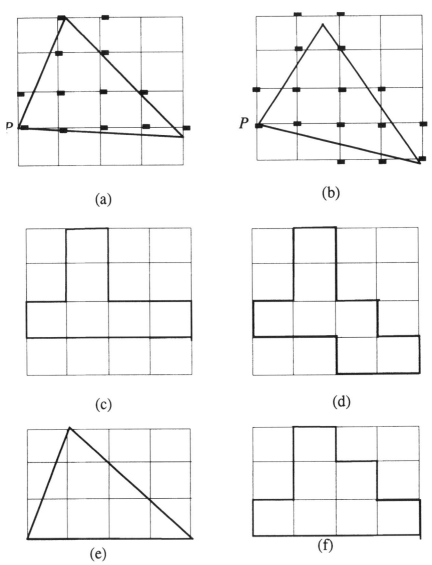

(a)

(b)

(c)

(d)

(e)

(f)

Figure 3 *Effect of rotation on chain codes.*

To achieve scale normalization, we scale all shapes so that their major axes have the same length. When grid cell size is decided, the number of cells in the basic rectangle of each shape is fixed. For example, if there are four cells along the major axis, the basic rectangle of a shape with eccentricity of 4/3 covers 12 grid cells. For instance, in Figure 3, the eccentricity of the best rectangle enclosing the triangle is 4 x 3. After we orient the rectangle along the major axis, we have Figure 3(e). The corresponding chain code representation is shown in Figure 3(f). The unique shape number of this triangle is 00033103313133.

The shape number obtained this way is unique, invariant to scale and rotation. Note that the order of the resulting shape number is not necessarily equal to n, depending on the boundary curvature. This is especially true when n is large.

3.6 Unique Chain Code

So far, we have obtained the unique shape number for each boundary. Shape number is unique and indicates the direction change of chain code segments relative to the previous segment. Because it reflects the direction change instead of direction itself, it is not natural to use. But it can be noted that the starting point of the shape number is unique regardless of the orientation of the resampling grid. This point is the starting point of the flattest (smoothest) region of the boundary. It is natural to think that since this point is unique the chain code with this starting point may also be unique. But this is not true. Because chain code depends on the orientation of the grid space. Same shape number does not guarantee the same chain code.

To solve this problem, we ignore the original grid space after the shape number is found. We compute the unique chain code based on the shape number using the following algorithm: (1) Select the first digit as any number within the chain code direction range, say 0; (2) the second digit differs from the first digit by an amount determined by the first digit in the shape number; (3) the third digit differs from the second digit by the amount determined by the second digit in the shape number, and so on until the complete chain code is obtained. In step (1), any number within the chain code direction range can be used as the first digit. For example, for 4-directional code, the first digit can be any of 0, 1, 2, and 3. This is possible because any digit within the direction range appears at least once in a chain code because the boundary is closed. In order to obtain a unique chain code, we fix the first digit to be 0. The following example illustrates the above procedure. Suppose the shape number is 0003003031133313313 and the first digit of the chain code is 0. Then the second digit should be 0 because there is no direction change as indicated by the first digit in the shape number. For the same reason the third and fourth digits are 0s also. The fifth digit is 3 because there is a direction change of 3 as indicated by the fourth digit in the shape number. We continue this process to obtain the unique chain code of the boundary: 000033322123212101. It should be noted that the last digit of the shape number is not used, because it reflects the direction change between the last digit and first digit of the chain code.

Let us summarize what we discussed so far. Given a shape boundary, we carry out rotation and scale normalization. From the normalized shape we obtain a chain code. The smallest first difference of the chain code is the shape number of the shape. The unique (or normalized) chain code can be obtained from the shape number. Both shape number and the normalized chain code are invariant to translation, scale and rotation, and can be used to represent shapes.

4. Unique Binary Sequence and Similarity Measure

4.1 Shape Binary Sequences

The unique chain code is invariant to translation, rotation and scale, but the lengths of chain codes of similar shapes can be different. Thus it is difficult to compute shape distance or similarity directly based on the unique chain code. So we need an alternative representation based on which we can calculate shape similarity.

We note that the relationship between the grid space and shape after the above normalization is also invariant to translation, scale and rotation (except $180°$ rotation which we will consider later). If we assign 1 to each grid cell covered by the shape and 0 to each grid cell not covered by the shape, and read these 1's and 0's from left to right and top to bottom, we will have a binary sequence for each shape which is invariant to translation, scale and rotation. For example the binary sequence for the shape in Figure 3(f) is 010001101111. We call this representation region-based representation.

The rectangular grids of all shapes have the same number of cells along the x axis. The number of cells in y direction depends on the eccentricity of the shape, the maximum number being the same as that in x direction. So the binary sequences of shapes with different eccentricities have different lengths.

4.2 Similarity Measure

The next issue is how to measure similarity between shapes based on their binary sequences. As the binary sequence indicates the cell positions covered by a shape, it is natural to define the distance between two shapes as the number of cell positions not commonly covered by these two shapes. Note that $180°$ rotation and other shape operations will be considered later. Based on the shape eccentricities, there are the following three cases for similarity calculation.

- If two normalized shapes have the same basic rectangle, we can bit wise compare the binary sequences of these two shapes and the distance between them is equal to the number of positions having different values. For example, if shapes A and B have the same eccentricity of 4 and binary sequences 11111111 11100000 and 111111111111100 respectively, then the distance between A and B is 3.

- If two normalized shapes have very different basic rectangles, i.e, they have very different minor axis lengths, there is no need to calculate their similarity as we can safely assume that these two shapes are very different. For example, if the eccentricities of shapes A and B are 8 and 2 respectively, i.e., the lengths of minor axes are 1 and 4 cells, then we can assume that these two shapes are quite different and there is no value to retrieve the shape. The difference threshold between minor axes depends on applications and cell size. Normally, if the lengths of minor axes of two shapes differ more than 3 cells, these two shapes should be considered quite different.

- If two normalized shapes have slightly different basic rectangles, it is still possible these two shapes are perceptually similar. We add 0's at the end of the index of the shape with shorter minor axis so that the extended index is of the same length as that of the other shape. The distance between these two shapes is calculated as in the first case. For example, if the length of the minor axis and binary sequence of shape A are 2 and 11111111 11110000 and the length of the minor axis and binary sequence of shape B are 3 and 11111111 111111000 11100000 respectively, then we should extend the binary number for shape A to 11111111 11110000 00000000. The distance between A and B is 4.

To facilitate the above similarity calculation during retrieval, shape eccentricity is stored together with the unique binary sequence. They together form the index of a shape.

4.3 Shape Operation Consideration

A shape has two possible orientations aligning the major axis along the x-axis with 180° rotation. In addition to the 180° rotation of shapes, the other two operations which will results perceptual similar shapes are horizontal and vertical flips. Figure 4 shows perceptually similar shapes after 180° rotation and horizontal and vertical flips.

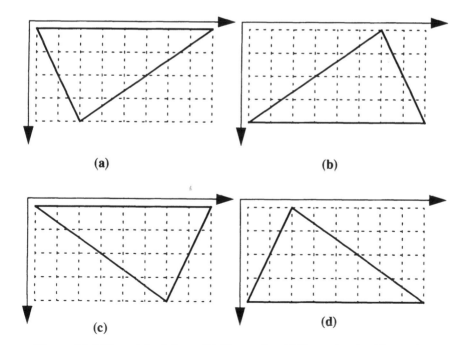

Figure 4 (a) The original shape (b) Shape after 180° rotation (c) Shape after horizontal flip (d) Shape after vertical flip

To take into account of these three operations we need four binary sequences to represent each shape. To save storage space, we still store one binary sequence for each shape but we generate four binary sequences for each query shape during retrieval. In this case, perceptually similar shapes resulted from $180°$ rotation and horizontal and vertical flips can be retrieved.

4.4 Summary of Index and Retrieval Processes

In the above we have described the region-based shape representation which is invariant to translation, scale, rotation and mirror operations, and similarity measure. In this subsection, we summarize the shape indexing and retrieval process. In a retrieval system, all shapes in the database are indexed. During retrieval, the query shape is also indexed. Then the query index is compared with shape indexes in the database to retrieval similar shapes.

Each shape in the database is processed and indexed as follows.

1. The major and minor axes and eccentricity of each shape are found.

2. The shape is rotated to place the major axis along the x direction, and the shape is scaled so that the major axis is of a standard fixed length.

3. A grid space with fixed cell size is overlaid on top of the normalized shape.

4. 1's are assigned to cells covered by the shape and 0's to other cells. By reading these 1's and 0's from left to right and top to bottom, we obtain a binary sequence for the shape.

5. The binary sequence and the length of the minor axis are stored as the index of the shape.

During retrieval, the following steps are used to represent the query shape and carry out similarity comparison.

1. The query shape is represented by its minor axis length and binary sequences using the same procedure as in the above index process. But note there are four binary sequences for each query to take into account $180°$ rotation and horizontal and vertical flip operations.

2. For efficiency reason, these four binary sequences are only compared with binary sequences of shapes in database with the same or similar eccentricities.

3. The distance between the query and a shape in the database is calculated as the number of positions with different values in their binary sequences.

4. The similar shapes are displayed or retrieved in the increasing order of shape distance.

The above outlined approach is simple and similar to the way we normally compare shapes. To compare two shapes, we prefer that they are of same or similar size (scale normalisation). Then we will rotate one of the shapes over the other so that they are in the similar orientation (rotation normalisation). Finally we determine how much they differ based on how much they do not overlap. The region-based approach incorporates all these steps.

5. Experimental Results

To study the retrieval performance of the above described region-based shape representation and similarity measure, we implemented a prototype shape retrieval system. To compare its retrieval performance with the more established FD-based method, we also implemented an FD-based method using radii as shape signature as described in [15].

Our experimental image database have 160 two dimensional planar shapes. Each shape in the database are indexed. Three index files, corresponding to the region-based indexes with cell size of 12x12, and 24x24 pixels, and FD-based index, are created. For each query, three types of indexes are also calculated and they are used to compare with indexes in their corresponding index files to obtain shape distances. Note that for each of the region-based methods, four indexes are obtained. Shapes are retrieved (shape name are returned) in the increasing order of distances.

The retrieval performance is measured using recall and precision, as commonly used in information retrieval literature [18, 19]. Recall measures the ability of retrieving all relevant or similar information items in the database. It is defined as the ratio between the number of relevant or perceptually similar items retrieved and the total relevant items in the database. Precision measures the retrieval accuracy and is defined as the ratio between the number of relevant or perceptually similar items retrieved and the total number of items retrieved. Recall and precision are used together to measure the retrieval effectiveness as precision varies depends on required recall. So we normally use a precision-recall curve to show a retrieval system's performance.

The detailed experimental results can be found in [20]. The main points of the experimental results are summarized below.

First, the shape distance measure described in this paper conforms with human perception in general.

Second, the use of smaller cell size produces better retrieval performance than the use of larger cell size in the proposed region based method, as shown in Figure 5, though more storage and computation power are required for the case of the smaller cell size.

Third, the indexing and retrieval method described in this paper has higher performance than FD-based method, as shown in Figure 5.

Fourth, our method has lower storage and computation requirements than FD-based metho.

Precision

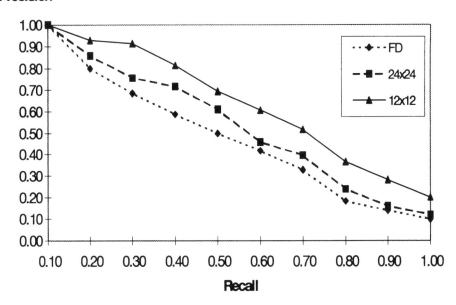

Figure 5 Retrieval performance comparison of the region-based method using cell size of 12x12 and 24x24 pixels and the FD-based method

6. Conclusion

In this paper we extended the basic chain code concept to obtain the unique chain codes for shape boundaries. This itself is quite significant because the unique chain code is invariant to translation, rotation and scale. It can be used to describe and index shapes,

Based on the chain code normalization process, we then derived the unique binary number which is suitable for shape index. The distance and similarity measures are calculated from the unique binary numbers. Using this approach, the index is compact and the retrieval operation is simple. Thus it should be suitable for large image database applications.

Our experiments show that the proposed region based shape representation and similarity method compares favourably to FD-based methods in both retrieval effectiveness and efficiency. Below, we look at the relationships between the region-based method and other closely related shape representations and similarity measure. One concern with any shape representation and similarity measure is its sensitivity to noise. So we briefly discuss the noise effect on the proposed approach.

One can think of the method introduced in this paper as an extension to pixel wise comparison techniques used in crude image recognition systems, but with three major improvements. First, grid cells are used instead of pixels in the index and retrieval process, leading to high efficiency. Second, our method is orientation independent. Third, our method is scale independent. We believe that by combining this method with texture and colour based methods, a very high performance image retrieval system can be achieved.

A closely related work is reported by Jagadish [14]. In his method, shapes are decomposed into a number of variable size rectangles, and two pairs of coordinates for each rectangle are used as the representation of the shape. The major differences between his method and our method are as follows. First, our representation is invariant to shape scale, translation, rotation and mirror operations, whereas his method is not invariant to rotation and mirror operations. Second, we decompose a shape into a number of fixed size squares (cells) whereas variable size rectangles are used in Jagadish's work. Thus it is difficult to do decomposition and more data are required for representing these rectangles in his technique. Third, it is easier to compute shape similarity in our approach.

Compared to methods based on curvature, significant edges and points [8, 13], our method has the following advantages. First, our normalisation is more natural and accurate. Second, it is easier to calculate shape similarity in our approach.

It appears that the retrieval performance of the region based approach is sensitive to noise on shape boundaries. This is because noise may change the position of the major axis thus change the binary sequence dramatically. But it may not be a serious problem considering the following. It is likely that the chance that noise affects the major axis is very low. If the noise does not affect the major axis, our method may actually perform better than other methods. This is because slight noise may not change the binary sequence but may change the boundary properties such as curvature, significant edge and points. So overall, the retrieval performance of the proposed approach under noise may be still comparable or better than other methods. This is partially proved in our experiments as some shapes in our database are "noisy" versions of others. Of course, until a comprehensive test is carried out, we cannot draw a definite conclusion. Also, for image retrieval applications, the retrieval is not based on exact match, a slight change in retrieved shape order due to noise may not be very important.

References

[1] Jain, R. (ed.), "NSF Workshop on Visual Information Management Systems: Workshop Report", Proceedings of the Conference on Storage and Retrieval for image and Video Databases, SPIE Proceedings Series, Vol. 1908, 1993, pp. 198-218.

[2] Jain, R., Pentland, A. P. and Petkovic, D., "Workshop report: NSF-ARPA Workshop on Visual Information Management Systems", June 1995, URL: http://vision.ucsd.edu/papers/ VimsReport95. html.

[3] Lu, G., Communication and Computing for Distributed Multimedia Systems, Artech House, 1996.

[4] Chua T S et al, "A concept-based image retrieval system", Proceedings of 27th Annual Hawaii International Conference on System Sciences, 4-7 January, 1994, pp.590-598.

[5] Niblack W et al, 'QBIC Project: querying images by content, using colour, texture, and shape', Storage and Retrieval for image and Video Databases, SPIE Proceedings Series, Vol. 1908, 1993, pp. 173-187.

[6] Wu, J. K., et al, "STAR - A multimedia database system for trademark registration", Proceedings of First International Conference, ADB-94, Vadstena, Sweden, June 21-23, 1994, pp. 109-122.

[7] Lam, C. P., Wu, J.K., and Mehtre, B., "STAR - a system for trademark archival and retrieval", Second Asian Conference on Computer Vision, December 5-8, Singapore, pp. III-214 - 217

[8] Jain, A. K and Vailaya, A., "Image retrieval using color and shape", Second Asian Conference on Computer Vision, December 5-8, Singapore, pp. II-529- II-533.

[9] Gonzalez, R.C. and Wintz, P., Digital Image Processing, 2nd edition, Addison-Wesley, 1987.

[10] Pitas, I., Digital Image Processing Algorithms, Prentice Hall, 1993.

[11] Mohamad, D., Sulong, G. and Ipson, S. S., "Trademark matching using invariant moments", Second Asian Conference on Computer Vision, December 5-8, Singapore, pp. I-439 - I-444.

[12] Cortelazzo, G. et al., "Trademark shapes description by string-matching techniques", Pattern Recognition, Vol.27, No.8, pp. 1005-1018, 1994.

[13] Mehrotra, R. and Gary, J. E, "Similar-shape retrieval in shape data management", Computer, September 1995, pp. 57-62.

[14] Jagadish, H. V., "A retrieval technique for similar shapes", Proceedings of ACM SIGMOD, Colorado, May 1991, pp.208-217.

[15] Kauppinen, H., Seppanen, T. and Pietikainen, M., "An experimental comparison of autoregressive and Fourier-based descriptors in 2D shape classification", IEEE Transactions on PAMI, vol.17, no. 2, Feb. 1995, pp. 201-207.

[16] Sajjanhar, A. et al, "An experimental study of moment invariants and Fourier descriptor for shape based image retrieval", Technical report, Gippsland School of Computing and Information Technology, Monash University, 1996. (Copies of the report can be obtained from Atul Sajjanhar on atuls@fcit.monash.edu.au)

[17] Scassellati, B. et al, "Retrieving images by 2D shape: a comparison of computation methods with human perceptual judgements", Storage and Retrieval for

image and Video Databases II, 7-8 Feb. 1994, San Jose, California, USA, SPIE Proceedings Series, Vol. 2185, pp.2-14.

[18] Frakes, W. B. and Baeza-Yates. R. (ed.), Information Retrieval: Data Structures and Algorithms, Prentice Hall, 1992.

[19] Salton, G. and McGill, M. J., Introduction to Modern Information Retrieval, McGraw-Hill Book Company, 1983.

[20] Lu, G. and Sajjanhar, A., "Region-Based Shape Representation and Similarity Measure Suitable For Content Based Image Retrieval", Technical report, Gippsland School of Computing and Information Technology, Monash University 1996. (A copy of the report can be obtained from Atul Sajjanhar on atuls@fcit.monash.edu.au)

Content-Based Retrieval Using Random Verification of 1D Cellular Automata Images

Zhi J. Zheng and Clement H.C. Leung

Department of Computer and Mathematical Sciences, Victoria University of Technology, PO Box 14428, MCMC Melbourne, Vic 8001, Australia

Abstract. A 2D map is proposed for random verification of 1D cellular automata image sequences for image retrieval. Two statistical quantities are used to measure the variations between current and next 1D cellular automata images for a given function, which provides a framework for random verification of cellular automata image sequences in 2D maps. Two sample sets of chaotic behaviour of 1D cellular automata image sequences and their maps are illustrated and compared.

1 Introduction

The next generation of database systems will be required to support a substantial level of visual and image content, and the ability to identify and retrieve images efficiently will be an important requirement [5]. To efficiently provide support for content-based retrieval, the problem of feature extraction an indexing will need to be addressed. In our previous studies [13, 14, 15], different feature indices (such as probability vectors) have been proposed for 2D binary images on hexagonal and rectangular grids. To demonstrate the usefulness of feature indices in practical environments, it is normally necessary to have a large amount of images organised by the proposed feature indices. To collect a large amount of images organised by specific indices will be very costly. Using random numbers, however, it is possible to generate large numbers of testing sample sets [4, 7, 8, 9]. Under different mathematical models, fractals [2, 3], chaos [1, 2] and cellular automata [4, 7, 8, 9] are useful tools for generating families of 1D and 2D sample images from initial images and mathematical equations. This will provide an ideal controlled environment to test and compare different indexing schemes for content based retrieval. Since random sequences may have totally different behaviour, it is necessary to have many applications to determine whether the image sequences are sufficiently random. For answering how random is random, we would like to use map structure for verification, which provides an efficient way for comparing random sequences.

2 Random Verification of Image Sequences on 2D Map

A balanced approach for the classification and transformation of 2D binary images on regular plane lattices has been proposed in [10, 11, 12, 13, 14].

The measures discussed in this paper provide further developments of those in [12, 13, 14, 15]. In meaningfully measuring the variation complexity of a sequence of images using the balanced approach on 1D binary images, a number of definitions are required.

Let X^t denote a 1D binary image with N points at time t and x^t be a given point on X^t, $x^t \in \{0, 1\}$. For an image sequence $\{X^t\}_{t \geq 0}$ generated from a given function f, we have

$$X^{t+1} = f(X^t). \tag{1}$$

By considering the pair of relationships between the successive images X^t and X^{t+1}, and letting N^t (or $\tilde{N}^t$) denote the number of 1 (or 0) points on X^t, $N = N^t + \tilde{N}^t$; and ΔN^t (or $\Delta \tilde{N}^t$) denote the number of variation of $1 \rightarrow 0$ (or $0 \rightarrow 1$) points from $X^t \rightarrow X^{t+1}$, it can be seen that the following *master* equations in difference form hold,

$$N^{t+1} - N^t = -\Delta N^t + \Delta \tilde{N}^t; \tag{2}$$
$$\tilde{N}^{t+1} - \tilde{N}^t = -\Delta \tilde{N}^t + \Delta N^t. \tag{3}$$

In measuring quantities for both $1 \rightarrow 0$ (or $0 \rightarrow 1$), two statistical measures denoted by μ^t and $\tilde{\mu}^t$ can be defined,

$$\mu^t = \Delta N^t / N; \tag{4}$$
$$\tilde{\mu}^t = \Delta \tilde{N}^t / N \tag{5}$$

which may be regarded as the fractions of points changed from the respective states. Since the values of the sum on both measures satisfies $0 \leq \mu^t + \tilde{\mu}^t \leq 1$, if each pair of measures corresponds to a point in 2D space, many possible points can be represented within the triangular area of the $[0, 1]$ segment as described by the inequality.

$$0 \leq \mu^t + \tilde{\mu}^t \leq 1 \tag{6}$$

Thus, using the transformation of equations (4) and (5), a pair of two images X^t and X^{t+1} determines a pair of two variations μ^t and $\tilde{\mu}^t$.

On noting both μ^t and $\tilde{\mu}^t$ lie within the unit interval $[0,1]$ and assuming their independence, we may represent them as a 2D map as shown in Figure 1.

From Figure 1(a), it can be noted that this map is roughly similar to the Ulam-stein map [6] for the quadratic transformation. In Figure 1(b), the main diagonal line of the map $\mu^t = \tilde{\mu}^t$ is illustrated. All points on the line have a pair of equal values for the two variations.

Different points of the map correspond to different values of the two measures. Let $g(\mu^t, \tilde{\mu}^t)$ be an updating function on the triangular region in Figure 1(a). Let

$$g(\mu^0, \tilde{\mu}^0) = 0, \forall \mu^0, \tilde{\mu}^0 \in [0, 1].$$

A new point $g(\mu^t, \tilde{\mu}^t)$, $t > 0$ can be renewed using

$$g(\mu^t, \tilde{\mu}^t) = \begin{cases} C_0, & \text{if } g(\mu^{t-1}, \tilde{\mu}^{t-1}) = 0; \\ g(\mu^{t-1}, \tilde{\mu}^{t-1}) + C_1, & (\text{mod } 256), \text{ otherwise} \end{cases}$$

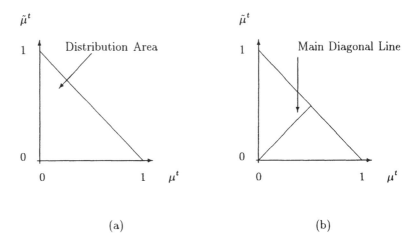

Fig. 1. 2D Map. (a) Triangular distribution area (b) main diagonal line

where C_0 is a constant odd number, and C_1 is a constant even number. Under such mechanism, the points and their values distributed on the map represent global information of the image sequence on evolution. This makes it possible to represent the map as a greyscale or pseudo-colour image. Different densities of the points would illustrate random behaviour of the image sequence. This will be particularly useful in the verification of different behaviour of chaotic image sequences.

3 Equilibrium Conditions of Chaotic Sequences

There are significant differences in chaotic behaviour between continuous and discrete systems. For a finite dimensional cellular automata image sequence, it has to be a quasi-chaotical sequence [8, 9]. Such sequence is expected in a fixed point or a limited circle eventually after a long period. Because expected lengths of limited circles for chaotical sequences are propotation to 2^N. It is useful for most random verification schemes to process a sub-image sequence to determine possible behaviour of the sequence.

Determining equilibrium conditions using 2D map has been investigated in [15]. In adopting a statistical approach, it is essential to determine the equilibrium conditions of a chaotic sequence.

In each individual transforming procedure, two independent measures generally result in $\tilde{\mu}^t \neq \mu^t$. For processing chaotic image sequences, it is necessary to investigate its equilibrium condition. Since $\tilde{\mu}^t$ and μ^t are direct quantitative measures of variations of the images, for an image sequence $\{X^t\}_{t=0}^T$ using equation (2), we have following equations.

$$N^T - N^{T-1} = -\Delta N^{T-1} + \Delta \tilde{N}^{T-1}$$

$$\cdots$$
$$N^{t+1} - N^t = -\Delta N^t + \Delta \tilde{N}^t;$$
$$\cdots$$
$$N^1 - N^0 = -\Delta N^0 + \Delta \tilde{N}^0$$

Summing both sides of the equations, we have

$$N^T - N^0 = \sum_{t=0}^{T-1} (N^{t+1} - N^t)$$

$$= \sum_{t=0}^{T-1} (-\Delta N^t + \Delta \tilde{N}^t)$$

$$= - \sum_{t=0}^{T-1} \Delta N^t + \sum_{t=0}^{T-1} \Delta \tilde{N}^t$$

Since $N^T, N^0 \leq N$, a global constraint for the sequence can be obtained for any T,

$$0 \leq | \sum_{t=0}^{T-1} \tilde{\mu}^t - \sum_{t=0}^{T-1} \mu^t | \leq 1 \tag{7}$$

Denote $\frac{1}{T} \sum_{0 \leq t < T} \tilde{\mu}^t$ by $\bar{\tilde{\mu}}^T$ and $\frac{1}{T} \sum_{0 \leq t < T} \mu^t$ by $\bar{\mu}^T$, then for the image sequence,

$$\lim_{T \to \infty} | \bar{\tilde{\mu}}^T - \bar{\mu}^T | \leq 1/T \to 0, \tag{8}$$

and in the limit, we have

$$\bar{\tilde{\mu}} = \bar{\tilde{\mu}}^\infty = \bar{\mu} = \bar{\mu}^\infty \tag{9}$$

From equation (9), it is evident that a chaotic image sequence has to have a pair of equal measures for the mean densities of the variation sequence. Since all sequences of cellular automata satisfy this condition, a general equilibrium condition is,

$$\bar{\mu} = \bar{\tilde{\mu}} = 0; \tag{10}$$
$$\text{and} \quad \bar{\mu} = \bar{\tilde{\mu}} > 0. \tag{11}$$

Under such conditions, if an image sequence is a chaotic sequence, it satisfies equation (11). Sequences may exhibit different behaviour depending on both the transforming function and initial configuration. For any image sequence, the measures $\bar{\mu}$ and $\bar{\tilde{\mu}}$ provide invariant characteristics for the sequence.

Because equation (7) is an intrinsic constraint for any sequence of the two statistical measures of cellular automata image sequences, a chaotic equilibrium sequence needs to have points concentrated on the main diagonal line or distributed around both parts separated by the main diagonal line in the map.

4 Chaotic Image Sequences and Their Maps

To show the usefulness of this new map for random verification, two sets of chaotic image sequences are selected from $k = 2, r = 1$ cellular automata. To illustrate different properties under a large number of iterations, two rules (rules 73 and 165) [9] are selected from the function set with 256 functions under the same initial configuration. Corresponding to Wolfram's four classes [8, 9], both 73 and 165 are in class III (exhibits chaotic aperiodic behaviour).

Each sequence will be represented by at most three maps undertaking 256, 2560 and 25600 times of iterations. There are a total of 6 images (256 by 64) and 6 corresponding maps plus two greyscale maps given in Appendix A.

For the two rules, there are significant differences among their image sequences and corresponding maps. It is a common question to ask how random is random for a given image sequence. Since each point on the map corresponds to a pair of variations, a sufficiently random sequence may have a large number of distincting points distributed on the map. In general, the larger the areas of points distributed on the map, then more random behaviour of image sequences is expected.

From the random variantions of image sequences, the image sequence of rule 73 has less random behaviour than rule 165. There are several invariant parts on the images of rule 73. From a visual aspect, complexities of the two image sequences have significant differences. Both rules 73 and 165 provide somewhat chaotic image sequences, and the points are concentrated on a certain area around the diagonal line.

Chaotic images and their maps are generated by a system of 2D map for visualising cellular automata image sequences implemented on an SGI Indy Workstation.

5 Conclusion and Further Work

Using the two variation measures, it is possible to construct a 2D map for random verification of a given image sequence of 1D cellular automata. All equilibria are represented by points concentrated around the diagonal line of the new map and all invariant sequences will be convergent to the origin of the map. They can be used for the verification of different behaviour over a long period of times for an initial image and function for cellular automata. This construct can provide new insight into the detailed investigation and classification of invariant properties relating to content-based image retrieval for chaotic image sequences. Since the map representation is a new structure, it is necessary for further investigation to be carried out on the systematic exploration of chaotic image sequences, especially for 256 rules of $k = 2, r = 1$ cellular automata image sequences and more complicated structures. More structural information may be revealed from such investigations.

References

1. R. Artuso, P. Cvitanović and G. Casati, *Chaos, Order and Patterns,* Plenum Press 1991
2. J. Briggs, *Fractals: The Patterns of Chaos,* Edward Berko, 1991
3. K. Falconer, *Fractal Geometry: Mathematical Foundations and Applications,* John Wiley & Sons 1990
4. E. Jen, Editor, *1989 Lectures in Complex Systems,* Addison-Wesley, 1990
5. R. Jain (ed.), NSF workshop on Visual Information Management Systems, *SIG-MOD RECORD,* Vol. 22, No.3, 57-75, 1993
6. P.R. Stein, "Iteration of Maps, Strong Attractors, and Number Theory – An Ulamian Potpourri," in *From Cardinals to Chaos, Reflection on the Life and Ledgacy of Stanislaw Ulam,* Cambridge University Press, 91-106, 1989
7. G. Weisbuch, *Complex Systems Dynamics,* Addison-Wesley, 1991
8. S. Wolfram, *Theory and Applications of Cellular Automata,* World Scientific 1986
9. S. Wolfram, *Cellular Automata and Complexity,* Addison-Wesley, 1994
10. Z.J. Zheng and A.J. Maeder, "The Conjugate Classification of the Kernel Form of the Hexagonal Grid," *Modern Geometric Computing for Visualization,* Eds by T.L. Kunii and Y. Shinagawa, 73-89, Springer-Verlag 1992
11. Z.J. Zheng and A.J. Maeder, "The Elementary Equation of the Conjugate Transformation for Hexagonal Grid," *Modeling in Computer Graphics,* Eds by B. Falcidieno and T.L. Kunii, 21-42, Springer-Verlag 1993
12. Z.J. Zheng, *Conjugate Transformation of Regular Plane Lattices for Binary Images,* PhD Thesis, Monash University, 1994
13. Z.J. Zheng and C.H.C. Leung, "Quantitative Measurements of Feature Indexing for 2D Binary Images of Hexagonal Grid for Image Retrieval," *Proc. IS& T/SPIE Symposium on Electronic Imaging,* Vol. 2420, pp 116-124, 1995
14. Z.J. Zheng and C.H.C. Leung, "Rapid Content Based Indexing for Image Retrieval," *Proceedings of International Workshop on Multimedia Database Management Systems,* IEEE Computer Science Society, pp 38-45, 1996
15. Z.J. Zheng and C.H.C. Leung, "Visualising Global Behaviour of 1D Cellular Automata Image Sequences in 2D Map," *Physica A,* 3-4 (1996), pp 785-800.

Appendix A

The 8 maps are illustrated in Pictures (A)-(H) respectively and 6 sets of sample images are shown in Pictures (a)-(f) for the last 256 1D images in each image sequence. The binary images are illustrated as 2D images in 256 by 64 matrices. Map images are represented as 256 by 256 matrices. The initial image is a 1D array with 64 points.

Pictures (a),(b) and (c) are three sub-image sequences of rule 73 for the last 256 images on the first 256, 2,560 and 25,600 iterations, and Pictures (A),(B) and (C) correspond to three 2d maps of rule 73 under the first 256, 2,560 and 25,600 iterations respectively.

Pictures (d),(e) and (f) are three sub-image sequences of rule 165 for the last 256 images on the first 256, 2,560 and 25,600 iterations, and Pictures (d),(e) and (f) correspond to three 2d maps of rule 165 under the first 256, 2,560 and 25,600 iterations respectively.

Finally Picture (G) is a greyscale picture of the map (C) for Rule 73 and Picture (H) is a greyscale picture of the map (F) for Rule 165 respectively under the first 25,600 iterations from the initial image.

The following notations are used,

R 165 (F 256) :   Using Rule 165, the map is generated by the first 256 iterations from the initial image;

R 165 (L 256/257) :   Using Rule 165, the sub-image sequence illustrated is the last 256 images from the image sequence with a total of 257 images.

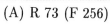

(A) R 73 (F 256)

(B) R 73 (F 2560)

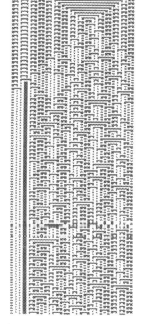

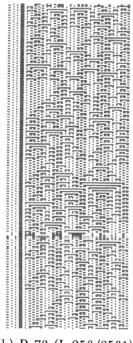

(a) R 73 (L 256/257)

(b) R 73 (L 256/2561)

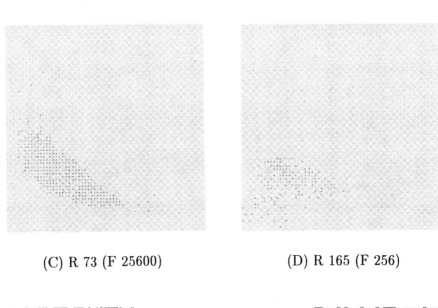

(C) R 73 (F 25600)   (D) R 165 (F 256)

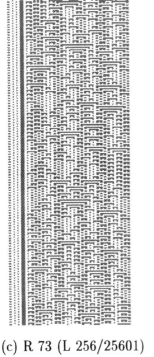

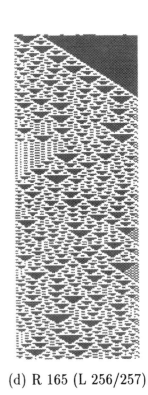

(c) R 73 (L 256/25601)   (d) R 165 (L 256/257)

(E) R 165 (F 2560)

(F) R 165 (F 25600)

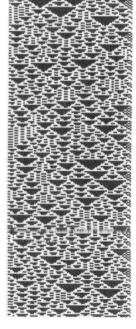

(e) R 165 (L 256/2561)

(f) R 165 (L 256/25600)

(G) R 73 (F 25600)

(H) R 165 (F 25600)

Extracting Complex Tissues of MRI Brain Images Using Conjugate Transformation for Medical Visual Information Systems

Z. J. Zheng[1], C. Pantelis[2], C.H.C. Leung[1], M.T.H. Wong[2] and D. Velakoulis[2]

[1] Victoria University of Technology, PO Box 14428, MCMC Melbourne, Vic 8001, Australia

[2] Mental Health Research Institute of Victoria , Corner Oak Street & Poplar Road, Parkville, Vic 3052, Australia

Abstract. In designing efficient, reliable and valid filters to process complex MRI brain images, a new established system, conjugate transformation, is proposed to construct smoothing filters in this paper. The smoothing filters constructed by the new method can perform 7.5-10.2 times faster than traditional erosion, dilation, opening and closing filters using multiple complex masks. This method is especially preferable for organising multiple complex patterns as a combinatorial mask to peform higher operations recursively. Speed-up ratio analysis for such smoothing filters is provided and recursive results of sample images in erosion, dilation, τ-closing and reversion are illustrated.

1 Introduction

The search for structural and functional abnormalities in the brains of patients with schizophrenia has been accelerated by the appearance of new techniques, such as Magnetic Resonance Imaging (MRI) and Positron Emission Tomography (PET). Previous studies with Computerised Axial Tomography (CAT) have provided only limited information concerning the nature of the underlying neurological basis of functional disorders such as schizophrenia. In neuroimaging, the reliable and valid classification of brain tissue into cortical grey matter, subcortical grey matter, white matter and cerebrospinal fluid (CSF) is essential for the volume estimation of these components. Volume changes have frequently been interpreted as evidence for pathology [6]. The classical technique is manually to outline cross sections of a particular structure on consecutive slices of brain scan, estimating the area by pixel counting and computing the volume by multiplying slice thickness by the summation of areas. Others have attempted 3-compartment segmentation (grey, white, CSF) involving image pre-processing to correct radio frequency inhomogenity [6], using fuzzy logic [2] or boundary pixel locking algorithms [6] in handling ambiguous boundaries resulting from partial volume artefact, assigning criteria range for different tissues [5] and using discriminant function analysis and 'training classes' [3]. We have been trying a 4-compartment segmentation using semi-automatic procedures [7]. This procedure provides a practical scheme to segment brain volumes into cortical and subcortical grey matter, white matter and Cerebro-spinal fluid (CSF). This segmentation provides useful information for examining the volume of cortical and subcortical regions. To perform such extraction more efficiently, it is necessary to investigate automatic segmentation techniques of MRI brain images. This current attempt uses conjugate transformation to improve the reliability, validity and speed of the classification exercise.

A number of automatic segmentation methods have been used in MRI with limited success [1] during the past decade. In an automatic system for MRI segmentation using fuzzy clustering technology, Clark and colleagues [2] has shown that, using a combination of fuzzy clustering, mathematical morphology and knowledge based techniques, it is possible to extract automatically complex tissues forming distinct segments. This system has some essential functions that meet our requirements. In their approach, the following components are included:

(1) Extracting a set of binary images from an original image as a relevant feature image set using grey-scale measures;

(2) 2D morphological operations on feature binary images, filters for different purposes: expansion, extraction, smoothing and so on using dilation, erosion, opening and closing;

(3) Quantitative measures for feature images, giving the number of feature points, percentages of relevant features between two relevant images such as distinction of grey matter and white matter;

(4) Fuzzy control policies for the extraction and combination of relevant information from sets of feature images according to the operations (1), (2) and (3)

From an image analysis viewpoint, the key component of the system developed by Clark *et. al.* [2], is the use of 2D mathematical morphology to implement different filtering functions. To extract complex tissues in practical situations, many morphological filters are required, and it is well known that some intrinsic difficulties exist in designing proper filters to extract complex patterns, especially the extraction of fine-structures using morphological schemes. For example, in extracting precise curves in arbitrary directions, it is necessary to construct a τ-opening operation, select multiple masks and perform recursive operations of erosion and dilation [4]. It is necessary for such operations to take a time proportional to the number of selected masks. Considering our MRI image analysis requirement to extract more refined structures of brain tissues in detail, it is essential to establish more suitable schemes in representing complex tissues.

2   Proposed Approach

To improve the reliability, validity and speed of classification, a new image analysis technique, namely conjugate transformation [8,9,10,11], will be employed instead of standard mathematical morphology techniques to extract complex tissues from MRI brain images.

This new scheme can be used to represent essential geometric structures in binary images for complex components such as extracting precise curves, separating pure block components and constructing highly efficient smoothing filters. Using conjugate transformation, it is feasible to design faster procedures for extracting these complex geometric components directly. Many functions requiring a complicated τ-opening (or τ-closing) operation in morphological operations can be implemented in a simple form using conjugate transformation. This technique requires merely a fraction of the time necessary for traditional methods [10]. In general, a speed-up ratio of about 8 can be observed when using conjugate transformation instead of morphological operations for smoothing filters of binary images on a rectangular grid. Here, a family of smoothing filters is constructed using both morphological and conjugate schemes. Results are provided in both speed-up ratios and sample images.

3   Inner Structure of Conjugate Classification

This section explains the reason behind smoothing filters and the inner structures of the conjugate classification. More details concerning the inner structure can be found in [10]. The conjugate classification for the hexagonal grid has been established by Zheng and Maeder [8] and further investigated by Zheng in [9,10]. The balanced approach for regular plane lattices is described elsewhere [10,11]. Only the third level of the conjugate classification is relevant for smoothing filters. This classification using the three invariants (x,p,q) can be briefly summarised as follows.

Let X denote a binary image on a given grid, and $x \varepsilon X$ be a given point of the image. The simplest scheme for the rectangular grid of nine points (3x3 window) is used as structuring form. The kernel form is a regular form composed of nine grid points for which one point x is at the central position with eight neighbouring points $x_0 - x_7$ around it. The kernel form can be denoted by $K(x)$ or K (Figure 1).

The kernel form $K(x)$ of the rectangular grid is a point x with eight neighbouring points around it. When each point is allowed to assume values of only 0 or 1, there is a total of 2^9 states. From the state set $K(x)$ of 512 states and the inclusion relation of set theory, one can use a hierarchy of 7 levels to represent the conjugate classification [10]. Each level contains 512 states and each node is a subset of states. No two nodes in the same level contain the same state. Let $K(x)$ be the root, then the first level can be divided into one state set G and one conjugate state set $\tilde{G}$ dependent on

$$K^8(x) = \begin{matrix} x_0 & x_1 & x_2 \\ x_7 & x & x_3 \\ x_6 & x_5 & x_4 \end{matrix} = (x, x_7, \cdots, x_i, \cdots, x_1, x_0) = (x_8, x_7, \cdots, x_i, \cdots, x_1, x_0),$$

$$x_i \in \{0, 1\}, \qquad 0 \leq i \leq 8, \qquad x \in X.$$

Fig. 1. *The Kernel Form of Rectangular Grid*

the value $x \in \{0, 1\}$ of the central point x. The second level of 18 nodes can be distinguished by $\{_p G\}$ and $\{_p \tilde{G}\}$, the number of connections, $0 \geq p \geq 8$; that is, the number of eight neighbouring points with the same value of the central point. The third level of different nodes is denoted by $\{_p^q G\}$ and $\{_p^q \tilde{G}\}$ related to $0 \geq q \geq 4$ which corresponds to the number of branches, (the number of runs of the eight neighbouring points with the same value of the central point in each state). In short, the conjugate classification using three invariants is a hierarchy of four levels, which has one (root), two, eighteen and thirty-six nodes respectively. Each node of the hierarchy is a class of states with 1-3 calculable parameters. The symbols (x, p, q) are used to denote a node of three calculable parameters of this classification. For convenience, each node is called a class.

3.1 Two Pseudo-triangles of Pattern Classes

The hierarchical structure of the conjugate classification provides a flexible framework for supporting different applications. The structure of the third level of the conjugate classification for pattern classes is shown in Figure 3(a) for two specific classes and in Figure 3(b) for two pseudo-triangles.

Thirty-six feature classes $\{_p^q G\}, \{_p^q \tilde{G}\}$ can be conveniently represented by $\{A, ..., R\}$ and $\{a, ..., r\}$ representing classes in another two pseudo-triangles respectively as shown in Figure 4.

3.2 Relevant Pattern Classes for Smoothing Filters

In relation to smoothing operations, it is required to use a collection of specific nodes in two geometric clusters G_s or $\tilde{G}_s$ respectively, where $G_s = \{A, C, D, E\}$ and $\tilde{G}_s = \{a, d, c, d\}$. From a structural viewpoint, node A or a represents 1 (or 0) isolated cluster; node C or c describes 1 (or 0) line-end cluster and nodes $\{D, E\}$ or $\{d, e\}$ may be interpreted as 1 (or 0) spur clusters in processed image. Using these clusters, it is possible to decompose different noises in a binary image into combinatorial forms of defined feature clusters.

In Figure 3(a), it is shown that each node may contain multiple states. In two geometric clusters, fixed numbers of states are involved.

Let $|\alpha|$ denote the number of states in α . There are $|G_s| = |\tilde{G}_s| = 25$ states in one cluster where $|A| = |a| = 1, |C| = |c| = |D| = |d| = |E| = |e| = 8$

$$\begin{array}{c} {}_{2}^{1}G = \left\{ \begin{pmatrix} 1\,1\,0 & 0\,1\,1 & 1\,0\,0 \\ 0\,1\,0, & 0\,1\,0, & \ldots\,1\,1\,0 \\ 0\,0\,0 & 0\,0\,0 & 0\,0\,0 \end{pmatrix} \right\}; \end{array}$$

$$\begin{array}{c} {}_{3}^{1}\tilde{G} = \left\{ \begin{pmatrix} 0\,0\,0 & 1\,0\,0 & 0\,0\,1 \\ 1\,0\,1, & 1\,0\,0, & \ldots\,0\,0\,1 \\ 1\,1\,1 & 1\,1\,1 & 1\,1\,1 \end{pmatrix} \right\}. \end{array}$$

(a)

$${}_{0}^{0}G \qquad\qquad\qquad\qquad {}_{8}^{0}G$$
$${}_{1}^{1}G\,{}_{2}^{1}G\,{}_{3}^{1}G\,{}_{4}^{1}G\,{}_{5}^{1}G\,{}_{6}^{1}G\,{}_{7}^{1}G$$
$${}_{2}^{2}G\,{}_{3}^{2}G\,{}_{4}^{2}G\,{}_{5}^{2}G\,{}_{6}^{2}G$$
$${}_{3}^{3}G\,{}_{4}^{3}G\,{}_{5}^{3}G$$
$${}_{4}^{4}G$$

$${}_{0}^{0}\tilde{G} \qquad\qquad\qquad\qquad {}_{8}^{0}\tilde{G}$$
$${}_{1}^{1}\tilde{G}\,{}_{2}^{1}\tilde{G}\,{}_{3}^{1}\tilde{G}\,{}_{4}^{1}\tilde{G}\,{}_{5}^{1}\tilde{G}\,{}_{6}^{1}\tilde{G}\,{}_{7}^{1}\tilde{G}$$
$${}_{2}^{2}\tilde{G}\,{}_{3}^{2}\tilde{G}\,{}_{4}^{2}\tilde{G}\,{}_{5}^{2}\tilde{G}\,{}_{6}^{2}\tilde{G}$$
$${}_{3}^{3}\tilde{G}\,{}_{4}^{3}\tilde{G}\,{}_{5}^{3}\tilde{G}$$
$${}_{4}^{4}\tilde{G}$$

(b)

Fig. 2. The third level of conjugate classification for rectangular grid (a). two nodes in eight states; (b) two pseudo-triangles of pattern classes.

```
A                  B          a                  b
    C D E F G H I            c d e f g h i
      J K L M N                j k l m n
        O P Q                    o p q
          R                        r
```

Fig. 3. Two pseudo-triangles in the 36 letters

3.3 Speed-up Ratios between Morphological Operations and Reversion

Dilation and erosion are essential operations of mathematical morphology. It is well-known that an essential operation uses one state as mask in one operation that needs a time equivalent to once look-up table operation. To construct complex operations involving N states $(N > 1)$, it is necessary to employ τ-operations. Under the current framework of mathematical morphology, a τ-operation takes N times longer than an essential operation [4]. Different from the two essential operations of morphology, conjugate scheme uses only one operation, reversion, as the essential operation. Two specific state sets determine a specific operation. Dilation and erosion are only special cases of reversion.

Different selected state sets construct different functions. Since conjugate classification classifies the entire state set of the kernel form into two pseudo-triangles as nodes, it is more convenient to use n nodes as a united mask directly instead of those N states. From [10], the Speed-up ratio is

$$S_p(N, n) = 2 \times 9 \times N/(4 \times 8 + 7 \times n), \tag{1}$$

where N is the number of states involved and n is the number of classes for the N states. The speed-up ratio equation has been verified in [10] using an SGI workstation and is found to be highly accurate in practical environments.

Two cases need to be considered for comparisons.

Case 1. once recursion of dilation (or erosion) for G_s (or $\tilde{G}_s$) states, $N = 25, n = 4$,

$$S_p(25, 4) = 2 \times 9 \times 25/(4 \times 8 + 7 \times 4) = 7.5, \tag{2}$$

Case 2. once recursion of τ-opening (or τ-closing) for both G_s and $\tilde{G}_s$ states, $N = 50, n = 8$,

$$S_p(50, 8) = 2 \times 9 \times 50/(4 \times 8 + 7 \times 8) \geq 10.2. \tag{3}$$

4 Use of Smoothing Filters

To show the results for the proposed scheme, 14 sample images are selected for the smoothing filters mentioned and these are shown in Figure 5. Picture (a) is the original MRI brain image in grey scale; picture (b) is a threshold binary image for extracting grey matter from picture (a). Using picture (b) as the initial image for different smoothing filters, pictures (c)-(e) are results of reversion operations involving both and states under one, four, and ten times of recursions respectively. Picture (e) has a better smoothing effect than pictures (c) and (d). Pictures (f)-(h) show the results of dilation merely involving states and pictures (i)-(k) are three results of erosion involving only states under corresponding recursions. Compared with the smoothing effects of pictures (f)-(h), pictures (f)-(h) have smoothed black components and pictures (i)-(k) have smoothed white components. The smoothing effects of pictures (f)-(k) cannot be compared with those of pictures (c)-(e). Under morphological framework, it is feasible to use erosion then dilation for τ–opening operation or dilation then erosion for τ–closing operations. Pictures (l)-(n) show the results of τ–closing under 1, 4, and 10 times of multiple dilations then another 1, 4, and 10 times of multiple erosions respectively. Compared with pictures (c)-(e) and pictures (l)-(n), there are only minor differences between three pairs of pictures under the same recursions. In this special case, τ–opening results are similar to τ–closing omitted here.

In relation to the speed-up ratios in practical images, the conjugate scheme is superior to traditional schemes. Smoothing filters constructed using it will play a key role in the extracting of complex tissues from MRI brain images in further medical image analysis applications and the construction of medical visual information systems.

References

1. J.C. Bezdek, L.O. Hall and L.P. Clarke, "Review of MR Image Segmentation Techniques using Pattern recognition," Medical Physics, 20(4):1033-1048, 1993.
2. M.C. Clark, L.O. Hall, D.B. Goldgof, L.P. Clarke, R.P. Velthuizen and M.S. Silbiger, "MRI Segmentation Using Fuzzy Clustering Techniques," IEEE Engineering in Medicine and Biology, 0739-5175/94, pp 730-742, Nov./Dec. 1994.
3. G. Cohen, N.C. Andreasen, R. Alliger, S. Arndt, J. Kuan, W.T.C. Yuh, J. Ehrhardt, "Segmentation techniques for the classification of brain tissue using magnetic resonance imaging," Psychiatry Research: Neuroimaging;45:33-51, 1992.
4. E.R. Dougherty. An Introduction to Morphological Image Processing, SPIE Optical Engineering Press 1992.
5. T.L. Jernigan, S. Zisook, R.K. Heaton, J.T. Moranville, J.R. Hesselink, D.L. Braff, "Magnetic resonance imaging abnormalities in lenticular nuclei and cerebral cortex in schizophrenia," Arch Gen Psychiatry, 48:881-90, 1991.
6. K.O. Lim, A. Pfefferbaum, "Segmentation of MR Brain Images into cerebrospinal fluid spaces, white and gray matter," Journal of Computer Assisted Tomography, 13(4):588-93, 1989.
7. C. Pantelis, R. Coppola, M. Gourovitch, P. Christo, E. Fuller Torrey and D.R. Weinberger, "Procedure for Volumetric Analysis of Brain MRI Images by Segmentation into CSF Spaces, Cortical Grey, Cortical White, and Subcortical Grey Matter using a Semi-automated Multi-level Threshold Technique," Schizophrenia Research, 9(2,3), 206, 1993.
8. Z.J. Zheng and A.J. Maeder. "The Conjugate Classification of the Kernel Form of the Hexagonal Grid, Geometric Computing for Visualization," Eds by T.L. Kunii and Y. Shinagawa, Springer-Verlag, pp 73-89, 1992.
9. Z.J. Zheng and A.J. Maeder. "The Elementary Equation of the Conjugate Transformation for Hexagonal Grid," Modeling in Computer Graphics, eds by B. Facidieno and T.L Kunii, Springer-Verlag, pp 21-42, 1993.
10. Z.J. Zheng, Conjugate Transformation of Regular Plane Lattices for Binary Images, PhD Thesis, Department of Computer Science, Monash University, 1994.
11. Z.J. Zheng and C.H.C. Leung, "Rapid Content based Indexing for Image Retrieval," Proceedings of International Workshop on Multimedia Database Management Systems, IEEE Computer Science Society, pp 38-45, 1996.

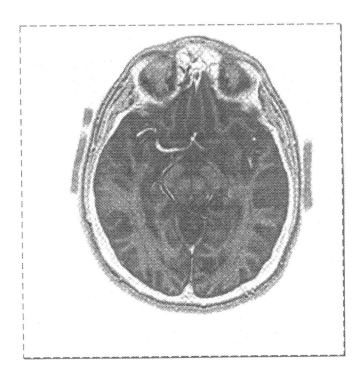

(a) Original Image (greyscale)

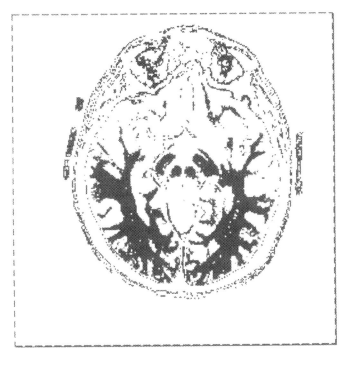

(b) A Binary Image of Grey Matter

(c) ACDEacde1

(d) ACDEacde4

(e) ACDEacde10

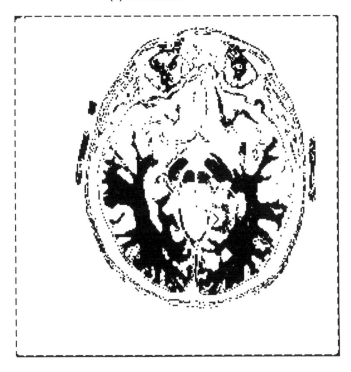

(f) acde1

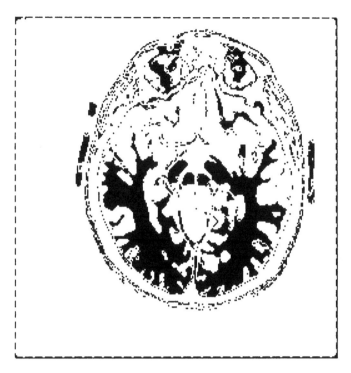

(g) acde4

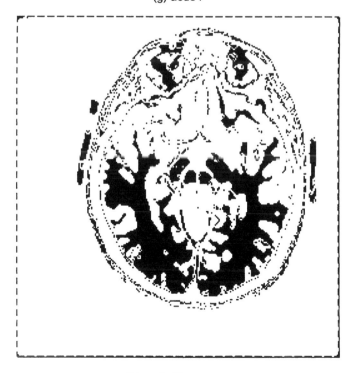

(h) acde10

(i) ACDE1

(j) ACDE4

(k) ACDE10

(l) acde1ACDE1

(m) acde4ACDE4

(n) acde10ACDE10

Figure 5. Different Smoothing Filters. (a) original; (b) a binary image of grey matter; (c)-(e) reversions; (f)-(h) dilations; (i)-(k) erosions and (l)-(n) τ-closings for 1,4 and 10 times from picture (b)

A Uniform Framework for Feature-Based Indexing and Retrieval in Visual Information Systems

M. C. Lee and Donald A. Adjeroh

e-mail: [mclee, donald]@cs.cuhk.edu.hk
Department of Computer Science and Engineering,
The Chinese University of Hong Kong,
HONG KONG.

Abstract. Feature-based indexing is one method that can be used to provide the needed access to first-hand, unbiased primary subject matter in visual information systems. The diversity and dynamism of user information needs and the inherent characteristics of visual information however make the process of indexing quite challenging and thus some unique approaches are required. From an analysis of the special nature of visual information, and of user information needs, the paper identifies the requirements for providing acceptable levels of performance in visual information retrieval. To meet the identified requirements, the paper proposes a uniform indexing framework, which is hierarchical, general and extensible, supporting both multiple indices and multilevel indices, while providing the needed constructs for similarity and relevance grouping. Candidate features that meet the requirements of robustness and uniform indexing at the various levels of the index hierarchy as may be needed in the uniform framework are also indicated.

1 Introduction

The recent popularity of applications involving visually- stimulated information such as digital libraries, video-on-demand, image archives, picture galleries, etc. has made visual information management a significant aspect of the more general area of multimedia information systems. Like in traditional databases, the importance of indexing in visual databases, (or visual information systems [1], VIS) requires no further elaboration. Unlike in traditional databases however, visual databases have some unique properties which make it implicit to search for more efficient and effective mechanisms for access to their content. Visual databases are typically characterized by huge volumes of data, various types of data (video, images, paintings, maps, etc.), and can be accessed based on various visual cues (e.g. shape, colour, texture, etc.). Further, from the information retrieval point of view, the various typology of user information needs, which is inherently dynamic, make it necessary to consider the ultimate users in developing appropriate indexing mechanisms. VIS also make new implications on traditional

---

[1] In this work, we use visual databases and visual information systems synonymously.

performance measures - retrieval efficiency, retrieval effectiveness, and indexing efficiency. In particular, performance levels acceptable to users of small-scale databases, as measured by recall and precision, may be unacceptable to users of huge-volume, integrated VIS. Thus, rather than the usual dichotomy placed on retrieved (relevant) and non-retrieved (non-relevant) documents, groups of perceived relevant information items may be preferred, and this brings up new issues like visual similarity evaluation and relevance ranking.

Some of the above problems have been recognized, and efforts are being made to address them from various quarters. For instance, in response to the need to access image content from a multiplicity of dimensions, some recently reported systems (QBIC [13] and CORE [39]) have used various features such as shape [16], colour [15, 25, 36] and texture as indices. Other features, such as geometric invariants [14], symbolic signatures [6], and spatial information [8, 18] have also been proposed. Apart from images, various approaches have also been suggested for content-based access to other types of visual data, especially video. These methods have however treated visual information in an isolated manner, making it difficult in providing transparent retrieval across the different forms of visual data, and in combining the various features, for instance in relevance ranking.

The diversity of visual information types however calls for a uniform indexing framework (in addition to fast indexing and retrieval mechanisms). Such a framework should provide uniform indices across the multiple sources (or types) of visual information, and should also be able to support the various conceptual levels at which users may wish to consider the visual content, (for instance, objects in a video frame, or at the shot level). In addition, the need to support the various typology of user information requirements - such as those with holistic or specific information needs - also requires that such a framework provides indices at varying levels of indexing exhaustivity and specificity, and that the multiple dimensions (shape, colour, texture, etc.) with which users "think about" visual information be put into consideration. And all these should be in the context of a truly integrated visual information system, incorporating an eclectic collection of visual data types, rather than the current approach of treating the various visual information sources in isolation.

Our objective is thus to provide such a uniform indexing framework, for a truly integrated VIS. In contrast to other similar proposals, [19, 34], the framework we present is hierarchical and general, and can support both objective feature-based indices and subjective attribute-based descriptors. It also supports the various types of user information need, and uses multiple indices at various levels of the hierarchy to provide access to the visual information content at different conceptual levels, including object-level access. The next section briefly explores current efforts that are related to the proposed framework. In section 3, the various issues that affect the performance of a truly integrated VIS are characterized, based on which we identify the requirements for an indexing system for visual information retrieval. Section 4 presents the uniform indexing framework that meets the identified requirements. Suitable features for the framework are described in section 5, and section 6 concludes the paper.

2 Related Work

Integrated visual databases typically contain an eclectic collection of visual data types - video, images, pictures, paintings, etc., thus posing serious challenges to easy and meaningful non- subjective access to their contents. The need for indexing in traditional database systems has long been recognized, as evidenced by the rigorous research effort in developing structures to support indices for traditional and image databases (see [5, 32] for a survey). Likewise, workers in information retrieval have long known the huge impact which effective indices could have on retrieval performance. In fact, it has long been pointed out that indexing is the major problem and the costliest bottleneck in information retrieval [12]. With visual databases playing a central role in visual information systems (VIS), the need for effective indices to the huge volumes of data becomes even more acute. It is therefore apparent that, as opposed to the isolated treatment of indexing and retrieval in most currently available proposals, an improved performance in visual information retrieval systems would demand a simultaneous consideration of both the problems of indexing and of retrieval. This line of thought is also supported by views of information retrieval as a matching problem [4, 9]. Ciaccia, et al. [9] considered the problem of retrieval as a massive similarity matching problem, while in [4], the problem was viewed as that of matching the semantics of the underlying information representation (the index) with the user's 'anomalous states of knowledge' (i.e. the usually unclear user's information need). There have also been some recent reports on the inherent relationship between indexing and retrieval performance in traditional information retrieval [35].

The need for models to support VIS have equally been realized and some proposals have been made, especially in the context of multimedia databases. Klas et al [22] identified a set of requirements for multimedia information management and proposed a number of primitives to support the requirements in an object-oriented framework. Dittrich [10] also proposed the object-oriented data model as a possible framework for handling multimedia data. Klinger and Pizano [23] supported visual databases by identifying 'visual structures' and providing descriptive data for such structures, in an approach that Ennser [11] has called the *visual-linguistic* paradigm. They also proposed the use of the entity- relationship data model for the support of the identified structures. More recently, Leung and Zheng [26] proposed the use of the relational model for modelling descriptive data about image contents. Data models for video have also been proposed [30], and efforts have also been made in providing query support for visual/video databases [20, 21]. Interestingly, Hwang and Subrahmanian [21] also proposed query support for object-level access to the video information. Obviously, this is premised on the assumption that indices for such objects are available. However, currently, notwithstanding the positive impact of such fine-grained access on retrieval in visual databases, few of the reported visual indexing and retrieval systems provide access at such fine-grained levels.

Apart from the reported work in [26], most of the others concentrated on the database aspects, rather than the indexing and retrieval problem. Without discounting the problem posed by the diversity of visual information content, visual information retrieval requires a uniform indexing framework for fast and effective access. This need has also been recognized in [22, 28], and a few proposals have recently been made [19, 27, 34]. The proposals so far have however focused on the use of subjective attribute descriptors for image contents, and we are yet to see proposals for truly content-based integrated VIS, incorporating video, images, pictures, paintings, etc. Moreover, models supporting feature-based indices which are automatically extracted from the visual information are still lacking. The aim of this work is to fill this void by providing a uniform indexing framework appropriate in a truly integrated visual information retrieval system. With such a framework, retrieval can be performed transparently across the various types of visual information, using the various cues with which users think about visual information contents, while operating uniformly at the various levels of the VIS hierarchy. Such a framework thus provides the needed mechanisms for the support of object-level queries as would be required by the query model proposed in [21]. Indices in the framework are extracted off-line, before the retrieval stage, and thus the approach differs from the dynamic indexing methods suggested in [7, 29].

Unlike other proposed uniform models for indexing [19, 34], the framework we present is hierarchical and general, and can support both objective feature-based indices and subjective attribute- based descriptors. To support the various types of user information need, the framework supports indexing of visual databases using multiple indices at various levels of the hierarchy, and thus provides access to the visual information content at different levels, including object-level access. Such an indexing framework will however raise some new issues in multidimensional similarity matching, similarity clustering, relevance clustering, and unification of indices.

3 Purpose of Indexing and Retrieval in VIS

To highlight the need for a uniform indexing framework for visual information retrieval, it is useful to first describe the unique requirements an indexing and retrieval system should meet for it to be useful in the context of visual information systems. The proposed methods are motivated by some techniques in traditional information retrieval, and thus we start with a brief description of the characteristics of such information retrieval systems.

3.1 Characteristics of Indexing and Retrieval Systems

The primary purpose of indexing in an information retrieval system is to provide representations (called *indices*) for the information so as to facilitate the search for (i.e. *retrieval* of) such information. Retrieval then involves the use of the indices to extract the required information in response to some user query. The indices are usually constructed for only some selected documents (called *relevant documents*), deemed to be potentially useful for the users of the information system, say based on the application area, or on the indexer's experience. Then, the perceived relevant documents must be described using some attributes and/or some keywords (*index terms*). It is obvious that the selected relevant documents, the attributes used, and the keywords could be subjective, and could also depend on the anticipated users of the information system. Thus, it may be difficult to identify any one correct set of indices that is universally acceptable for any given document. Notwithstanding, some objective measures for making decisions on the relevant documents or the index terms have also been proposed, typically based on frequency counts, position, and context [24, 31].

A document is viewed as being *relevant* to some user request if it can provide some information to satisfy the user's information needs. It then means that a relevant document may or may not be understood by some particular user, (for instance, it could be in a different language), but to some others, the information contained in the document can be helpful in meeting their request. Thus, in addition to relevance, other more restrictive measures are sometimes used to judge the "suitability" of the selected documents. Examples here include *pertinence* (appropriateness for the user, e.g. a relevant document may not be pertinent to a user if the user does not understand it), and *utility* (usefulness to the user, e.g. a pertinent document may not possess utility if the user already knows its content). To avoid the philosophical nature of some of these issues, terms such as relevance, utility or pertinence are often used synonymously to indicate a document that could be useful (in a broad sense) in satisfying some user information need [24].

The performance of an indexing and retrieval system is measured primarily by three factors: *indexing efficiency, retrieval effectiveness* and *retrieval efficiency*. The first parameter is more relevant to the indexer, while the others are of more importance to the user, though all could be affected by certain capabilities provided by the indexing system, such as the matching strategy. Indexing efficiency measures how fast the indexing process can be performed, which usually depends on the time required for feature extraction and matching. The retrieval efficiency is an indication of the system response time to user queries. It depends on various factors, such as complexity of user query, clarity of request, size of the database, index exhaustivity, and the specific index used (i.e. the index structure, and the matching strategy). Retrieval effectiveness is a more often used measure since it gives us some idea of how far we can rely on the results produced by the system. The effectiveness is determined by two factors: *precision* - the proportion of the total items retrieved which are relevant, and *recall* - the proportion of relevant documents retrieved out of the total relevant documents in the database. While precision shows the ability to retrieve relevant information, recall indicates the ability to avoid non-relevant information. The two measures are usually diametrical, and an improvement in one often results in some sacrifice on the other. Thus, rather than using the dichotomy whereby documents are considered as retrieved or not retrieved, relevant or not relevant, etc., some systems provide a relevance/similarity ranking of the search results.

Clearly, measuring effectiveness in such situations could involve other strategies, different from precision and recall, for instance by comparing the system ranking to an ideal ranking.

The performance in terms of effectiveness depends on certain characteristics of the indexing system, namely indexing correctness, exhaustivity, specificity, completeness, and consistency [24, 31, 35]. *Indexing correctness* refers to the absence of an index term which should have been present, and the presence of one that should have been absent. In a way, it measures the completeness of the indexing, by indicating the presence of the correct descriptors, and the absence of erroneous descriptors. This factor is directly related to the initial step of conceptual analysis (in which the potential user needs for the document are analyzed), and the subsequent translation of the results of the analysis into a specific set of index terms. *Exhaustivity* basically indicates the number of items used to index a document, and expresses the extent to which the descriptors cover the concepts involved. *Specificity* on the other hand shows the various conceptual levels at which the document is indexed. Thus a document indexed at a high level of specificity will involve fewer index terms and will essentially cover the major subject matter of the document. Like precision and recall, specificity and exhaustivity have an opposing relationship, as an increase in one tends to reduce the other. While generally, specificity and exhaustivity are affected by the number of index terms, the relationship is not straightforward, for instance, the addition of one or more index terms could increase either the specificity or exhaustivity, depending on the new meanings that can be constructed from the new index term(s).

The implication of retrieval correctness on the performance is quite obvious. On the one hand, exhaustivity and specificity tend to have impact on different aspects of effectiveness. High exhaustivity will lead to high recall but low scores in precision with longer response time, since more comprehensive searches will be involved, and possibly more non-relevant documents would be retrieved. The converse is true for specificity. However, high specificity may not be advisable in environments where broad searches may be required or where the user is probably not sure of what he wants, or how to go about it.

3.2 Nature of Visual Information

In developing a framework for indexing in VIS, it may be beneficial to consider the characteristic nature of visual information from an information retrieval point of view. In this context, we look at visual information from different perspectives, such as information overload, inadequacy of textual descriptions, the issue of relevance, multiplicity of sources, multiplicity of visual cues, and huge volumes of data.

Visual information is typically represented in the form of pictures or image sequences. If one is to go along with the old saying that *a picture is worth more than a thousand words*, then the limitation of textual description of a visual experience and the amount of information available from such an experience become more apparent. It therefore means that because of the possible information overload, the user may not be able to structure his request very concisely and may require some help cues to guide him during information retrieval. The limitations of textual descriptions also imply that content-based, non-subjective access to the visual information may be needed to satisfy the user needs.

Like in traditional information retrieval, the problem of relevance takes an even more acute dimension in visual information retrieval systems. Just as a given image can be described in several ways, the relevance of an image or an object in the image could vary drastically across different users or environments. This shows the inherent unpredictability of the potential utility, pertinence or relevance of a visual information item. The problem is exacerbated by the multiple dimensions (or visual cues) from which the contents of an image can be considered. A user may be interested in one or more of the visual attributes of the image contents, such as colour, shape, texture, etc. A visual information retrieval system should therefore provide access points to the information content based on the various cues or modalities with which the user "thinks about" visual information. This calls for multiple indices to the same visual infomration content, and also requires support for both content-based and descriptive attribute-based access to the visual information. It can be argued that content-based features (such as colour, shape, texture, etc.) extracted directly from the image provide us with a first-hand, unbiased information with respect to the primary subject matter. To avoid the difficulty involved in providing universally acceptable descriptors of the image content, some researchers have proposed that indexing can be based almost exclusively on the factual, primary subject matter [11].

Another aspect of visual information systems is the multiplicity of sources of visual information. A VIS could support various image types such as pictures, photographs, paintings, animation, video sequences, etc., usually emanating from different types of applications and devices. However, one positive aspect of this is that, in terms of content, (the primary subject matter), the various forms of visual information are similar, especially when viewed as mere images. Thus uniform content based indices can be derived for various types of visual information, regardless of the source, (at least for some selected application areas).

The usually huge volumes of data involved also imply that some unique considerations may have to be made to ensure good performance. For instance, the need for short response time, coupled with the presence of multiple index features, may call for faster methods for matching the indices. Further, traditional measures of effectiveness such as precision and recall could have new implications in visual information retrieval. For instance, while for a small database, a user may be willing to view say 100 images to find 9 useful ones (a precision of 9/100), the same user may not be happy to be inundated with 1000 images with only 90 useful items. This, combined with the problem of relevance, imply that, instead of classifying items as retrieved/not retrieved or relevant/not relevant, groups of potentially pertinent images could be retrieved and the results ranked according to their relevance or similarity so that the user will have a final say on which information items would best suit his purpose. It is therefore important that, to facilitate the retrieval process in visual information systems, the indexing mechanism provides some methods for similarity and relevance grouping of the information content.

When indexing is based on content-based features, the problems of relevance (what to index), indexing correctness, exhaustivity, and specificity (all of which affect the overall performance), take a new turn. In this situation, the role of index terms in traditional information retrieval is taken up by the particular indexing features used. Thus, the number of different features used in the indexing will come into play, and, in addition to retrieval efficiency and effectiveness, the indexing efficiency will also have to be considered.

Notwithstanding the foregoing, we can still use some ideas from automatic text retrieval to decide which images could be relevant. Lancaster [24] has given some broad guidelines for making such decisions in traditional text retrieval systems. Also Shatford [33] has treated the issue of relevance as a problem of deciding what to index, and thus made some suggestions. Based on these suggestions, and in the context of visual information retrieval, we provide the following guidelines for choosing relevant images or objects from the visual database: (i) include all visual information items known to be of potential interest to the users (ii) include all objects which could be of interest to the users of the VIS and which are represented substantially in the image or video (iii) index each of these as specifically as possible based on anticipated user needs (iv) index only a part that is not implicit in a whole (v) index only something that is clearly delineated, unless its presence is unusual and noteworthy.

3.3 A Classification of User Information Needs

In text information retrieval, the conceptual analysis stage identifies the relevant documents and is directly related to the anticipated user needs. Thus, the performance of an information retrieval system depends heavily on the result of this analysis. The same is still true for retrieval in VIS. Moreover, user idiosyncrasies, coupled with the characteristic nature of visual information (in particular the issue of relevance, and the multiple dimensions in which visual information content can be considered) make it necessary to consider the users of the final visual information retrieval system.

Guidivada et al [19] have classified users of an image retrieval system into *naïve, casual,* and *expert* users. A naïve user is one who is not used to the image domain or characteristics. A user who is quite familiar with the image domain and characteristics, but performs retrieval only occasionally was classified as a casual user. An expert user is equally familiar with the image characteristics, but performs retrieval operations frequently. Though a familiarity with the system may help the users to formulate their queries more concisely, unarguably, there could be situations in which all the above categories could be seeking the same information, with the same level of detail. In fact, the same individual, say the expert user, could have different information needs at different times in his interaction with the system, say based on the previous results. Thus, from the indexing point of view, it may be more useful to categorize users based on the perceived *information needs*[2], rather than on their familiarity with the system or frequency of use, which tends to portray a fixed classification of the individual users.

Such a categorization scheme has been used by Simonnot and Smaïl [34], in which user information needs were classified as *thematic, connotative, exploratory, and precise.* In addition to these, we introduce *holistic* information needs and *browsing* needs, while relating the information needs to the probable dimensionality (i.e. number of index features) that would be involved in satisfying such needs. Thematic information need concerns a broad theme, and user information needs can be viewed as being at the categoric level [17]. This requires medium levels of both exhaustivity and specificity and low dimensionality. As an example, a user may specify that he wishes to retrieve visual information items with a specific category of shapes, colour, etc. Users with precise information needs have very good idea of the specific information they require, and thus such a situation calls for high levels of specificity. Exploratory searches are needed in response to a user's request for a short overview of the contents of the VIS. Like in thematic search, this could also require medium levels of exhaustivity and specificity, but in addition, the multiple dimensions of visual information may play a more important role here, calling for medium dimensionality. Connotative query involves subjective features, and thus would require both content-based features and descriptive attribute-based information.

Holistic information need requires detailed information and calls for high exhaustivity, in addition to a consideration of the various dimensions of visual information. Browsing needs can be applied to any of the above probable user information needs, and concerns the mechanisms of information presentation rather than indexing. But, since a user with a browsing need typically has little idea of the information he seeks, browsing needs have a better probability of being satisfied when indexing is performed with high exhaustivity and high dimensionality. In fact, a catch-all approach for visual information retrieval could be to index the visual information contents as exhaustively as possible, using many dimensions (i.e. many index features). The selection of the actual level of exhaustivity and the number of features to be involved in satisfying a particular request can be then be decided at retrieval-time - based on the perceived user information needs - for instance, as expressed by the user.

The above scheme stipulates no particular rigid classification upon the users. A user's information need can change from one mode to another even during the same retrieval session with the system. For instance, a user with a browsing need may turn into a holistic user based on results from the browsing, and further, based on the results of the holistic search, he may require more precise information on a particular object or image. This flexibility captures the inherent dynamism in user information needs, and also indicates the need for mechanisms for query reformulation and use of relevance feedback in visual infor-

---

[2] A detailed discussion on motivations for user information needs and user information seeking behaviours can be found in [38].

mation retrieval systems. Exploratory and browsing information needs may also make the provision of mechanisms for similarity grouping and relevance ranking more mandatory, while connotative information need may be more easily satisfied with some form of relevance grouping.

3.4   Requirements for Indexing and Retrieval in VIS

The preceding discussions have shown that the characteristic nature of visual information would have a great impact on the performance of any visual information retrieval system. The problem of pertinence or relevance has a direct impact on retrieval effectiveness. In turn, what is deemed relevant depends on the conceptual analysis stage and the expected needs of the user. Apart from relevance, the indexing correctness is another factor which directly affects the performance. For visual information, the concept of indexing correctness now transcends the usual meaning of absence of a required descriptor and presence of an unrequired descriptor. Since the features used in the indexing now represent the descriptors, it then means that we must also consider correctness in terms of such features, especially their *discriminative capability*. For instance, one may wish to know how a given index feature indexes (i.e. represents) the same object under various changes in view condition, (such as scale, rotation, illumination, and occlusion), or the distance between the two indices for the same image (or object) under such changes, etc. On the other hand, the distace between two different objects as measured by the same index feature will also be considered.

The problems of indexing exhaustivity and specificity can also be related to the number of features used. It then implies that multiple-feature indices are required to capture more "descriptors" as may be needed to support queries which are based on any of the multiple visual cues or dimensions with which visual information contents may be considered. It should be a possible to assign weights to each of the features, to indicate their relative importance in a given application, or to a given user. Also, indexing should involve the various types of visual data, such as video, images, paintings, photographs, etc. It is expected that regardless of the type of medium, when an object or an image appears in two or more media, the system should be able to retrieve (and present) the objects/images in the various media in response to a general query on the object/image. Moreover, the user need not know the particular type of medium, (e.g. video or static images) where the object/image of interest is located. Support for such transparent retrieval mechanisms in a truly integrated VIS calls for a uniform framework for indexing the various relevant objects and images in the entire database. Furthermore, the huge volumes of data involved in a typical VIS makes it more beneficial to seek ways of indexing the different forms of visual information in a uniform manner.

Although it could be quite difficult to formulate a model that is general enough to describe all types of applications, it is possible to find some class of applications that can be supported by a uniform framework [19]. The intrinsic similarity of the particular index features from the different types of visual data can be harnessed to approach this problem. Also, a multilevel framework, in which an entire video is viewed as a sequence of key/representative frames can be useful in this regard. Thus, video sequences, images, pictures, paintings, etc. can all be handled homogeneously, for instance, by use of some uniform abstractions - as long as we can find effective features to represent the various visual information items at these abstraction levels. This then implies that object-level indices for access to the relevant objects in the video or image can be provided. This will in turn lead to an improvement in indexing performance and an increased probability of satisfying the various types of users, especially those with holistic or with precise information needs.

In summary, for an effective access into the contents of a visual database, the user may require the following facilities: (i) content-based access to specific visual information (ii) content-based access to groups of visual information (iii) object-level feature indices (iv) attribute-based indices (v) multilevel indices, and (vi) multiple indices to the same information.

On the side of the indexing system, in addition to meeting the above user needs, the following may also be required: (i) uniform indexing framework for supporting the various types of visual information (ii) robust features for the indexing (iii) mechanisms for efficient extraction of the indices (iv) techniques for efficient similarity evaluation using the indices, and (v) methods for similarity and relevance clustering

At retrieval time, there should be strategies in place to provide the user with the following: (i) ranked retrieval results (ii) query reformulation, and (iii) browsing interface.

In the following section, we propose methods for meeting the above requirements. We concentrate on providing a uniform framework with content-based multiple indices, multilevel indices, similarity grouping and relevance clustering. Apart from a brief discussion on relevance clustering and searching, we do not consider the retrieval-time problems such as query reformulation and browsing mechanisms further in this paper.

4 A Uniform Indexing Framework

A uniform indexing framework was pointed out as a possible way of addressing the problems of long indexing time, and multiplicity of information sources in the usually large-volume visual databases. Moreover, the user of a VIS may only be concerned with whether the system can satisfy his information needs, and not necessarily the type of medium - video or images - where the information is stored. We argue that rather than treating the various types of visual information in isolation, for some class of applications, it is possible to find features which can be used to represent the information content in a uniform manner, and possibly at various levels of abstraction. (Guidivada et al [19] have identified areas like art galleries and museums, interior design, architectural design, and real estate marketing as belonging to such a class). Such features should provide the same index representation for the same object, regardless of whether it appears in say a video or a picture. By the same token, a static image should have the same index as say a key frame from a video, if the contents of the two are visually similar. A consequence of the above is that the index features should be largely invariant within the same media under changes in various view conditions, and also across different visual media.

The need for a uniform framework in VIS has long been recognized [22, 28]. However, only recently have some proposals started to emerge [19, 27, 34]. Unfortunately, the proposals so far seem to have concentrated on the retrieval side, neglecting the long identified inherent problematic part of retrieval systems - indexing [12]. Further, the proposals have only adressed the issues related to attribute-based descriptors and the semantic aspect of visual information. The scheme we propose is general, hierarchical, and extensible, and provides facilities to incorporate various forms of indices as may be required for improved retrieval performance, in the light of the special nature of visual information, and the various categories of user information needs.

4.1 A *Textbook* Metaphor

We use a *textbook* metaphor to capture the inherent hierarchical structure of the information content in an integrated visual information system. A textbook typically comes with an index to its contents. The indices show the page location of the perceived relevant items (keywords) within the text. Also, the table of contents provides us with another level of abstraction for the information content, in terms of chapters(or parts) and page numbers. This hierarchical conceptual structure embodied in the textbook metaphor is illustrated in Figure 1. It could be observed in Figure 1(a) that a chapter may have only one page, and a page may or may not have any item deemed relevant enough for the purpose of indexing. Conceptually, it is also possible for a book to be of a single chapter, or even one single page.

It is simple to visualize how the textbook metaphor extends to visual information systems as shown in Figure 1(b-d). First, a video sequence is considered as a sequence of images. The temporal nature of video is used to partition[3] the video into its constituent shots, which are represented as a set of key/representative frames called *index frames*. Then from the information retrieval viewpoint, the VIS is just a set of images. We distinguish between two types of images: *image* - one with one or more relevant objects, and *pictures* - an image with no distinguishable relevant object. The picture thus represents visual information items such as paintings and photographs, which may need to be treated as a whole. In our model, we use the generic term index frames to refer to both images and pictures, and also to video keyframes.

To support multilevel access to the visual content, indices are provided at the various levels of the hierarchy - shot level (for video), frame level, and object level. And, multiple indices using various index features are provided where appropriate. Uniformity in the framework is achieved by mandating that any index used at a given level of the hierarchy should provide invariant indices across

---

[3] We do not consider video partitioning here. See [1, 3] for some methods.

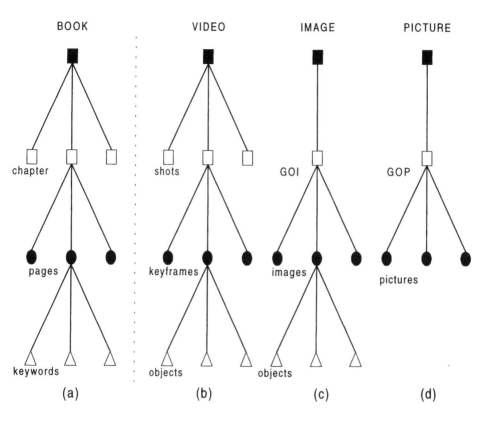

BOOK   VIDEO   IMAGE   PICTURE

chapter   shots   GOI   GOP

pages   keyframes   images   pictures

keywords   objects   objects

(a)   (b)   (c)   (d)

Fig. 1. Textbook metaphor for different types of visual information. GOP − Group of Pictures; GOI − Group of Images.

any visual information item belonging to that level. That is, the index features have to be such that a key frame can be compared with an image or a picture for similarity; and an object from an image can be compared with one from a keyframe using the same indices. Moreover, a group of similar pictures (GOP) which can be represented as a single picture, or group of similar images (GOI) (also represented as a single image) can be compared with the representation of a video shot, since they are all at the same level of the hierarchy. Figure 2 shows the textbook metaphor for representing the visual information contents in an integrated VIS.

Clearly, the number of indices needed at each index level increases as we go down the hierarchy. For instance, an object can be described using various features such as colour, shape, texture, etc., but the video shot may have only the key frames as its index. It is also obvious that certain index features may apply at one level, but not at the other, or to some type of index frame. For example, a shape feature may be more applicable to an image or an object, but not to a picture. However, certain features, such as colour ratio features and geometric constraints can be applicable at various levels of the hierarchy

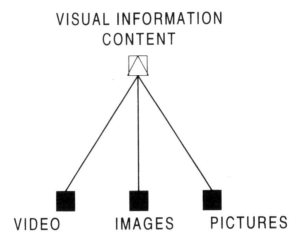

Fig. 2. Textbook metaphor for an integrated visual information system.

4.2 Formal Definitions

Index An index is a representation with which the information content at a given level of the index hierarchy can be accessed. The index could be *logical*, represented as mere numeric values, such as histograms. The logical index is typically extracted automatically based on some image analysis activities, and could include such features as shape, colour ratios, texture, geometric information, spatial information, etc. The logical index may or may not have any physical/visual meaning to the user of the VIS. The index could also be *descriptive*, (example, descriptive metadata), and is used to indicate subjective information such as semantic or contextual information, and some other information which may not be easily extracted automatically, for instance dates, copyright information, etc. We distinguish between the logical and descriptive indices, and refer to the former as *feature-based indices*, and the later as *attribute-based descriptors*. Major emphasis is placed on feature-based indices in this work.

Index Object An index object (or just object) is a visually-distinguishable structure in an index frame which is deemed to be relevant. To support the multiple modalities in which the visual information content can be accessed, each object is represented with multiple indices. An index object is a 5-tuple defined as follows:

$O_I = (O_{ID}, S_{IF}, S_{AD}, F_{ID}, Loc)$

where O_{ID} is the identity of the object; S_{IF} is a set of feature-based indices used to represent the object; S_{AD} is a set of attribute-based descriptors used to describe the object; F_{ID} is the frame identity of the index frame containing the object; Loc is the coordinate location of the object in the image or frame.

The index object identity is the property that distinguishes the object from all other index objects. Each object has two types of identities - the *logical ID* and the *physical ID*. The logical ID is unique for any given *distinct* index object in the database and independent of the physical location of the object. The physical ID indicates the physical location of an index object, such as to which index frame it belongs. For the same object appearing in two different frames, the logical ID would be the same, but each appearance in a different frame will have a different physical ID. Thus apart from the identification of the objects, the IDs also serve as a fast mechanism for retrieval, especially for exact matches.

F_{ID} serves as an indirect mechanism to know the type of visual information to which the object belongs, - video or image. In this respect, the index objects can also be classified into *video objects* and *image objects*, based on F_{ID}.

S_{IF} represents the objective content-based indices which are automatically extracted from the object. On the other hand, S_{AD} is used to capture the subjective attributes (metadata) which are used to describe the object. Thus, semantic and context information can all be incorporated using this tuple, and at any level in the index hierarchy (see other definitions). Standard methods used in text databases can be used to process such information. However, for visual information systems, there is also the problem of *index unification* - unifying the semantics of the objective feature-based indices and those of the descriptive metadata.

Index Frame The index frame(or just frame) is a generic term used to represent various types of visual information - such as video key frames, images, pictures, paintings, etc. It also serves as a collection mechanism for the index objects. An index frame is a 5-tuple defined as:

$$F_I = (F_{ID}, S_{IF}, S_{AD}, S_{IO}, Par)$$

where F_{ID} is the identity of the index frame; S_{IF} is a set of feature-based indices used to represent the frame; S_{AD} is a set of attribute based descriptors used to describe the frame; S_{IO} is a set of child index objects. If S_{IO} is null, F_I is called a *simple index frame* (e.g. a picture), otherwise it is a *complex index frame* (e.g. an image); Par is the parent shot or video. If Par is defined, F_I is a key frame for some video shot. Otherwise it is a static image or picture.

Although the index frame provides a collection mechanism for the index objects, this should not be construed to imply the usual notions of class and inheritance as used in object-oriented data modelling. The only inheritance by the objects from the frame is the parent video or shot (where it exists). Thus, objects belonging to the same index frame may not have much else in common, apart from the fact that they have the same parent frame. It is also worthy to note that our index objects are not the same as "objects" as used in object-oriented databases. Here, we are not concerned with object-oriented issues like object state, object values, and inheritance (except as pointed out above). Moreover, our notion of video object is quite different from the video object used by Oommoto and Tanaka in the OVID project [30], where the video object actually corresponds to a video shot.

Extensibility in the framework is provided by use of S_{IF}, S_{AD}, and S_{IO}. S_{IF} and S_{AD}, provide facilities for modifying the specific index features attached to an index object or to an index frame. Thus new indices can be introduced at will. Similarly, with S_{IO}, the frame type can change from a complex frame to a simple frame and vice versa. Since multiple indices are used, it is obvious that the introduction of a new index feature to the system will call for appropriate mechanisms to extract similar or corresponding indices for user query, and also for techniques for comparing the objects or index frames based on the new index feature. Further, when a new index is attached to an object or a frame, it may be necessary to re-check the database, since some new items may become similar to the object or frame based on the new feature. This may have implications on the *is-similar-to* relationship described in the next section.

Visual Information Object A visual information object (or just visual object) is any indexed information item in the database with its own identity. Examples could be a video object, an image object, a video shot, a group of pictures, etc.

Visual Information System In our model, each object belongs to one or more frames. An image database or picture database is just a set of such frames. A video sequence is an ordered set of video scenes/shots. Each scene is in turn represented by a set of video abstractions, such as the keyframe, which is also represented as an index frame. A video database is thus equally treated as a collection of such sequence of index frames, (the sequence information can be incorporated as part of the frame identification). Therefore, from an indexing and retrieval point of view, the visual database (or visual information system, VIS) is a multiset, containing both sequences of index frames and ordinary collection of index frames, and also a collection of video objects and image objects. In effect, the visual information content is captured by a collection of visual objects. Although index objects are inherently derived from some index frames, both the index frames and the index objects have their own identities and indices, and a user can make requests requiring direct access to any of them. The index frames and index objects are viewed as a first class entities in our model. Thus, in terms of content, the visual information system can be described with a 5-tuple:

$$VIS = (F_{IS}, F_{IC}, O_I, S_R, R_R)$$

where $F_{IS} = \{F_{I_{s_1}}, \ldots, F_{I_{s_n}}\}$ is the set of simple index frames; $F_{IC} = \{F_{I_{c_1}}, \ldots, F_{I_{c_m}}\}$ is the set of complex index frames; $O_I = \{O_{I_1}, \ldots, O_{I_k}\}$ is the set of index objects; S_R represents the *similarity relationships* between the index objects and also between the index frames in the database. It contains all the *similarity-sets* in the system. R_R represents the *relevance relationships* between the index frames and/or the index objects. It contains all the *relevance-sets* in the system. While the members of a similarity set have to be at the same level of the index hierarchy, members in the relevance-set do not necessarily have to be at the same level in the hierarchy.

Using the above model, the problem of indexing in VIS has then been reduced to just providing effective indices for both the index objects, and the index frames, to facilitate easy access to the various levels of the VIS hierarchy. For video, depending on user request, the access could be up to the shot level, or even the entire video sequence (the root node in Figure 1(b)). Migrating from the object level to the entire video sequence level should then be a simple matter, since an index object automatically inherits the parent video or shot from its parent frame.

5 Relationships in the Framework

The framework we propose can be viewed as a quasi object-oriented framework. As indicated earlier, the index frame is not the same as the class construct as used in object oriented systems. Thus the frame does not necessarily provide a strong inheritance mechanism for the index objects, and the various objects belonging to a frame need not have any thing in common, except the fact that they belong to the same frame, and probably the same video sequence. For example, unlike the class construct in object-oriented data modelling, the index frame does not necessarily hold similar objects. The proposed model however provides some mechanisms for relating different visual objects. The first is the use of the logical and physical object IDs which provide fast access to the same object in possibly different types of media, (example video and images). Some other mechanisms used to establish relationships in the model are based on similarity clustering and relevance clustering.

5.1 Similarity Clustering

An important facility for establishing relationships in the framework is the *is-similar-to* construct which is used to establish relationships between different objects or frames, regardless of their location. Relationships between objects or between frames are derived automatically at indexing time based mainly on their (visual) similarity as indicated by the feature based indices used, or based on the attribute-based descriptors. The is-similar-to relationship between two objects or between two frames is defined in a similar fashion as follows:

$$\text{is-similar-to } (O_{I_1}, O_{I_2}) = (O_{I_1}, O_{I_2}, [I_{F_1}, D_1], \ldots, [I_{F_k}, D_k]); \ D_i \leq \tau_i$$
$$\text{is-similar-to } (F_{I_1}, F_{I_2}) = (F_{I_1}, F_{I_2}, [I_{F_1}, D_1], \ldots, [I_{F_m}, D_m]); \ D_i \leq \tau_i$$

where (O_{I_1}, O_{I_2}) and (F_{I_1}, F_{I_2}) are respectively the related index objects and index frames; I_{F_i} is the ith index feature involved in the similarity relation; D_i is the distance between O_{I_1} and O_{I_2} (or between F_{I_1} and F_{I_2}) based on and the specific distance measure used; τ_i is the similarity threshold for the ith feature.

Thus for each index object (or frame), there could be a set of other objects (frames) with which it is involved in an is-similar-to relationship. We call this set the *similarity set* (or *similarity cluster*) for the object (or frame). The is-similar-to relationship thus provides fast access to groups of images or objects based on their similarity. The scheme would require a preliminary similarity threshold with which objects or frames can be automatically grouped at the time of indexing. The threshold can also serve as a method to deactivate the similarity clustering when it is not needed (example by simply setting the threshold to zero for some types of distance metric).

It may also be observed that by ranking the set of objects (or frames) in a similarity cluster, the user need for ranked retrieval results can be satisfied in an efficient manner, at least for the user with a non-holistic information need. It is also important to notice that when the distance measure used to obtain D_i is a metric, and depending on the specific feature involved, the is-similar-to relationship between say A and C can be derived indirectly from the previous similarity relationships between A and B, and between B and C, if these are already known. More significantly, the concept of similarity set can be generalized to a *similarity matrix*, which will hold similarity information between an object (or frame) and all other objects (or index frames) in the database. In this case, the choice of thresholds would be made at retrieval time, rather than at the indexing stage. However, in this situation, storage of the indices could become a major issue on its own, considering the huge volumes of data involved in visual information systems and the possibly multiple feature indices that will be needed.

5.2   Relevance Clustering

Another important construct for forming relationships between the visual objects (both index frames and index objects) is the *is-relevant-to* construct. This is used to establish a relationship between objects and/or images regardless of their location and their position in the index hierarchy. Unlike in similarity clustering, relevance clustering is performed at retrieval time, based on a given query. The idea is that a set of visual information items that the user found relevant in satisfying his information need can be grouped together for future use. The relevance cluster could be automatically or manually generated, and can relate to visual information items at different levels of the index hierarchy. The is-relevant-to relationship between a visual object and other visual objects is defined as follows:

$$is\text{-}relevant\text{-}to\ (V_O) = ([V_{O_1}, Subj_1], \ldots, [V_{O_k}, Subj_k])$$

where V_O is the visual object in question; V_{O_i} is the ith visual object involved in the relevance relation; $Subj_i$ is the subject of the query for which V_{O_i} is found relevant to V_O. An object could be relevant to another object on more than one subject.

For each visual information object, there could be a set of other visual objects with which it is involved in an is-relevant-to relationship. We call this set the *relevance set* (or *relevance cluster*) for the visual object. Similarity clustering is basically static, independent of user information needs, and is derived mainly from the features used for indexing. Relevance clustering on the other hand is dynamic, and supports the differences in users' query request (even for the same object), by grouping visual objects based on user interaction patterns and the information items the users indicated as being relevant in satisfying their information needs. The idea of relevance clustering is more in line with the dynamic indexing techniques proposed in [7, 29].

An object may not be in the similarity set of another given object (example depending on the features used), but could be a member of the relevance cluster. For instance, two objects which are entirely different visually may have the same meaning (e.g. works of art). Also, the relevance relationship has the capability to relate between visual objects at different levels of the index hierarchy. For instance, a picture of a city may or may not be visually similar to say the key frames used to index a documentary video of the same city. But the picture and the index frames could be related with a relevance relationship, using the city name as the subject. Thus, while the is-relevant-to and the is-similar-to relationships have the same objective of speeding up the search for a query item, relevance clustering goes further to reduce the intrinsic limitations of strictly content-based indexing (i.e. indexing based only on primary subject matter). Moreover, it also helps in reducing the problematic issue of mismatch between user information needs, the query input, and the retrieved results.

Like in the overall framework, relationships between the objects or frames also brings about the issue of assigning importance to the indices when multiple indices are used. While this can be achieved by use of some weights, the particular weights should be derived based on certain considerations, such as, the specific application, the index level, an analysis of past user interactions, etc. It could also be left to the user to decide.

6 Retrieval/Searching in the Framework

After the indexing, the next question is how to retrieve information from the database using the indices. The problem then becomes how to search the database using the extracted indices. The retrieval performance therefore will be primarily affected by two issues: the search strategy used, and the methods used in matching the indices. The problems of similarity matching and how to cut down the huge computational requirement and thereby improve the response time have been considered in a separate discussion [2]. Here, we briefly describe how non-sequential search can be performed using the proposed framework.

The search methods can depend on the index structures and the organization methods used to store the indices. And for visual information systems, with the huge data volumes and multiple indices, index organization could become an important issue. Various approaches are being investigated for this purpose, based mainly on methods from traditional database management [5], and image databases[32]. In the uniform framework, the two clustering constructs can form a basis for non-sequential search using the indices.

At the beginning, searching is performed sequentially, until a similarity match is found for the target query. From this point, the search path is switched to the similarity set of the matching object, and the elements of the similarity set are matched with the target. If another match is found among the members of the similarity set, the search is further switched to the elements in the similarity sets of the new matching objects. The process is continued recursively in this manner until the user terminates the search, or the entire database has been searched.

Whenever a match is found, the contents of the relevance set is checked and the query terms are compared to see if the contents of the relevant set could be useful in the current query. If so, the similar objects along with the members of the relevant set(s) will be retrieved. With appropriate mechanisms for query reformulation, the user can modify the initial query for a more specific search. It is also conceivable that, as some similar objects are found, the search can continue in the background while the already found relevant documents are presented to the user. Therefore, in a way, the search or retrieval is directed by the contents of the similarity and relevance clusters. Thus, the retrieval performance especially the response time can be greatly influenced by the mechanisms used to populate the relationship clusters.

7 Suitable Features for the Framework

The preceding sections have described a general and uniform framework which provides multiple access and multilevel indices for retrieval in visual information systems. It should however be pointed out that the overall performance - retrieval effectiveness and efficiency, and indexing efficiency - will still be affected by the underlying features used for the indices. Although the retrieval efficiency is now independent of the specific domain or visual information type, it still depends on the matching strategy used for each element of the multiple indices, and the number of such indices involved in responding to the user query. On the other hand, the extraction of the feature-based indices still needs to be efficient without sacrificing robustness.

The basic requirement for index features in the framework is that they meet the conditions of uniformity of access, invariance, fast extraction, and fast matching. Fast extraction and fast matching are needed to ensure efficiency in indexing and during the retrieval stage. For uniformity of access, the index should provide a uniform representation for the visual information items across different domains and at the same level of the index hierarchy. For example, the features used should provide uniform indices for a picture, an image and a video frame; or for an image object and a video object. Moreover, it would also be desirable if the same feature can provide uniform indices across hierarchies, for instance, for a video object and an image.

The requirement for invariance is a usual condition for feature-based indices. It can also help in meeting the other requirement for uniformity of access. In visual information systems, images of the same scenery may be captured under various changes in view conditions, such as illumination, direction of view, partial occlusion, etc. Moreover, a video shot of the same scenery may be taken under conditions different from that at the time the picture was taken. The indices for the two are however required to be very similar, regardless of the changes in view condition. The invariance condition ensures that the indices in the framework are largely invariant to such changes, thus ensuring robustness of the indices.

The foregoing therefore implies that features such as mere colour indices (colour histograms) may not be suitable for the framework, since this is not invariant under illumination changes. Also, the computational cost in extracting and matching certain features (such as shape) may make such features less appealing. Suitable features for the proposed framework could include colour ratio features [15, 25], geometric invariant features [14]], spatial indices [18], and the conjugate invariants proposed in [40]. However, for a better discriminative capability, the conjugate invariants may have to be extended into more general invariants, rather than the current form which is based on only binary conjugates. It is also obvious that some features could be more suitable at a certain level of the hierarchy than others. For example, shape features could be suitable at the lowest level of the hierarchy, but not at higher levels. Thus, the position of the visual object on the index hierarchy will also affect the features that could be used, and more features become suitable as we go down the hierarchy.

8 Conclusion

The vast amount of information often contained in a visual database will have little or no utility if we do not have indices for effective and efficient retrieval of such information. Feature-based indexing provides us some ways to access first-hand, unbiased primary subject matter in such situations. We have proposed a uniform indexing framework that meets the various requirements for efficient and effective feature-based access in truly integrated visual information systems. The uniform framework was motivated by the characteristic nature of visual information, and the various types of user information needs in a VIS environment. In particular, the framework provides support for multiple and multilevel indices to the visual content, and facilities for similarity and relevance grouping.

Among the unique aspects of the proposed model are the relationship constructs and the facilities for extensibility. One possible interesting use of the extensibility and generality offered by the proposed framework is the incorporation of facial databases in the VIS. In this case, the features used in face recognition [37] can serve as the feature indices, and thus a user can just submit the picture of a given person as a query, (for instance a politician or sportsman under study) and the system retrieves all the appearances of the individual in the visual database, including video shots, paintings, and pictures having the individual. This will definitely make use of such relationships as the is-similar-to relationship, since the person's face may be changing over time, but could still have some similarities which would be in the similarity set for the matching pictures. With the relevance relationship, other important information items that may be related to the person can also be retrieved, even when such are not necessarily similar to the input picture of the individual.

References

1. D. A. Adjeroh, and M. C Lee, "Robust and efficient transform domain video sequence analysis: an approach from the generalized colour ratio model", accepted, Journal of Visual Communication and Image Representation.

2. D.A. Adjeroh and M.C. Lee, "Probabilistic similarity evaluation using fast incremental matching with optimal premature termination", Submitted.

3. G. Ahanger and T.D.C. Little, "A survey of technologies of parsing and indexing digital video", Journal of Visual Communication and Image Representation 7, 1, 26-42, 1996.

4. N.J. Belkin, R.N. Oddy, and H.M. Brooks, "ASK for information retrieval", Part I & II, Journal of Documentation, 38, 51-71, 145- 164, 1982.

5. E. Bertino and P. Foscoli, "Index organizations for object- oriented database systems", IEEE Transactions on Knowledge and Data Engineering, 7, 2, 193-209, 1995.

6. S-K Chang, Q-Y Shi and C-W Yan, "Iconic indexing by 2D strings", IEEE Transactions on Pattern Analysis and Machine Intelligence , 9, 3, 413-428, 1987.

7. S-K Chang, "Toward a theory of active index", Journal of Visual Languages and Computing, 5, 101-118, 1995.

8. S-S Chen, "Content-based indexing of spatial objects in digital libraries", Journal of Visual Communication and Image Representation 7, 1, 16-27, 1996.

9. P. Ciaccia, F. Rabitti, and P. Zezula, "Similarity search in multimedia database systems", Proc., 1st International Conference on Visual Information Systems, Melbourne Australia, 107-115, 1996.

10. K. Dittrich, "Object-oriented data model concepts", in A Dogac, M.T Ozsu, T. Sellis (eds.), "Advances in Object-Oriented Database Systems", NATO ASI series, 29-45, 1994.

11. P.G.B. Enser, "Pictorial information retrieval", Journal of Documentation, 51, 2, 126-170. 1995.

12. R.A. Fairthorne, "Automatic retrieval of recorded information", Computer Journal, 1, 1, 36-41, 1958.

13. M. Flickner et al, "Query by image and video content: the QBIC system", IEEE Computer, 23-31, Sept. 1995.

14. D. Forsyth, J.L. Mundy, A. Zisserman, C. Coelho, A. Heller, and C. Rothwell, "Invariant Descriptors for 3-D Object Recognition and Pose," IEEE Transactions on Pattern Analysis and Machine Intelligence , 13, 10, 971-991, 1991.

15. B.V. Funt and G.D. Finlayson, "Color constant color indexing," IEEE Transactions on Pattern Analysis and Machine Intelligence , 17, no. 5, 522-529, 1995.

16. 14. W.I. Grosky and Z. Jiang, "Hierarchical approach to feature indexing," Image Vision and Computing, 12, 5, 275-283, 1994.

17. M. D. Gross, "Indexing visual databases of designs with diagrams", in A. Koutamanis, H. Timmermans, and I. Vermeuten, (eds.), Visual Databases in Architecture, Avebury, Aldershot, 1- 14, 1995.

18. V. T. Gudivada and V. V. Raghavan, "Design and evaluation of algorithms for image retrieval by spatial similarity", ACM Transactions on Information Systems, 13, 2, 115-144, 1995.

19. V.T. Gudivada, V.V. Raghavan, and K. Vanapipat, "A unified approach to data modeling and retrieval for a class of image database applications", in V. S. Subrahmanian and S. Jagodia (eds.) Multimedia Database Systems: Issues and Research Directions, Springer-Verlag, Berlin, 37-78, 1996.

20. S. Hibino and E.A. Rundensteiner, "A visual query language for identifying temporal trends in video data", Proc., International Workshop on Multi-Media Database Management Systems, New York, USA, 74-81, 1995.

21. E. Hwang and V.S. Subrahmanian, "Querying video libraries", Journal of Visual Communication and Image Representation, 7, 1, 44-60, 1996.

22. W. Klas, E.J. Neuhold, and M. Schrefl, "Visual databases need data models for multimedia data", in T. L. Kunii (ed), Visual Database Systems, Elsevier Science Publishers B.V. (North- Holland), 433-462, 1989.

23. Klinger A and Pizano A, "Visual structure and data bases", in, T.L. Kunii (ed.), Visual Database Systems, Elsevier Science Publishers B.V. (North-Holland), 3-25, 1989.

24. F.W. Lancaster, Indexing and Abstracting in Theory and Practice, University of Illinois, USA, 1991.

25. M. C. Lee and D. A Adjeroh, "Indexing and retrieval in visual databases via colour ratio histograms", Proc., 1st International Conference on Visual Information Systems, Melbourne Australia, 309-316, 1996.

26. C. H. C. Leung and Z. J. Zheng, "Image data modelling for efficient content indexing", Proc., International Workshop on Multi-Media Database Management Systems, New York, USA, 143-150, 1995.

27. D. Lucarella and Z. Antonella, "A visual retrieval environment for hypermedia information systems", ACM Transactions on Information Systems, 14, 1, 3-29, 1996.

28. M.H. O'Docherty and C.N. Daskalakis, "Multimedia information systems - the management and semantic retrieval of all electronic data types", The Computer Journal, 34, 3, 225-238. 1991.

29. B. J. Oommen and C. Forthergill, "Fast learning automaton-based image examination and retrieval", The Computer Journal, 36, 6, 542-553, 1993.

30. E. Oomoto and K. Tanaka, "OVID: design and implementation of a video-object database system", IEEE Transactions on Knowledge and Data Engineering, 5, 4, 629-643, 1995.

31. G. Salton, Automatic Text Processing: The Transformation , Analysis and Retrieval of Information by Computer, Addison- Wesley Publishing Co., 1989.

32. H. Samet, "The quadtree and related hierarchical data structures", ACM Computing Surveys, 16, 2, 187-260, 1984.

33. S. L. Shatford, "Some issues in the indexing of images", Journal of American Society of Information Science, 45, 8, 583- 588, 1994.

34. B. Simonnot and M. Smaïl, "Model for interactive retrieval of video and still images", Proc., International Workshop on Multi- Media Database Management Systems, New York, USA, 128-135, 1995.

35. D. Soergel, "Indexing and retrieval performance: the logical evidence", Journal of American Society of Information Science, 45, 8, 589-599, 1994.

36. M.J. Swain and D. Ballard, "Colour Indexing," International Journal of Computer Vision, 7, 1, 11-32, 1991.

37. M. Turk and A. Pentland, "Eigenfaces for recognition," Journal of Cognitive Neuroscience, 3, 1, 71-86, 1991.

38. T.D. Wilson, "On user studies and information needs", The Journal of Documentation, 37, 1, 3-15, 1981.

39. J.K Wu, A. N. Desai, B.M Mehtre, C.P. Lam, and J.Y. Gao, "CORE: A content-based retrieval engine for multimedia information systems", Multimedia Systems, 3, 23-41, 1995.

40. Z. J. Zheng and C.H.C. Leung, "Automatic image indexing for rapid content-based retrieval", Proc., International Workshop on Multi-media Database Management Systems, New York, 38-45, 1996,

Navigational Exploration and Declarative Queries in a Prototype for Visual Information Systems[1]

Lutz Wegner, Sven Thelemann, Jens Thamm, Dagmar Wilke, Stephan Wilke
Universität Kassel, FB Mathematik/Informatik, D-34109 Kassel, Germany[2]

Abstract. We introduce ESCHER, a prototype database system for visual information systems based on the extended non-first-normal-form data model. The nested table approach is the paradigm for the graphical interface which allows browsing, editing and querying the database. Interaction is achieved by fingers generalizing the well-known cursor concept. Apart from explaining this navigational interaction and the necessary system support for „real-time" feed-back, we focus on interactive query formulation for nested tables in a QBE-like fashion. Emphasis is on ad-hoc queries by casual users which are typical for visual information systems. The paper closes with examples of non-textual data types which are seamlessly integrated into the data model and the interface.

1 Introduction

In his invited talk at the 1995 Conference on Very Large Data Bases in Zurich, Switzerland, David DeWitt created quite a commotion when he asked „Database Systems: Road Kill on the Information Superhighway?" — pointing out that most information systems, like the Web [4], employ servers without DB-technology [8]. Thus, trusted database concepts, like e.g. integrity constraints, views, declarative queries, a clear separation of conceptual and internal schemas etc., are missing in today's systems as evidenced in the high number of dangling references in the Web.

Similarly, it has been argued that the present hypertext paradigm for Visual Information Systems (VIS) in the Internet will not succeed in the long run because it is based on navigational exploration. Although the existence of search engines and autonomous agents can help in this context, it is quite likely that the growth of the Net will soon inhibit any useful searches unless very precise declarative queries can be issued against an improved system which e.g. permits query optimization and collection of references without loading of actual pages, as implemented in e.g. Hyper-G [19].

On the other hand, database development has not progressed enough to provide cheap, possibly public domain database servers for non-standard applications supporting complex objects, multimedia data types, interoperability, declarative que-

---

1. Revised and extended version of a contribution to the 1996 Int. Conf. on Visual Information Systems [37]
2. Work supported in part by SAP AG, Walldorf, Germany

ries and navigational user interaction modes. Stonebraker [27] argues that this will be the domain of the so-called object-relational DBMSs which by the year 2005 will have a market share of 1.5 times the one of relational DBMS and 150 times the one of object-oriented DBMS.

Within this framework, visual aspects will be of central interest which should not come as a surprise considering that even today most software projects spend more time and money on the interface than on all other components together. Accordingly, a recent editorial [25] predicts a \$3.79 billion market for visual development tools by 1999 which should be seen in perspective against todays relational market which rates at \$8 billion per year [27, p. 18].

In this paper we introduce ESCHER, a Visual Information System prototype supporting non-standard applications as encountered in science, engineering, tourism and the entertainment industry. ESCHER originated in 1987 as part of a joint research project with IBM Scientific Center Heidelberg and became operational in 1989 as a database editor [16, 29, 33, 34]. The underlying data model is an extension of the classical NF^2 (non first normal form) data model [1, 7, 26] which in turn predates what is now often called the object-relational model [27].

The user interface of ESCHER features tabular representations of hierarchical (nested, or NF^2-) "views" of database instances, including non-standard data types like pixel data. It provides the fundamental means of interaction for browsing and editing of complex objects, visual query formulation and query result display — which is the focus of this paper —, interactive schema design and computer supported cooperative work (CSCW) [35]. At present, ESCHER's representation and editing techniques for complex objects are being ported to a 4GL. They will become part of one of the next releases of a large business processing system. The research version of ESCHER is available as public domain software for IBM RS/6000, HP 9000 series, and LINUX-based machines under OSF/Motif. A port to SUN-machines is currently under way at La Trobe University in Australia.

The remainder of this paper is organized as follows. In Section 2 we describe ESCHER's tabular representations of schemas and tables. Section 3 discusses our approach to interaction by means of so-called *fingers*, which are a generalization of the well-known cursor concept. Section 4 will introduce ESCHER's QBE-like query formulation. In Section 5 we will then report on our implementation experiences with multimedia, which can be seamlessly integrated into ESCHER's nested table paradigm for the user interface. Section 6 compares our approach with related work from the extensive literature on visual editors and visual query formulation (see [3, 20] for additional references). Section 7 summarizes the paper.

2 A Tabular Approach

The most wide-spread method for information display, at the instance level, is by means of tables. Typical examples are listings of flight, train or bus connections, listings of TV-programs, office directories in buildings, etc.

Information about an entity is collected within one tuple (row) with attributes appearing as columns. Appearance of several entities, usually in some type of sort order, within one table provides desirable context information ("... there are several flight connections, which one is direct?") which is not available in form-based (tuple-at-a-time) representations.

When relationship information is included, say in a view created from normalized tables e.g. for a list of employees together with the projects they work on and the courses they have visited, (flat) tables can become cumbersome requiring one entry (row) for each possible combination in PROJECTS × COURSES. Arranging the entries in nested form can help, at least if the relationship is hierarchical, as indicated in Figure 1. It also shows ESCHER's way of displaying database instances with the structure of the table, also called the table *schema*, above the table.

#ENO	[ ]NAME		<>COURSES		{}PROJ	
	LAST	FIRST	CID	DATE	PID	#BUDGET
4711	Monari	Lisa	Unix SQL C++	4-89 10-92 5-93	Escher Herkul+	20000 175000
4712	?s?	?s?	<???>		{???}	
4713	Smith	Adam	NetAdmin	2-87	{}	
4714	Newcome	Rita	C++ Tcl/Tk	7-95 11-95	Escher	20000
4715	Fraser	John	<>		EWIN	?d?

Figure 1: A snapshot of the EMPLOYEE table

Alternative representations include graphs of all kinds where attribute values appear within nodes and relationships are expressed as arcs [17]. While this visualization method is very useful at the schema level, it becomes fast unmanageable — unless sophisticated lens and fading techniques are employed — when several dozens of instances are to be shown. Similarly, virtual rooms, bookshelves or orbits [15] permit visually appealing navigation, however, all at a high computational cost.

Tabular representations also include meta-data such as schemas and catalogues.

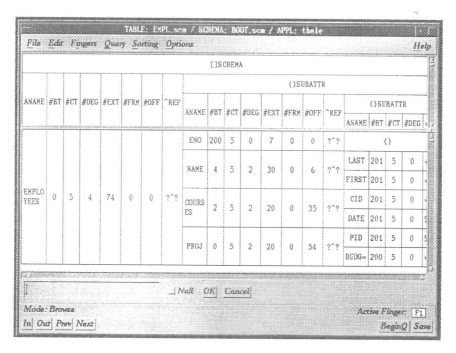

Figure 2: The EMPLOYEES-Schema under the BOOT-Schema

Figure 2 shows the schema of the EMPLOYEES-table of Figure 1 in a tabular representation underneath a meta-schema, called Boot-Schema in ESCHER. The name refers to the fact that it is the first schema which is loaded at system boot time. This schema also constitutes a fixpoint because it is the schema of all schemas including itself. Note that the tuples of the schema appear as sets in the meta-schema because attributes are unordered in relational theory. Accordingly, atomic attributes have an empty SUBATTRIBUTES-set (see e.g. the ENO-attribute).

Displaying this (infinite) meta-schema, which is implemented as a self-referential loop, is actually possible but omitted here. In general, being able to store meta-information within the system under consideration and being able to display this information visually not only facilitates the implementation phase but is also a good test of design consistency.

3 Interaction

Access to the data is provided by means of so called *fingers*. They generalize the cursor paradigm of graphics and text editors. They are displayed as a colored area which corresponds to the object a finger is currently pointing at. In a table more than one finger may point to objects, one of which is the *active finger* and is used for navigating through the table.

In Figure 1, finger F1 is the active one. The colored areas indicate that F1 is positioned on a NAME-tuple. Note that there are actually two colored areas: apart from the data object, the corresponding structure in the schema part is also shaded. The mode is *Browse* because atomic values cannot be entered for complex attributes. When the user descends to the atomic fields of this complex attribute, the mode-indicator will change to *Edit*-mode and the data entry widget at the lower left will become activated. Note also the way null values are shown: the entries ?s?, <???>, and {???} are null values of string, list, and set type.

Essential operations on fingers are the navigational operations "going into an object" (*In*, i.e. descending into the next deeper nesting level), "out to the surrounding object" (*Out*), "to the next object" (*Next*, staying on the same nesting level), and "to the previous object" (*Prev, Back*). These operations are also used internally, e.g. when the trees representing the query are matched against schema and table tree. At the graphical interface, the user navigates through the instances using the same basic finger operations, but may also use the mouse to move the active finger to the area of interest. The mouse click gets translated in a sequence of finger operations.

This poses some interesting problems, both for interaction semantics and for the required performance. Consider Figure 3 for possible mouse actions, where **X** denotes „single left button click", **XX** double-click, and **O** → **O** a „left-button-down-drag".

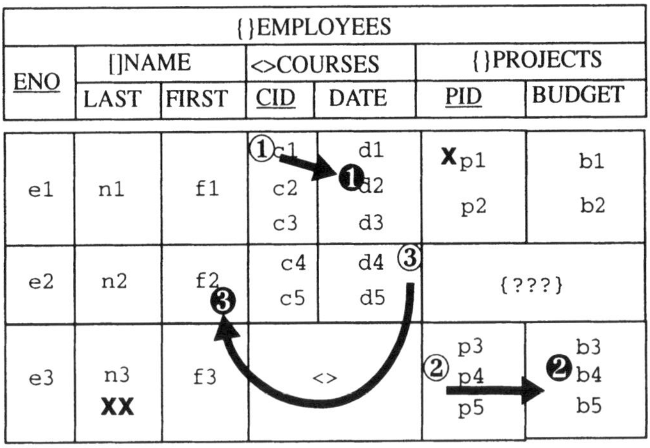

{}EMPLOYEES						
ENO	[]NAME		<>COURSES		{}PROJECTS	
	LAST	FIRST	CID	DATE	PID	BUDGET
e1	n1	f1	①c1 c2 c3	d1 ❶d2 d3	**X**p1 p2	b1 b2
e2	n2	f2 ❸	c4 c5	d4 ③ d5	{???}	
e3	n3 **XX**	f3	<>		② p3 p4 p5	b3 ❷b4 b5

Figure 3: Mouse Interaction Semantics

A single mouse click, as on p1 in Figure 3, causes the finger to move onto the atomic object (integer, text, boolean, pixel picture) on which the mouse cursor happened to rest at that time. Similarly, a double click permits updating of an atomic object, in our example entering a new last name for n3. The interaction mode then changes from browse to edit and a separate entry widget appears. Editing directly in place is under consideration but more difficult to implement.

A mouse drag is used to place the finger on the smallest syntactically valid object which encloses start and end point of the drag. The term „syntactically valid" refers to the fact that ESCHER cannot place fingers on subsets (sublists)

within set- or list-valued objects like PROJECTS or COURSES above or on sub-
ranges of attributes (projections) of tuples.

Thus, the move ① → ❶ places the finger on the set of courses {[c1, d1], ...,
[c3, d3]} of employee e1,② → ❷ places the finger on the tuple [p4, b4] and ③
→ ❸ places the finger on the entire e2 employee tuple.

The last move, which temporarily touches the e3 tuple, requires an extra com-
ment. As the cursor enters the e3 tuple, all of the table becomes colored in the color
of the active finger because the set of EMPLOYEES would be the proper syntactic
unit for this movement. As the cursor moves back into the e2 tuple, the color jumps
back to this tuple. Thus, the user receives immediate feedback as the mouse cursor
enters the territory of new objects. This implies for ESCHER that redrawing of the
visible part of the table with active finger shown as colored area must happen as
soon as the finger area changes and not only at „button-up-time"! This makes
mouse-initiated finger movements much easier to use than we can describe here.

On the other hand, having the ESCHER-finger follow the mouse cursor without
noticeable delay puts hard performance requirements on the system: normally the
employees table will consist of several thousand tuples and only a small portion
will be visible. While this is equally true for highlighting paragraphs in WYSI-
WYG text editors, ESCHER has to deal with variable size objects whose extension
is recursively defined and can change anytime due to insertions and deletions.

ESCHER solves the problem by drawing the visible portion from the inside to
the outside making some intelligent guesses about the object extensions and performing software clipping as soon as drawing reaches non-visible objects. Details

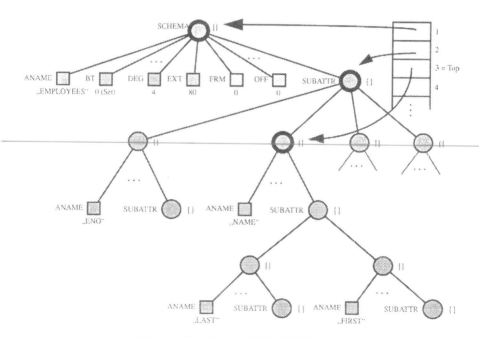

Figure 4: Tree for the EMPLOYEES-schema

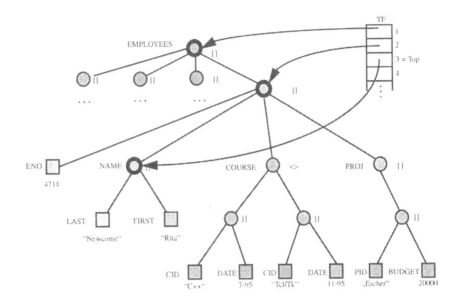

Figure 5: Object tree with stack for a table finger

of these clever heuristics can be found in [38, 39].

Fingers are also employed for cut-and-paste operations, in schema definitions, for query formulation as shown below in Section 4, and for many internal tasks, e.g. the just mentioned drawing of schema and table, for sorting and nest/unnest-operations, and for „catching" a mouse click, i.e. assigning it to the proper node in the object tree. Note also that fingers come in pairs as mentioned above. Figures 4 and 5 above illustrate this point again by showing a schema finger inside the schema tree, respectively inside the EMPLOYEES-table.

It should also be mentioned that the finger paradigm is not limited to a tabular representation. High-lighting or otherwise marking an object which has received the focus of interest is a familiar notion and is employed in many editors for vector graphics and in fact had been operational in ESCHER at one point for vector graphic interpretations of complex objects [24]. Moreover, as pointed out before in [33], fingers — unlike most iconic representations — are independent of a cultural context. This makes them especially valuable for Visual Information Systems which these days might operate world-wide.

At present, tasks like visual editing, sorting and duplicate deletion, export and import of tables, etc. are implemented through a library of some 150 C-functions which is called the *Object Manager*. The Object Manager (OM) in turn sits on top of the *Data Manager* (DM) which implements the typed complex objects of the OM as trees of untyped nodes (containers). The Data Manager relies on services of the *Record Manager* (RM) which stores byte strings in paged files using our own software-based pointer swizzling technique [36].

Thus, ESCHER is not implemented on top of any existing relational or object-oriented DBMS. Neither does it use a DBMS programming language nor does it offer one, at present. However, there are two proposals for such languages for ESCHER, called SCRIPT [22] and SCRIPT++ [30], the latter with an extensive operational semantics description.

Finally, a simpler interpretative navigational language which directly models OM-functions has been designed. As can be seen from the overview in Table 1, it is based on Tcl [21] with fingers treated as widgets. Ultimately, the scripting language will allow users to add own methods to types and to extend the interface through Tcl/Tk.

Table 1: Basic set of finger operations in Tcl

Command	Remark
finger .F T	constructor for finger F, viewed as a widget, which places F over table T
pop .F	move Finger F to enclosing object
push .F **-first** **-last** **-name** A	move finger F on first enclosed object move finger F on last enclosed object move finger F to attribute A (when previously on tuple)
go .F **-next** **-back** **-name** A	move finger F to next object (below, to right) move finger F to previous object (above, to left) move finger F to attribute A (from another attribute A')
put .F V	update value which finger F points to with new value V
get .F	return value which finger F points to
isfirst .F	return true iff finger F on first element of collection
islast .F	return true iff finger F on last element of collection
isempty .F	return true iff finger F on an empty collection
insert .F **-before** **-after**	inserts a null-object before finger F and move F onto element inserts a null-object after finger F and move F onto element
delete .F	delete object to which finger F currently points and move F to predecessor or to successor or, if neither exists, to enclosing object
fork .F1 .F2	create from finger F1 another finger F2; both currently point to the same object
free .F	release finger F
isatomic .F	return true iff finger F points to atomic object

4 Query Formulation and Query Result Display

As mentioned in the introduction, navigational exploration of information is typical of Visual Information Systems but is not sufficient in the long run. On the other hand, declarative queries in an SQL style are not suitable for the casual user either.

One solution is the use of a template to fill in values which must be matched by a query. The idea goes back to Zloof's landmark paper [40] introducing the QBE (Query-By-Example) language for the relational data model. Templates corresponding to relations of the database schema are filled in to express selection predicates. Variables (the "examples") express relational joins. Projection symbols specify the schema of the result table.

ESCHER follows the template paradigm but with some interesting modifications due to the complex object data model. For the following discussion, we assume the reader to be familiar with QBE as presented in e.g. [20, 40].

4.1 Query definition and execution

In ESCHER a typical query consists of the following steps:

(i) From the overall database schema, a *view table* is created which results in a new table with a nested structure, thus representing a nested view on the database.

This step uses a tool navigating over ER-like diagrams to create a nested view from existing (nested or flat) base tables. In our example, EMPLOYEES would become the root and PROJECTS and COURSES would be joined (nested) as sub-attributes into the view. Of course, it is an open question as to what extent the casual user may be allowed to create his or her own view tables of the database. Here we assume that the casual user may choose among a predefined set of nested base or view tables.

(ii) The user chooses a table of interest (the *query* table), say the EMPLOYEES-table from Figure 1. Such a table is either a base table or a view table created by step (i). The table is displayed on the screen and the user starts a query by clicking on the *BeginQ* button or selecting *BeginQuery* from the pull-down menu of the table window. This step corresponds to the FROM-part of a SELECT-FROM-WHERE query.

(iii) Now a dependent window appears on the screen with a QUERY template and schema. The QUERY schema corresponds to the structure of the query table. The QUERY template is initialized with a default value and edited for specifying the selection predicates in a QBE-like fashion. This will be explained in detail below. Step (iii) corresponds to the WHERE-part of a SELECT-FROM-WHERE query.

(iv) The user has to specify what is usually called the SELECT-part of the query. For that purpose he has the choice between two modes of query result display:
    – *Search mode*: The user positions the active finger to the substructure of interest in the QUERY schema. When the query is executed, the active finger in the window for the query table becomes the *query finger*. It is positioned on the first data object that "matches" with the select conditions as specified in

the QUERY template. Its structure is constrained by the structure given by the active finger in the QUERY schema. By clicking on the *Next* button the user can move the query finger to the next found data object and so on until the end of the table is reached. This is much in the tradition of well-known search utilities for text editors.

– *Filter mode*: By choosing the filter mode, the result of the query is shown in a RESULT table displayed in a separate window and only the "matching" tuples or values are filtered out and shown in the RESULT table. This is the way most database systems present the result of a query to the user.

(v) The definition of a query is finished by clicking on the *EndDef* button in the QUERY window. The query is then executed by clicking on the *RunQ* button.

The usual method to present the result of a query is, of course, to create a result table as in our *filter mode*. The *search mode* is particularly suitable for a browser like ESCHER because it shows the information in context. This situation is not uncommon in applications at which we aim with our DBMS. In tourism, e.g., the result of a query might be acceptable or not depending on the choice there is and the willingness of the customer to accept alternatives. In searching for a hotel, a particular offer becomes acceptable if the user sees that the price range is in general above his/her specified limit or that there is a very limited selection anyway. Similarly in flight and train connections, seeing the context outside the exact scope of a query can be very helpful, e.g. in a situation like " ... there are two connections leaving X between 8 and 10 am, but both involve changing trains twice; however, if you were willing to leave at 7:45 am, I could offer you a non-stop connection ...".

Finally it should be mentioned that queries can be saved for future reuse. Figure 6 below shows a snapshot from ESCHER with a query for employees who have either visited a course on *Unix* and *C++* and who work on project *Tasman*. Details are explained in Section 4.2 where similar queries are discussed.

4.2 Syntax and semantics of queries

We now turn to steps (ii) through (v) from above, especially to the syntax and semantics of the QUERY template, which specifies the selection conditions of a query. It will be shown how QBE-like queries correspond to a textual query. The textual representation then gives us the semantics of the graphical query. The textual query language for ESCHER is part of the proposed database programming language SCRIPT, which has especially been designed for ESCHER [22]. It is based on set and list former expressions whose semantics is assumed to be intuitively clear from the given examples.

We start with a simple query involving a conjunction of elementary conditions. An elementary condition is of the form $A \; \theta \; B$, where A and B are atomic path expressions, atomic literals, or atomic variables and θ is one of the comparison operators =, <>, <, >, <=, >=, and ~ (which compares a string value A with a regular expression B). The query

```
{ x.ENO | x in EMPLOYEES, y in x.COURSES, z in x.PROJ:
y.CID = "C++" and z.PID = "Escher"}
```

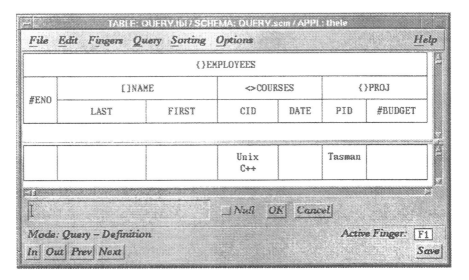

Figure 6: Searching for an employee with courses on $C++$ and Unix in project Tasman

asks for employees who have visited a C++ course and work in the project Escher (Figure 7 (a)). The already nested structure of the query table makes explicit join conditions unnecessary. Note that as in the case of relational QBE queries, the "="-operator is assumed when no explicit operator is given. The shaded area in the QUERY template of Figure 7 (a) corresponds to the .P-flag known from "flat" QBE [40]. In the given example this means: Whenever a combination (x, y, z) matches the selection condition, x.ENO is to be "printed". In *search mode* this implies moving the query finger to the just found x.ENO value in the query table.

The query

$\{$ x.ENO $\mid$ x in EMPLOYEES, y_1 in x.COURSES, y_2 in x.COURSES:
y_1.CID = "C++" and y_2.CID = "Unix" $\}$

asks for employees who have visited both a C++ and a Unix course. The corresponding QBE-query is (b1). In flat QBE, variables would have to be employed to express the query.

Query (b1) involves a set inclusion condition. In ESCHER-QBE an alternative syntax expresses set inclusion more directly, as shown in Figure 7 (b2), which is an alternative for Figure 7 (b1). The following *collection conditions* can be used: $A \ \theta$ B, where A and B are collections (sets or lists) and θ is one of the comparison operators $=, \subseteq, \supseteq, \subset, \supset$. Besides that, ESCHER-QBE supports the disjointness condition $A \cap B = \varnothing$ (A has none of B) and the non-disjointness condition $A \cap B \neq \varnothing$ (A has some of B). While editing the query template and depending on the position of the active finger the appropriate conditions (elementary or collection-oriented) can be chosen from a "conditions" menu. Figure 7 (c) illustrates the usage of the disjointness condition $A \cap B = \varnothing$. The query asks for those employees who do not work on Escher or Herkules.

So far we have only considered conjunctions of selection conditions. The query

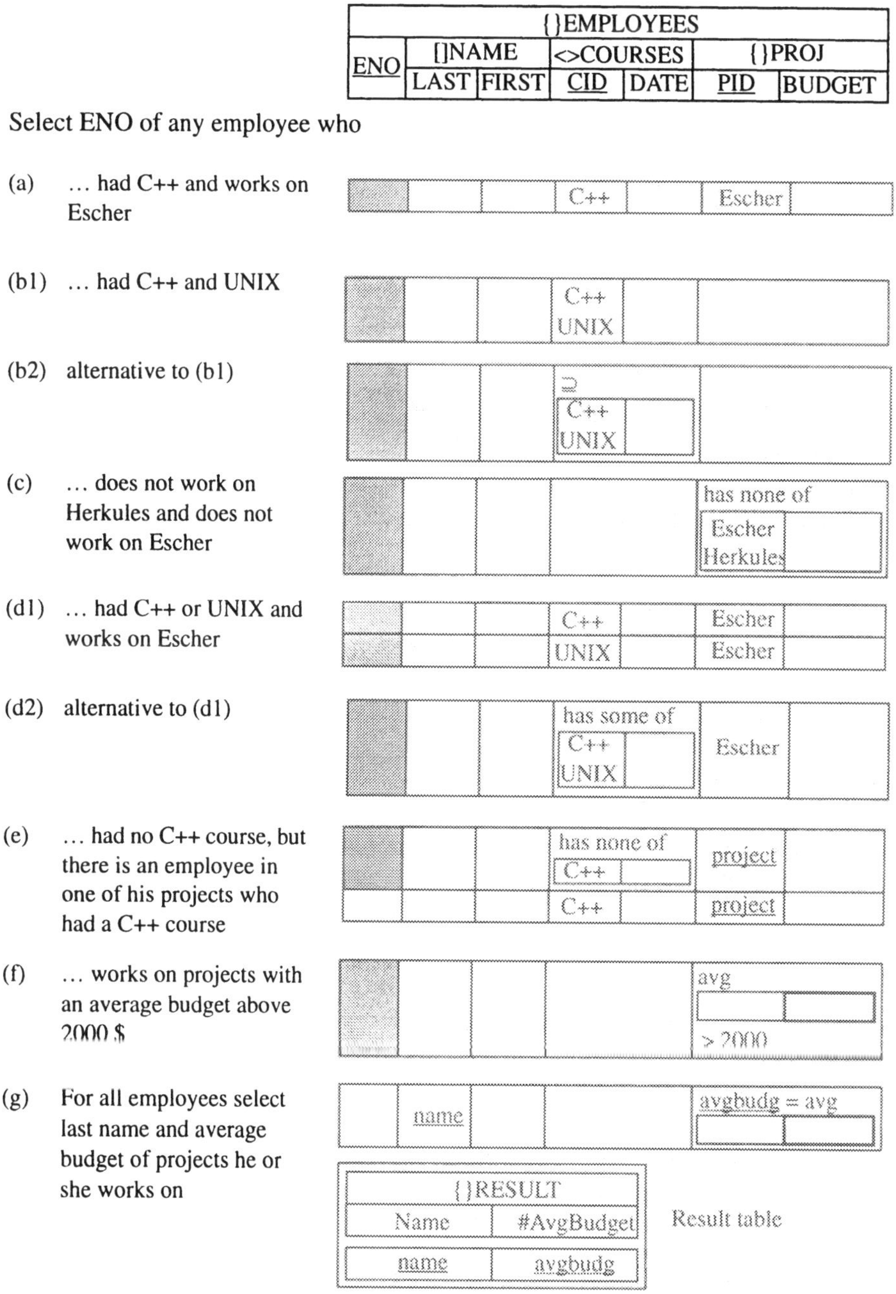
{}EMPLOYEES
ENO
[]NAME
LAST
FIRST
<>COURSES
CID
DATE
{}PROJ
PID
BUDGET
Select ENO of any employee who
(a) … had C++ and works on Escher
C++
Escher
(b1) … had C++ and UNIX
C++
UNIX
(b2) alternative to (b1)
⊇
C++
UNIX
(c) … does not work on Herkules and does not work on Escher
has none of
Escher
Herkules
(d1) … had C++ or UNIX and works on Escher
C++
Escher
UNIX
Escher
(d2) alternative to (d1)
has some of
C++
UNIX
Escher
(e) … had no C++ course, but there is an employee in one of his projects who had a C++ course
has none of
C++
project
C++
project
(f) … works on projects with an average budget above 2000 $
avg
> 2000
(g) For all employees select last name and average budget of projects he or she works on
name
avgbudg = avg
{}RESULT
Name
#AvgBudget
name
avgbudg
Result table

Figure 7: Sample queries

{ x.ENO | x in EMPLOYEES, y in x.COURSES, z in x.PROJ:
(y.CID = "C++" or y.CID = "Unix") and z.PID = "Escher"}

involves a disjunction and asks for employees having visited a C++ *or* a Unix course. The query is equivalent to

{ x.ENO | x in EMPLOYEES, y in x.COURSES, z in x.PROJ:
y.CID = "C++" and z.PID = "Escher"} ∪
{ x.ENO | x in EMPLOYEES, y in x.COURSES, z in x.PROJ:
y.CID = "Unix" and z.PID = "Escher"}

This gives us a first ESCHER-QBE formulation of the query, as shown in Figure 7 (d1). Here, two ENO fields are marked, which corresponds to the union of the two sub-queries (flat QBE would employ two .P-flags). Another solution is shown in Figure 7 (d2): The query can be restated with an non-disjointness condition $A \cap B \neq \emptyset$ (A has some of B). This solution has the advantage that the condition z.PID = "Escher" needs to be formulated only once.

Up to this point we could avoid the use of variables (i.e. the *examples* in QBE-languages), because the nested structure of the query table already contains implicit joins. Case (e) in Figure 7 involves a join with the same table: "Find all employees who had no C++ course but work on a project which has an employee who participated in a C++ course". In order to express the join we introduce the variable project (an underlined name distinguishes a variable from other entries). The textual version of the query is

{ x.ENO | x in EMPLOYEES, y in EMPLOYEES, z_1 in x.PROJ, z_2 in
y.PROJ,
u in y.COURSES: {"C++"} $\cap$ {c.CID | c in x.COURSES} = $\emptyset$ and
z_1.PID = z_2.PID and u.CID = "C++"}

In ESCHER-QBE functions having a set- or list-valued argument may become part of a query. This includes common aggregate functions like count, sum, avg, min, max. The query of Figure 7 (f) asks for employees working for projects with an average budget above 2.000 K\$. Its textual counterpart is

{x.ENO | x in EMPLOYEES: avg({y.BUDGET | y in x.PROJ}) > 2000}

If the elements of a collection are tuples, which is the most common case, then the argument to an aggregate function is specified by highlighting the relevant tuple attribute in a tuple template positioned below the aggregate function name.

If the function value, i.e. derived information, is to become part of the query result output, then *filter mode* must be chosen. In that case variables have to be used for connecting the QUERY templates with a separate RESULT table. Figure 7 (g) shows how a result table consisting of (name, average budget)-pairs is constructed. The result of applying an aggregation function can be assigned to a variable:

avgbudg = avg({y.BUDGET | y in x.PROJ})

The variables name and avgbudg are used to construct tuples to be inserted in the RESULT table. The textual version of the query is given by

RESULT := {[Name: x.NAME.LAST, AvgBudget: avg({y.BUDGET | y in
x.PROJ})] | x in EMPLOYEES}

Finally it is shown how ESCHER supports the notion of continued queries. The query

   {x.COURSES | x in EMPLOYEES: x.ENO = 4711}

returns the complete list of courses for the employee with ENO 4711. When executing the query a unique (ENO is a key!) COURSES-list is found and in search mode the active finger is positioned on this list. We could now query for particular courses, say after a certain date, within the new scope of courses of employee 4711. As in „flat" QBE, more complex selection conditions can be entered in separate condition boxes.

Before we compare the approach above with existing example-based query formalisms, we like to point out our current status with regard to non-standard data types.

5 Multimedia Extensions

ESCHER is designed to include various non-textual data types, like pixel pictures, vector graphics, sound, and video. Presently, ESCHER features import, export, storage, and display of GIF (up to 256 colors), JPG (true color) and XBM (bitmap) pixel pictures. As an example, Figure 8 shows a nested table for a hotel information system with the cursor positioned on a hotel in Hamburg. The placement of the cursor might result from running a query formulated in a QBE-like fashion with "Hamburg" entered in the city-field as explained in Section 4.

Of course, a pixel-valued attribute can participate in the usual editor operations, like cut-and-paste. It could also be moved to a QBE-template to serve as search criteria except that search conditions for pictures have not been defined. Also the usual finger operations could operate inside a pixel picture, i.e. to clip part of the picture and to zoom (stepwise IN/OUT finger operation). Picture data are of little interest for query formulation unless particular algorithms for feature extraction are considered which are outside the scope of this paper.

On the other hand, pictorial data can easily be used to enhance the information content of query results. The obvious case is to make the picture(s) integral part of the selected tuples, as with x-ray pictures in medical information systems, floor-prints and pictures of houses for sale in the real estate business, or hotel pictures in a tourist information system. Depending on the weight of the picture, the remaining textual information can be considered as an annotation of the picture which can guide the search or conversely, the picture is simply an add-on.

Continuing along this line of design, a pixel picture can be used to transform textual information, e.g. a hotel location when a street plan is added to the city tuple in the hotel example above. Moving the finger to a particular hotel creates a corresponding marker in the street plan. Again, this falls well within ESCHER's tabular visualization paradigm but needs extra application support.

Finally, QBE-like queries is of interest as part of network browsing, e.g. in the Web. As a preliminary step, we have implemented ESCHER's display style for NF^2 tables using HTML (see Figure 9). As for query formulation, however, HTML provides insufficient interaction expressiveness to support ESCHER's finger paradigm.

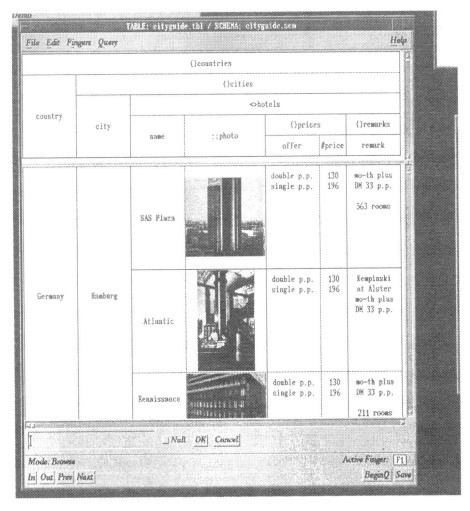

Figure 8: Screen shot for hotel application

Interested readers should visit our WWW-server at http://www.db.informatik.uni-kassel.de/ .

6 Related Work

As pointed out in [20], QBE directly implements the domain relational calculus of Codd. To handle universal quantification, QBE introduces limited set operators. It extends the calculus by permitting simple aggregation functions like *Sum*, *Max*, *Min*, and *Average*. However, as QBE has no scoping concept, the operators are not powerful enough to express all relational calculus queries without naming and saving intermediate queries. Finally, QBE in its original form has no provisions for

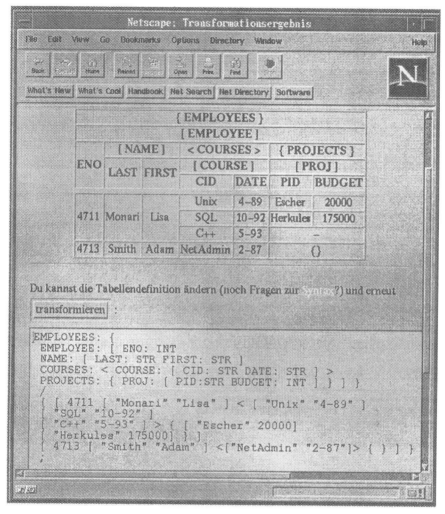

Figure 9: The EMPLOYEES-example as generated HTML-table

tables which are not in first normal form.

Several languages extend QBE as summarized in [20]: Aggregates-by-Example, Summary-Table-by-Example, Query-by-Statistical-Relational-Table, Time-by-Example, Generalized-Query-by-Example, Office-by-Example, Formanager, The Natural Forms Query Language, System-for-Business-Automation, PICQUERY, and Query-by-Pictorial-Example.

In particular, Generalized-Query-by-Example (GQBE) addresses nested tables since the language supports relational, hierarchical and network data models. Queries in GQBE look similar to queries in ESCHER as can be seen from the following table which has the task to "find all the names of personnel having at least one boy and one girl as children" [20, p. 33].

Table 2: Generalized-Query-by-Example

| PERSONNEL-N | pname | sex | CHILDREN | | |
			ename	sex	age
	P.*george*		mike	M	
			annie	F	

Formanager addresses the problem of nested tables by introducing an algorithmic concept with programs and subprograms. ESCHER has no programming constructs for QBE-like queries but can store queries and can chain queries where subsequent queries occur in the scope of the result finger as set by the previous query.

Almost all of the above mentioned example-based languages support aggregate functions and have condition boxes. Aggregates-by-Example, Summary-Table-by-Example and Time-by-Example also provide unrestricted set operations which we feel is the cleanest way of dealing with collection data.

Finally, Office-by-Example supports image objects much in the way ESCHER does, i.e. for viewing and editing, but not for query formulation. To handle feature extraction and geometrical queries, systems like PICQUERY and Query-by-Pictorial-Example provide highly specialized functions. In general, combining multimedia data types with an NF^2-algebra might be a promising step towards more formalized computational models for multimedia systems [10, 14].

On the browser side, interfaces similar to ESCHER which are suitable for the casual user are the form-based approaches [11, 12]. Other browsers navigate along the arcs of a graph which represent entities and relationships or class hierarchies [2, 5, 17]. They do not support the skeleton approach of QBE.

A language for specifying interfaces to nested relational databases can be found in [9] while a visual language approach to interfaces is presented in [6]. Stack-based query languages similar to our Tcl-extension are proposed in e.g. [28].

The strength of ESCHER is then that it combines a powerful browser for the nested relational model with a QBE-like querying facility thus making set operations a natural part of the interface. Moreover, other non-standard data types are easily integrated and can enhance result output as required for Visual Information Systems. Last, but not least, most queries shown in this paper are operational.

7 Conclusions

In this paper we presented an interactive ad-hoc query facility for an extended NF^2 data model as implemented by the database prototype ESCHER. Defining a query can be divided into 5 steps as indicated in Section 4. In step (i) of the query formulation, a suitable view is created from the global database schema leading to a view table with a local schema. The steps (ii) through (v) show how the user specifies selection conditions in the QUERY template being the core of the QBE-like query facility. The semantics of this interactive query definition was given in detail. For the discussion, it had been assumed that all necessary information for queries was contained in a single query table. If this is not the case, part (i) has to be resumed by extending the query table.

Through several examples we have indicated that complex queries are possible and we claim that QBE-queries in the context of nested relations are easier to understand than those of „flat" QBE. We have omitted examples for queries across several tables, although they add to the expressive power of the query language.

In summary, we aim at the *casual* user who is mainly interested in "simple" ad-hoc queries on pre-defined query tables. In particular, we see ESCHER's QBE-like query facility as a type of autopilot for flying over "data space". By entering appropriate coordinates, ESCHER will direct the user to the target area from where he or she can navigate to make "a visual landing" on a specific data tuple.

Future work on ESCHER will focus on concurrency to permit computer supported cooperative work [35] where the multiple finger paradigm is a natural starting point but must be enhanced by extended transactional concepts.

References

[1]   S. Abiteboul, N. Bidoit. Non First Normal Form Relations. An Algebra Allowing Data Restructuring. Rapp. de Recherche No. 347, INRIA, Rocquencourt, France, Nov. 1984

[2]   A. Auddino, Y. Dennebouy, Y. Dupont, E. Fontana, S. Spaccapietra and Z. Tari. SUPER: A Comprehensive Approach to Database Visual Interfaces. In [13], pp. 365-380.

[3]   C. Batini, T. Catarci, M.F. Costabile, S. Levialdi. Visual Query Systems. Tech. Rep. No. 04.91 (March 1991), Dipartimento di Informatica e Sistemistica, Universita degli Studi di Roma "La Sapienza"

[4]   T.Berners-Lee et al. The World-Wide Web, CACM 37:8 (1994) 76-82

[5]   Daniel Bryce, Richard Hull: SNAP: A Graphics-based Schema-Manager. In: Stanley B. Zdonik, David Maier (eds.): Readings in Object-Oriented Database Systems. San Mateo (CA): Morgan Kaufmann, 1990 537-550

[6]   S.-K.Chang, G.Costagliola et al. Visual-Language System for User Interfaces, IEEE Software 12:2 (March 1995) 33-44

[7]   P. Dadam, K. Küspert, F. Andersen, H. Blanken, R. Erbe, J. Günauer, V. Lum, P. Pistor, G. Walch. A DBMS Prototype to support extended NF^2 relations: An integrated view on flat tables and hierarchies. Proc. ACM SIGMOD Conf. on Management of Data, Washington, 1986, pp.356-366

[8]   David DeWitt. Database Systems: Road Kill on the Information Superhighway, Invited Talk (not included in proceedings), 21st VLDB, Zurich, Switzerland (1995)

[9]   G.-J. Houben, J. Paredaens. A Graphical Interface Formalism: Specifying Nested Relational Databases, Proc. of the IFIP TC2 Work. Conf. on Visual Database Systems, Tokyo 1989, Elsevier Science Publ., Amsterdam (1989) 257-276

[10] T.Käppner and R.Steinmetz. Computational Models for Distributed Multimedia Applications, in: Computer Science Today, Jan van Leeuwen (Ed.), Springer LNCS 1000, Berlin-Heidelberg-New York, 592-607

[11] H. Kitagawa and T.L. Kunii. The Unnormalized Relational Data Model For Office Form Processor Design, Springer, Berlin-Heidelberg-New York (1989)

[12] Kitagawa et al. Form Document Management System SPECDOQ. Proc. ACM SIGOA Conference on Office Information Systems, Toronto, Canada, June 25-27, 1984 (published as SIGOA Newsletter, Vol. 5, Nos. 1-2), 1984, pp. 132-142

[13] E. Knuth and L.M. Wegner (eds): Proc. IFIP Work. Conf. on Visual Database Systems, Budapest, Hungary, 30.9-3.10.1991, Elsevier Science Publishers (North-Holland), 1992

[14] S.Koshafian and A. Brad Baker. Multimedia and Imaging Databases, Morgan Kaufmann, San Francisco, CA, 1996

[15] Uwe Krohn. VINETA: Navigation through Virtual Information Spaces, Proc. Advanced Visual Interfaces '96, Gubbio, Italy, May 27-30, 1996, ACM Press, 49-58

[16] K. Küspert, J. Teuhola, and L. Wegner. Design issues and first experience with a visual database editor for the extended NF^2 Data Model. Proc. 23rd Hawaii Int. Conf. System Science, January 1990, pp. 308-317

[17] M. Kuntz. A Versatile Browser-Editor for NF^2 Relations, Proc. 2nd Far-East Workshop on Future Database Systems, Kyoto, Japan (Apr. 26-28 1992), pp. 266-275

[18] M.Levene and G.Loizou. A Graph-Based Data Model and its Ramifications, IEEE TKDE 7:5 (1995) 809-823

[19] H.Maurer. Hypermedia Systems as Internet Tools, in: Computer Science Today, Jan van Leeuwen (Ed.), Springer LNCS 1000, Berlin-Heidelberg-New York, 608-624

[20] G. Özsoyoglu and H. Wang. Example-Based Graphical Database Query Languages, IEEE Computer 26:5 (May 1993) 25-38

[21] John K. Ousterhout. Tcl and the Tk Toolkit, Addison-Wesley, Reading, Mass., 1994

[22] M. Paul. Typerweiterung im eNF^2-Datenmodell. Ph.D. thesis (in German), Aachen: Shaker-Verlag, 1995

[23] C.Plaisant, D.Carr, and B.Shneiderman. Image-Browser Taxonomy and Guidelines for Designers, IEEE Software 12:2 (March 1995) 21-32

[24] A.Ramsay. A Graphics Interface for ESCHER, Project Report, Dept. of CS, The Univ. of Queensland, June 1992

[25] M.Snell: Industry Trends, Editorial IEEE Computer, March 1995, 8-9

[26] H.-J. Schek, M. Scholl. The Relational Model with Relation-Valued Attributes. Inf. Systems, Vol. 11, No. 2, 1986, pp. 137-147

[27] M.Stonebraker with Dorothy Moore, Object-Relational DBMSs: The Next Great Wave, Morgan Kaufmann Publishers, San Francisco, CA, 1996

[28] K.Subieta, C.Beeri, F.Matthes, J.W.Schmidt. A Stack-Based Approach to Query Languages, in Proc. 2nd Int. East/West Database Workshop, Klagenfurt, Austria, 25-28 Sept. 1994, J.Eder and L.A.Kalinichenko (Eds), Springer, London (1994) 159-180

[29] Sven Thelemann. Assertion of Consistency Within a Complex Object Database Using a Relationship Construct, Proc. 14th Int. Conf. Object-Oriented & Entity-Relationship Modeling, Bond Univ., Qld, Australia, Dec. 13-15, 1995

[30] Sven Thelemann. Semantische Anreicherung eines Datenmodells für komplexe Objekte, Ph.D. thesis (in German), Universiät Kassel, June 1996

[31] Sun Microsystems Computer Corporation. The Java Language Specification, Vers. 1.0 Beta, Oct. 1995

[32] Jens Thamm, Sven Thelemann, and Lutz Wegner. Visual Information Systems - A Database Perspective, Proc. DMS'96 - The Third Pacific Workshop on Distributed Multimedia Systems, (David Du and Olivia R. Liu Sheng eds.) June 25 - 28, 1996, The Hong Kong Univ. of Science and Technology, Clear Water Bay, Kowloon, Hong Kong, 274-285

[33] L.M. Wegner. ESCHER - Interactive, Visual Handling of Complex Objects in the Extended NF^2 Data Model. Proc. IFIP Work. Conference on Visual Database Systems, Tokyo (April 1989) 277-297

[34] L.M. Wegner. Let the Fingers Do the Walking: Object Manipulation in an NF^2 Database Editor. Proc. "New Results and New Trends in Comp. Science" (H. Maurer, ed.), Graz/Austria, June 1991, Springer LNCS 555 (1991), pp. 337-358

[35] L.Wegner, M.Paul, J.Thamm, and S.Thelemann. A Visual Interface for Synchronous Collaboration and Negotiated Transactions, Proc. Advanced Visual Interfaces '96, Gubbio, Italy, May 27-30, 1996, ACM Press, 156-165

[36] L.Wegner, M.Paul, J.Thamm, and S.Thelemann: Pointer Swizzling in Non-Mapped Object Stores, Proc. Seventh Australasian Database Conference (ADC'96), Melbourne, Australia, 29-30 January 1996, Rodney Topor (Ed), Australian Computer Science Communications 18:2, 11-20

[37] L.Wegner, S.Thelemann, S.Wilke, and R.Lievaart. QBE-like Queries and Multimedia Extensions in a Nested Relational DBMS, Proc. Int. Conf. on Visual Information Systems, Melbourne, Australia, 5-6 February 1996, C.Leung (Ed.), 437-446

[38] D. Wilke. Anforderungen und Konzepte der Handhabung komplexer Objekte in einem Datenbankeditor, Master's Thesis, Univ. Kassel, 1996 (in German)

[39] S. Wilke. Einsatz optimierter Visualisierungstechniken zur Darstellung komplexer Datenbankobjekte, Master's Thesis, Univ. Kassel, 1996 (in German)

[40] M. Zloof. Query-by-Example: A data base language, IBM Systems Journal 6 (1977) 324-343

Incorporating Typed Links
in a Visual Search Tool for Images on the Web

E. A. Rose

Massey University, Information Systems Dept.,

Palmerston North, New Zealand

E.A.Rose@massey.ac.nz

Abstract

This paper extends the query, search and browse algorithm (QSBA) [1], which provides a unified visual presentation of images found on the World Wide Web with typed links which can serve as a way to organise search results into recognisable patterns that can be visually explored more efficiently. User-defined relevancy criterion can be used to query typed links, in ranking search results and in varying the spatial organisation of result nodes based on semantic relationships. This visual search tool works with existing web indexers (manual and robot), browsing tools, and the HTML standard. A prototype system is currently under development.

1 Introduction and Motivation

The information hyperspace known as the World-Wide Web (WWW or the Web) has recently become an important source of information on a myriad of topics. The popularity of visual document browsing tools such as Mosaic [2] and Netscape [3] have helped to rapidly transform the Web from a hypertext information space to a hypermedia information space. The defacto Web policy of making software packages and browser add-ons readily available at low cost and the multi-platform nature of the Web have helped to further fuel the growth of this vast, distributed source of both visual and textual information.

This unprecedented, and largely uncontrolled growth also has its downside. Finding image information (aka visual information) is often very time consuming due not only to problems of limited bandwidth but also to inadequate search engines and indexing mechanisms for visual data on the Web. Robot-based search engines such as Lycos [4] and InfoSeek [5] as well as passive databases such as Yahoo [6] and the W3 Catalog [7] have been useful in providing a means of doing keyword searches of previously indexed web pages or sets of manually categorised web pages respectively, in addition to random browsing. Lycos[4] recently added the ability to restrict the results of keyword searches to visual data in the form of GIF, JPEG and MOV files. The result page of this type of search, shown in Figure 1, is a text based list of brief descriptions, each with a link which leads to an image or video file without the supporting textual information or context it originally appeared in. This can be problematic since the original context in which the image appeared may be of interest to the searcher as a source of related information for additional queries. A second problem is the need to browse each link to actually view the image. Similarly, Yahoo[6] has incorporated Excalibur's Visual Retrieval Ware [8] software into its Image Surfer option which is only available for a small set of indexed image

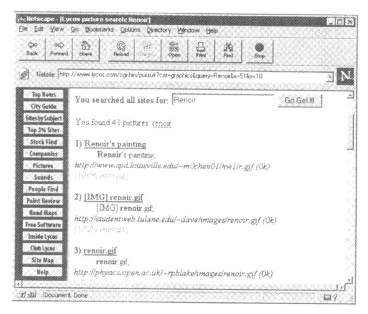

Fig. 1. Lycos Results Page, Search for Renoir Pictures

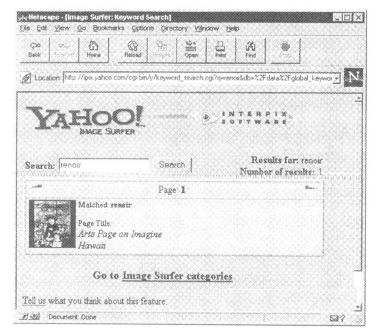

Fig. 2. Yahoo Image Surfer Results, Search for Renoir Pictures

files in a few categories. The Yahoo Image Surfer option allows the user to specify a relevancy weight (0 to 100) for the following visual search parameters: color content, texture content, grayscale shape and color shape as well as keywords. The result is a set of 4 to 24 (in multiples of 4) thumbnail links to images as shown in Figure 2, again without returning a link to the original context. The parameter choices are also somewhat technical for the average user. As only one image of a "Renoir" painting was returned however, the results were somewhat disappointing.

Previous research [9] suggests that browsing and querying exist on a continuum as hypermedia navigational techniques and therefore, a combination of both techniques ought to be explored in finding alternative ways of accessing both textual and visual information [10]. Searching the web in general is difficult since it is unstructured in the sense that nodes (HTML documents) and links which make up the Web do not have well-defined semantics in the form of a set of consistently defined node and link attributes which would facilitate both content-based and structure-based search respectively. Furthermore, there are no enforced standards for storage formats, available search engines use different ways of ranking results, the search space changes on a daily basis and some result links are out of date or "dangling".

QSBA, in an attempt to alleviate some of these problems, integrates searching for information in a casual manner without an a priori goal (aka browsing) with goal-directed search (aka querying). Techniques from the fields of information retrieval and database query languages are combined in order to allow a successively narrower or broader definition of the search space to be defined via computer-mediated, user specification of search parameters with hypermedia browsing.

The purpose of this work is to provide a mechanism which allows the user to find visual data stored on the Web and evaluate their relevance utilizing existing query and browse tools, enhanced with a transparent Hypertext Markup Language (HTML) [11] source search procedure. Typed links are proposed as a standard approach to adding greater semantics to the links between images and pages, within web pages and between pages. The search tool is referred to as a Query, Search and Browse Assistant (QSBA). In addition, the QSBA provides the user with a unified visual presentation, which combines the functionality of conversational and direct manipulation interfaces.

2   Exploratory Search Using Current Tools

Generally, existing search engines can be used to identify starting points on a particular topic. Keywords are entered and the search engine returns a possibly ranked list of Uniform Resource Locator (URL's) or links to web pages which were indexed on the specified keywords. Each item in the list is captioned with a brief description which varies depending on the search engine used.

The returned list must be browsed manually to see if any of the pages are relevant to the searcher. Selected links from the result hit list must often be traversed through several levels, with returns to the original list of hits to explore or browse additional paths until the desired information is located. The hit list serves as the root of a hierarchy of information that may possibly be relevant to the search task. If only a few relevant items are returned, the search engine seems fairly efficient. On the other hand, many irrelevant items may be returned and those which are ranked as most relevant may not be seen as such by the issuer of the initial query. The only way to determine the relevance to the user is for the user to browse each link until he/she tires of the process or finds enough relevant information.

To illustrate this point, an exploratory study utilising the Lycos and Yahoo search engines was performed to find image files of paintings by the French painter, Renoir. Each engine returned different results in terms of both content and ranking as shown in Table 1. Default options were used in both cases. Yahoo begins with the set of 14 categories shown in Figure 3 of which Art and Humanities served as the starting point. Yahoo orders by decreasing relevancy by giving greater weight to pages that contain all of the keywords, have matches in the <title> tag rather than in the body text or URL and that fall under more general categories. Given that many web page authors do not give "meaningful" titles to their pages, pages could be categorised in a number of ways, different search sites use different classification schemes and URL's don't always contain "meaningful" paths and filenames, searching can be problematic. Lycos orders search results by decreasing relevance to the keywords and performs an OR operation on them by default. Results containing all keywords appear higher on the hit list.

Table 1: Results of Exploratory Search

	Yahoo	Lycos
Index Type	Passive	Robot
Number of Hits (Site Search)	25	1855 (loose) 52 (strong)
Number of Hits (Category Search)	0	0 (loose) 0 (strong)
Number of Hits (Picture Search)	1	41 (loose) 41 (strong)
Search Options * - default option	-- **method**: intelligent*, exact phrase, match ALL, match ANY, person's name -- **area**:Yahoo Categories*, Sites, Today's News, Net Events -- **currency**: 1 day, 3 days, 1 wk, 1 mo, 6 mo, 3 yrs* -- **display**: 10, 20*, 50 or 100 matches/page	-- **method**: match ANY*, match ALL, match 2-7 words [also select loose*, fair, good, close or strong match] -- **area**: Sites*, Sounds, Pictures, By Subject (Lycos Categories) -- **currency**: Not available -- **display**: 10*,20,30 or 40 matches/page [also select summary, standard*, detail]

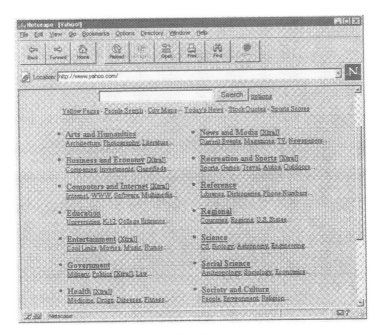

Fig. 3. Yahoo Initial Search Screen

Some of these problems can be seen by examining the search results in Appendix A. It is interesting to note that some sites which are indexed by both Yahoo and Lycos such as the "Web Museum, Paris" which resides at a number of mirror sites including sites whose URL's contain the word "Renoir" such as http://sunsite.nus.sg/wm/paint/auth/Renoir/ and http://sunsite.unc.edu/wm/paint/auth/Renoir/ and contains 26 different thumbnail images of Renoir paintings didn't appear via a category search in either case. However, 11 of the mirror sites do appear in the first 40 results of the Lycos site search but do not appear in the set of 41 image files in the Lycos picture search when using the keyword "Renoir". The word "Renoir" also appears in the <H1> tag on the Renoir page at several of these mirror sites. The Web Museum could be found using both Lycos and Yahoo when doing a search for either "WebMuseum" or "Web Museum".

Further examination of the results shows little commonality. The top ranked results in all three sets of URL's are different. Of the 25 URL's returned by Yahoo, 11 are relevant and one of them appears twice since it was indexed under 2 different categories, leaving 10 relevant sites. Of the remaining 14 irrelevant sites, one had a title of "Renoir Hotel", 3 represented the same bed & breakfast site with "/Renoir" in the path portion of the URL and 10 sites referred to pages where the server name in the URL contained "Renoir". Of the 41 pictures returned by Lycos, the first 24 are termed 100% relevant since they have "Renoir" in the title. Of these 24 sites, 22 also have "Renoir" in the image file name portion of the URL but they are not ranked higher than the 2 sites which match on title but not the URL. For the remaining 27 of the 41 hits, all but 3 matched on the URL and the last 2 were irrelevant. The first 40 of the 1855 (or top 52) Lycos site matches contain very few matches with the other two sets of results but do contain 11 of the "WebMuseum: Renoir" mirror sites ranked as 11, 15, 16, 22, 24, 29, 30, 34, 35, 37 and 39. These 11 URL's come from different sites and the similarity in title seems to have little bearing on the ordering.

The user must load each of the above sites and skim through them to find the desired image or to determine if there are no such images in which case a new search must be initiated. The QSBA as discussed in the next section, attempts to alleviate some of these problems.

3 Searching For Web Images with QSBA

The QSBA search process consists of three stages. First, manual querying of the Web indexers produces a set of entry-point links, or URL's. Next, the set of URL's is explored by a semi-automated search of HTML source code, which runs in the background and excludes irrelevant Web pages. Finally, if the searcher encounters a page with relevant images, or if the page's relevance is ambiguous, its contents, including the images, are uploaded into the Browser, and the user is asked to decide how to proceed. The following subsections provide a concise description of each stage.

3.1 Stage I – Querying Web Indexers

Currently, stage I produces an initial set of entry-point URL's, based on user-specified number and type of Web indexers, as well as the type of image retrieval desired by the user (i.e. find a particular subset of images, or perform an exhaustive search through a specified number of levels). If the objective is to find all images pertaining to a particular topic, the user may prefer to query all the listed robot indexers and have a union operation performed on the resulting URL's. On the other hand, a query which searches for one instance of a particular image on a well-defined subject, may be formulated such that a subset of manual indexers that specialize in this subject are accessed, and a pruning operation may be subsequently performed on the retrieved URL's to narrow the search.

The QSBA user interface (see Section 4), helps the user to formulate the query, then formats and parses it, and sends it to the user-selected Web indexers. The output URL's are post-processed based on the query criteria, and the finalized list is used to initialize the second stage of QSBA, namely, the semi-automated search. Note that rudimentary multi-indexer query writers have been recently implemented on the Web, either as a unified interface [12], or as simultaneous search [13].

3.2 Stage II – The Semi-Automated Search

In stage II, for each entry-point URL a semi-automated search is performed to identify the Web pages which may contain the desired image(s). The QSBA Searcher runs in the background. In the basic QSBA model, the Searcher assumes that each entry-point URL is the root of a hierarchical tree-like, or digraph-like, link structure. The Searcher retrieves the HTML source (text only) and examines it for the presence of visual data (i.e. file extensions .gif, .jpg, .jpeg, .mov), the presence of keywords from stage I in the page title (<title> ... </title>), section headings (<Hn> ... </Hn>), image file names, the values of the ALT attribute in (<IMG>) tags or image captions (<CAPTION>), as well as the existence of new, as yet untraversed URL's.

During this phase, two URL lists are maintained by the QSBA Searcher, a list of unexplored URL hierarchies, and a URL log. Each newly discovered URL is examined against these two lists and, if new, is appended to the appropriate element of the former. This eliminates duplicate URL's that appear in the results of current search engines. For each entry-point URL (root of hierarchy), the search is terminated, or paused, if one of the following conditions exists: (1) the original URL list returned by the existing search engines is exhausted; (2) the desired image or images have been found; (3) the user decides to terminate the search; or (4) a pre-selected number of examined pages emanating from a given URL has failed to uncover the search object, and has produced no new URL's. Hierarchies of URL's which do not contain any image files are discarded.

3.3 Stage III – Browsing and Decision-Making

The QSBA enters the Browse mode of stage III, whenever the Searcher thinks that the desired image(s) has been found, or when it cannot decide whether a particular intermediate page is relevant. Any existing Web browser which supports graphics/visual mode can be used in stage III. The Web browser is given the source HTML file of the page in question and displays it, including the upload of its image(s). At this point, the basic QSBA Browser interface provides the user with several options, or buttons, such as: Stop, Display All Pages, Next Entry-Point URL (i.e. re-enter Stage II), New Keyword (i.e. re-enter Stage I), etc. Depending on the user's selected choice, the search process either continues or stops and displays the collection of images as an HTML page of thumbnails and their associated context URL's as discussed in the next section.

4 QSBA User Interface Design

The QSBA user interface builds on the Netscape web browser and the HTML 2.0 <FORM> element, [11], to provide the user with a work space which unifies all three stages on a single screen. In stage I, the user is presented with a Web page containing form fields that allow the user to specify keywords and other search options as shown below in Figure 4a. Check boxes are used to specify search

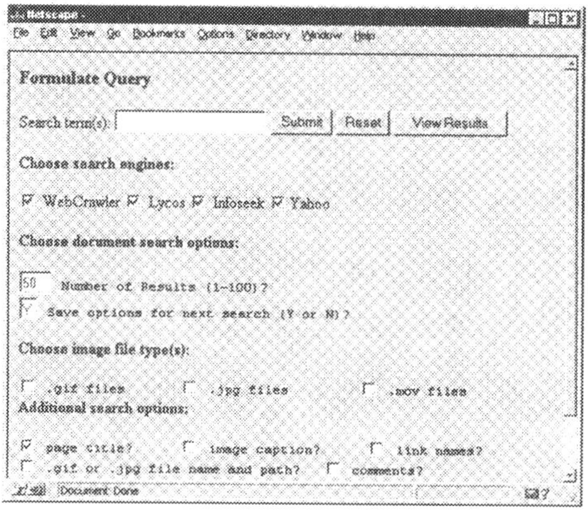

![Netscape Query Formulation Screen showing Formulate Query interface]

Fig. 4a. Query Formulation Screen

criterion based on document structure (i.e. image caption, title, etc.). The search can be halted by clicking the STOP button at any time. In stage III, check boxes appear next to each thumbnail as shown in Figure 4b, which allows the user to keep the image or discard it. The URL associated with the page where the image was found also appears under each thumbnail as a link so the user can browse these pages for additional information if he/she chooses to do so.

Fig. 4b. QSBA Results Screen

5 Limits of the Initial Prototype of QSBA

A initial prototype of QSBA is currently being enhanced to expand its functionality. The prototype is being developed using PERL and JAVA. While constructing the initial prototype[1] the following potential problems were identified:

- Some collections of web images are structured as cyclic graphs (e.g. Art-Deco Museum [14]). Sites such as the Tyrrell Museum [15] are both cyclic and have cgi-bin image maps which hide underlying URL's in the HTML source. This problem has been partially solved. The process of eliminating duplicates could also be used as a stop criterion to prevent looping through a cycle.
- Collections of images stored at ftp:// or gopher:// sites such as Sandra's Clipart [16], cannot be automatically-searched without retrieval and most images are compressed or tarred as well. Thumbnails of these files still can not be produced using QSBA.
- Web page author's have a great deal of freedom in terms of structuring pages, naming files, grouping "semantically similar" links and other design issues. The unstructured nature of such an environment, leads to ambiguities in file-names, titles, captioning, etcetera which can result in the retrieval of many irrelevant Web pages. Some of these problems can be alleviated by allowing the option to only include pages that contain keywords in certain HTML tags (`<title>`,`<Hn>`, `<caption>`, `<img>`, `<fig>`, `<cite>`) and eliminating sites that only match on server names and/or other body text.
- Sites such as the WebMuseum [17] have multiple mirror sites for large collections of images in order to distribute load, improve availability and reduce communication costs. Some mirror sites can be eliminated from the result set by looking for the phrase "mirror site" and ignoring the URL's listed immediately after these words.
- "Dangling" links can result in dead ends. This problem is difficult to solve since existing search engines are used and web sites may be moved or removed before the web search engine site updates its database.

6 Improving on the Initial QSBA Prototype with Typed Links

The initial QSBA prototype in [1] discussed six desirable extensions: eliminate non-content images such as logos from the results, provide ways to isolate other types of multi-media data, provide a mechanism to include or exclude documents written in particular languages, improve convergence criteria and ways of handling empty result searches, apply a combined set of search parameters from all included search engines to the union of results returned from all engines to further reduce the number of starting point URL's, enhance display capabilities of the interface to allow the user to match structural and content based attributes with visual attributes (color hue, color intensity, shape, size, etc.) as in [18][19][20]. In this paper, the extension of QSBA to utilise user-selected relevance criteria and a taxonomy of link types from linguistics work on discourse grammars is discussed. Typed links can be used to improve the ability to identify and filter result links and to improve visual display of the search results to reflect user specified relevance.

Figure 5 shows a hierarchy of link types adapted for visual data, with the leaf nodes making up the right- hand column. This approach builds on work such as [21] in the area of linguistics, on discourse grammars which have built taxonomies of relationship types between chunks of language. Word-Proposition links and Proposition-Proposition links have been replaced with Image-Page and Page-Page links in Figure 5. The linguistic taxonomy can be used to add well defined semantics to a hyperspace such as the Web. It can also be used to filter out subsets of interesting sites and links as subgraphs which form recognisable patterns (i.e. hierarchies, hypercubes, rings, directed-acyclic graphs) that can be searched more efficiently or used to group data in a visual display.

Ideally, the current HTML standard DTD would be modified to add an additional attribute to all tags which include link information (i.e. <A HREF=''URL'' TYPE=''lt''>) where ''lt'' is one of the link types in Figure 5 and the default is "ALL". The default refers to current, non-typed links. This would provide a standard means of adding additional semantics to a link traversal that could be used in automated searching algorithms. There may also be a strong relationship with user relevancy criteria which could be utilised both in the search process as well as in providing a means of ordering the result links based on user preferences for spatial groupings of information in the display.

Spatial orientation mechanisms such as hierarchies, nesting and proximity [22][23][24] are useful in helping the user to quickly view the nodes determined by the search to be most relevant according to user-specified criteria rather than criteria built into a particular Web indexer. Information about semantic relationships between returned nodes can also be determined quickly via visual placement on the screen. This can be used to return one thumbnail of a particular Renoir painting with associated links to the same or similar paintings located at other sites. The image files representing this painting may have a number of different characteristics such as being of different formats (GIF, JPEG), different sizes and different color depths. They may also originate in pages with different contextual information that may be of use to the user. There may also be relationships between different pages of images such as a temporal ordering based on when the works were created or a change in style used by the painter.

7 Architecture of QSBA

The QSBA environment is shown in Figure 6. The QSBA Interface utilizes the Netscape browser to provide a familiar interface and to take advantage of the large base of existing users and emerging standards in Web browsing tools. Existing Web indexers such as Lycos, Yahoo and WebCrawler are used in their current form to directly access Web pages using user-specified keywords. An HTML form viewable

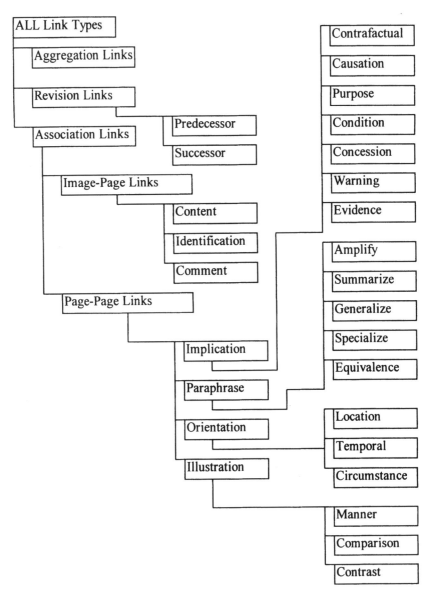

Fig. 5. Taxonomy of Link Types (based on [21])

in Netscape serves as the starting point for the search. Keywords and additional search parameters as discussed in section 4 are passed on to the QSBA searcher which formats and sends a query to each selected search engine. Results returned to the Searcher are sorted by relevance and duplicates are eliminated. The searcher displays the number of initial hits and automatically follows promising links stemming from each initial hit until no more relevant links are found within a distance of five pages or the user clicks the STOP button. At this point, thumbnails of relevant images are displayed so the user can make a comparison without loading separate pages for each image in order to do so.

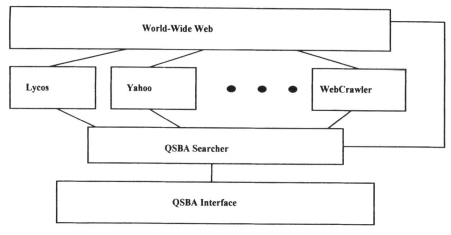

Fig. 6. QSBA Architecture

8 Related Work

A loose coupling of browsing and querying is built into the Netscape browser in the form of a "Search" button which links the user to a page of links to various search engine pages including the ones we have utilised in our study. Multi-engine searches such as Telstra's CUSI page provide a more convenient way of sending the same query to multiple engines using each engine's defaults by allowing the user to repeat the query using a new search engine by selecting it from a scrollable list and then clicking on the "Search" button. Unlike QSBA, however, the results are not combined and filtered for duplicate links, there is no special handling of images (creation of a page of thumbnails) or any facility in the interface to allow the user to specify relevance or change the ranking of results to reflect the user's mental model of what is relevant to them during a particular search situation.

[9] discuss a three-dimensional model of structural responsibility, target orientation and interaction method, which provides a framework for testing the ability of hypermedia information retrieval tools in meeting task needs. Structural responsibility can refer to the user or system depending on the task (i.e. navigation is unstructured from the user's perspective). A distinction is made between browsing and navigation. Browsing distinguishes between targeted and discovery based exploration whereas navigation emphasizes who is responsible for dealing with structure. This leads to the concepts of navigational query and navigational browse where the user handles structure and computer-mediated query and computer-mediated browse where the system handles structure. QSBA allows for navigational query and browse where the user acts as the agent of search by specifying a well-defined target or general neighborhood respectively. QSBA also supports computer-

mediated query and browse where the system acts as the search agent by eliminating duplicate or irrelevant URL's.

Overview diagrams [18] and the use of spatial collections by the VICKI spatial hypertext browser [19] are examples of existing mechanisms to visualize a large set of query results on a computer screen. VICKI also enables users to record their interpretation of external web materials by incorporating them into a larger user-defined context which utilizes the concept of collections to visually group related references to web pages and colors to indicate relationships between elements of a collection or within several collections. VICKI requires pre-processing of Web pages and manual classification of these pages in order to provide sufficient semantics to form collections which can be manipulated by VICKI. QSBA, on the other hand, utilizes existing browsers such as Netscape and the HTML standard rather than the development of a new non-standard application.

9 Summary and Conclusions

The Web can be characterized as a diverse network of heterogeneous linked nodes of information sometimes referred to as a hyperbase. Many different classes of users with varying skill levels in using Web browsers require access to the Web. The Web serves as both a navigational interface and a structuring mechanism blurring traditional distinctions between the database and its interface. Therefore, the metaphors contained in the interface must serve as a context for the selection of information, the visualization of the information and the structuring or linking of the information. The author's of information nodes are free to structure their Web pages using HTML (or one of its variants) in any manner they choose. The links that emanate from a particular page often have ill-defined semantics and the spatial positioning of links into groups by the author often results in groupings of links which do not form a cohesive unit of related information at a particular level of granularity thereby creating confusion for the information seeker.

Extending the HTML standard with typed links as discussed in section 6, would allow Web authors to associate additional semantics to the hyperspaces they create in the form of web sites. Making the extension a part of the HTML standard is advantageous since it would provide a uniform way for web developers to add relevant semantics to the links between pages and would also provide a uniform way for search engines to retrieve information based on more specific search criteria.

The freedoms allowed in terms of navigating the Web and structuring the information it contains must be balanced against the current problems of disorientation and information overload encountered when browsing the Web. We propose the QSBA search mechanism as one way of helping to alleviate these problems.

10 Future Work

QSBA is currently being prototyped and tested using the world-wide web (WWW) hypermedia database (hyperbase) and existing search engines such as the Infoseek,

Excite, Lycos and Yahoo. Experimental testing will need to be done to determine the effectiveness of typed links in increasing the percentage of relevant results returned by web search engines. Since typed links are not currently part of the HTML standard, sample data consisting of web pages designed using typed links will need to be prepared.

Different types of searches conducted by users with varying levels of expertise will also need to be conducted. Convergence criteria for ending the search will also need to be explored as will a mechanism for handling "empty result" searches.

References

[1] Rose, E. and Schloss, G. "QSBA: A Query, Search and Browse Assistant for Images on the Web", *Proc. of Visual 96 Conf.*, Melbourne, Australia, Feb. 1996.

[2] NCSA Mosaic™: URL = http://www.ncsa.uiuc.edu/SDG/Software/Mosaic/

[3] Netscape™: URL = http://home.netscape.com/

[4] Lycos™: URL = http://www.lycos.com/ or http://www.lycos.com/customsearch.html

[5] InfoSeek™: URL = http://www.infoseek.com/

[6] Yahoo: URL = http://www.yahoo.com/ (Image Surfer: http://ipix.yahoo.com/ cgi-bin/isurf.cgi?dbAlias=Computers_and_Internet/Multimedia/Pictures)

[7] CUI W3 Catalog: URL = http://cuiwww.unige.ch/w3catalog (by Ocsar Nierstratz and Universities of Bern and Geneva)

[8] Excalibur Visual Retrieval Ware: URL = http://www.excalib.com/

[9] Waterworth, J. A. and Chignell, M.H. "Exploring Multimedia Information", in *Multimedia Interaction with Computers*, Ch. 6, Ellis Horwood, 1992.

[10] Agosti, M. and Crestani, F. "A Methodology for the Automatic Construction of a Hypertext for Information Retrieval", in *Proc. of 1993 ACM Symp. on Applied Computing*, 1993.

[11] Berners-Lee, T. and Connolly, D. M. "HTML 2.0: HyperText Markup Language Draft",URL=http://www.w3.org/hypertext/WWW/MarkUp/ MarkUp .html

[12] Configurable Unified Search Interface (CUSI): URL = http://pubweb.nexor.co.uk/public/cusi/cusi.html (by Martijn Koster and Twente University)

[13] SavvySearch: URL = http://www.cs.colostate.edu/~dreiling/smartform.html (by Daniel Dreilinger)

[14] Schachner, M. "Art Deco and Art Nouveau Museums", URL = http://www.webcom.com/~tuazon/ajarts/arthp.html

[15] Hortensius, W. "Royal Tyrrell Museum Web Site" , URL= http://www.cuug.ab.ca:8001/VT/tyrrell/index.html

[16] Loosemore, S. J. "Sandra's ClipArt Server", URL = http://www.cs.yale.edu/homes/sjl/clipart.html

[17] Pioch, N. "The WebMuseum", URL = http://www.oir.ucf.edu/wm/

[18] Mukherjea, S. and Foley, J. "Visualizing the World-Wide Web with the Navigational View Builder", in the *Electronic Proceedings of the Third International Conference on WWW*, 1995.

[19] Marshall, C. and Shipman III, F. "Spatial Hypertext: Designing for Change, *Communications of the ACM*, August 1995, pp. 88-97.

[20] Ahlberg, C. and Shneiderman, B. "Visual Information Seeking: Tight Coupling of Dynamic Query Filters with Starfield Displays", in *Proc. of CHI*, 1994.

[21] Parunak, H.Van Dyke, "Ordering the Information Graph" , Chapter 20 in the *Hypertext/Hypermedia Handbook*, Software Engineering Press, McGraw-Hill, 1992.

[22] Kahn, P. "Visual Cues for Local and Global Coherence in the WWW", *Communications of the ACM*, August 1995, pp. 67-69.

[23] Shipman, F. and Moran, T. "Finding and Using Implicit Structure in Human-Organized Spatial Layouts of Information", in *Proc. of ACM CHI'95 Conf.*, May 1995, pp. 346- 353.

[24] Thuring, M., Hannemann, J. and Haake, J. M. "Hypermedia and Cognition: Designing for Comprehension",*Communications of the ACM*, August 1995, pp. 57-73.

APPENDIX A

Yahoo Hit List (Categories and Sites for Each)
Found 0 *Category* and 25 Site Matches for renoir.

Business and Economy: Companies: Arts and Crafts: Galleries: Virtual Galleries

1. Renoir International - limited edition prints and graphics from the works of Perre-Auguste Renoir, Rembrandt, Durer, and others.

2. Art@home - selection of prints for sale from Rembrandt to Renoir; includes on-line auction.

3. Masterprints Gallery Shop - Featuring Fine art Posters of works by Monet, Matisse, Rembrandt, Renoir,Van Gogh, Picasso, Degas and others.

Business and Economy: Companies: Apparel: T-Shirts: Specialty

4. Art T-shirts by XactImage - vanGogh, Monet, Degas, Renoir, Michaelangelo, daVinci...Beautifully printed on T-shirts and Sweatshirts.

Entertainment: People

5. Foraker, Andrew - I have pictures of paintings by Monet, Renoir and ...

6. http://renoir.vill.edu/~jergens/

7. http://renoir.vill.edu/~jergens/

8. http://renoir.vill.edu/~ppenney/

9. http://renoir.vill.edu/csc/s95/maley/rahul/

Business and Economy: Companies: Arts and Crafts: Posters

10. Art of Europe - prints of Rembrandt, Cezanne, Vermeer, Monet, Van Gogh, Renoir, Klimt and more, with moulding.

Business and Economy: Companies: Arts and Crafts: Reproductions

11. Heirloom Art - Reproduction paintings available. Manet, Monet, Renoir,

12. Isabelle Deco Gallery. Replicas are true copies on canvas of Van Gogh, Monet, Renoir,...

Regional: U.S. States: California: Cities: San Francisco: Business: Arts

13. Renoir International - limited edition prints and graphics from the works of Pierre-Auguste Renoir, Rembrandt, Durer, and others.

Regional: U.S. States: California: Cities: San Francisco: Lodging

14. Renoir Hotel

Regional: Countries: United Kingdom: Business: Companies: Arts and Crafts: Reproductions

15. Heirloom Art - Reproduction paintings available. Manet, Monet, Renoir, Regional: U.S. States: Washington, D.C.: Business

16. Art@home - selection of prints for sale from Rembrandt to Renoir; includes Business and Economy: Companies: Travel: Lodging: Bed and Breakfasts

17. Whistler British Columbia's Finest Bed and Breakfast http://www.whistler.net/accomadate/renoir/

Recreation: Sports: Volleyball: College: Men

18. Villanova University ,
http://renoir.vill.edu/~rojones/vball.html
Science: Zoology: Animals, Insects, and Pets:
Dogs: Breeds: English Setter
    19. English Setter,
http://renoir.vill.edu/~zegarski/setters.html
Regional:Countries:Canada:Business:Companie
s:Travel:Lodging:Bed and Breakfasts
    20. Whistler British Columbia's Finest Bed
and Breakfast
    http://www.whistler.net/accomadate/renoir/
Regional: Countries: Canada: Provinces and
Territories: British Columbia: Cities: Whistler:
Lodging
    21. Whistler British Columbia's Finest Bed
and Breakfast
    http://www.whistler.net/accomadate/renoir/
Regional:U.S.States:Pennsylvania:Cities:Villan
ova:Education:Colleges:Villanova University:
Athletics

22. Men's Volleyball Club,
http://renoir.vill.edu/~rojones/vball.html
Recreation: Automotive: Makes and Models:
Honda: Civic: CRX
    23. CRX Page,
http://renoir.vill.edu/csc/f93/vonhagen/html/crx
.html
Entertainment: People
    24. Lotlikar,
Nate,http://renoir.vill.edu/csc/f94/lotlikar/html/
nate.html
Regional: Countries: India: Education: K-12
    25. Hebron School - a small, residential,
Christian boarding school

http://renoir.vill.edu/csc/s95/maley/rahul/hebro
n.html

Lycos Hit List (Ranked Order)

You found 41 pictures: renoir.

1) Renoir's painting ,
http://www.spd.louisville.edu/~m0chen01/hw1/
r.gif (0k)
[100% relevant]
2) [IMG] renoir.gif,
http://studentweb.tulane.edu/~dave/images/reno
ir.gif (0k)
[100% relevant]
3) renoir.gif ,
http://physics.open.ac.uk/~rpblake/images/renoi
r.gif (0k)
[100% relevant]
4) Renoir, Pierre-Auguste, The Garden at 12
rue Cortot, Montm
http://www.ithaca.edu/hs/arthistory/ah1/image1
9/renoir1.jpg (0k)
[100% relevant]
5) renoir-les_parapluies,
http://www.grenet.fr/recre/gif/renoir-
les_parapluies.gif (0k)
[100% relevant]
6) Renoir, Pontneuf ,
http://149.160.3.48/My_Pictures/Renoir%2CPo
ntneuf.jpg (0k)

[100% relevant]
7) Renoir, La Loge
http://149.160.3.48/My_Pictures/Renoir_La_Lo
ge.jpg (0k)
[100% relevant]
8) renoir pontneuf
http://jasmine.esu10.k12.ne.us/~lexingto/Sando
z/images/renoir.pontneuf.jpg
[100% relevant]
9) Renoir, Madame Charpentier
http://149.160.3.48/My_Pictures/Renoir%2C
Madame_Charpentier.jpg
[100% relevant]
10) renoir dancer
http://jasmine.esu10.k12.ne.us/~lexingto/Sando
z/images/renoir.dancer.jpg
[100% relevant]
11) Renoir, Dance a Bougival
http://149.160.3.48/My_Pictures/Renoir_Dance
_a_Bougival.jpg (0k)
[100% relevant]
12) renoir bouquet
http://jasmine.esu10.k12.ne.us/~lexingto/Sando
z/images/renoir.bouquet.jpg

[100% relevant]
13) renoir-moulin_de_la_g
http://www.grenet.fr/recre/gif/renoir-
moulin_de_la_galette.gif (0k)
[100% relevant]
14) renoir parapluies
http://jasmine.esu10.k12.ne.us/~lexingto/Sando
z/images/renoir.parapluies.jpg
[100% relevant]
15) renoir ride
http://jasmine.esu10.k12.ne.us/~lexingto/Sando
z/images/renoir.ride.jpg (0k)
[100% relevant]
16) A Passion for Art: Renoir, Cézanne,
Matisse, and Dr. Barne
http://www.publish.com/0196/contest/disk2.jpe
g (0k)
[100% relevant]
17) renoir.moulin.de.la.galette.gif (52670 bytes)
http://newton.ex.ac.uk/Icons/gallery/renoir.mou
lin.de.la.galette.gif (0k)
[100% relevant]
18) renoir-on_the_terrace.gif
http://www.acm.uiuc.edu/rml/Gifs/Art/renoir-
on_the_terrace.gif (0k)
[100% relevant]
19) renoir-m_r_l.gif
http://www.acm.uiuc.edu/rml/Gifs/Art/renoir-
m_r_l.gif (0k)
[100% relevant]
20) Renoir, Le Moulin de la Galette
http://149.160.3.48/My_Pictures/Renoir%2CM
oulin_de_la_G.jpg (0k)
[100% relevant]
21) renoir in-the-meadow
http://jasmine.esu10.k12.ne.us/~lexingto/Sando
z/images/renoir.in-the-meadow.jpg
[100% relevant]
22) renoir.moulin.de.la.galette_trans1.gif
(52678 bytes)
http://newton.ex.ac.uk/Icons/gallery/renoir.mou
lin.de.la.galette_trans1.gif (0k)
[100% relevant]
23) renoir on-the-terrace

http://jasmine.esu10.k12.ne.us/~lexingto/Sando
z/images/renoir.on-the-terrace.jpg
[100% relevant]
24) renoir.moulin.de.la.galette_trans2.gif
(52678 bytes)
http://newton.ex.ac.uk/Icons/gallery/renoir.mou
lin.de.la.galette_trans2.gif (0k)
[100% relevant]
25)
http://www.hol.gr/wm/paint/auth/renoir/terrace.
jpg
[99% relevant]
26)
http://www.cnam.fr/wm/paint/auth/renoir/juggl
ers.jpg
[99% relevant]
27) [Renoir-Bild...]
http://www.phil.uni-
sb.de/FR/Kunst/Galerie/bougival.gif (138k)
[99% relevant]
28)
http://www.hol.gr/wm/paint/auth/renoir/renoir.j
pg
[99% relevant]
29)
http://mexplaza.udg.mx/wm/paint/auth/renoir/ju
gglers.jpg
[99% relevant]
30)
http://sunsite.unc.edu/louvre/paint/auth/renoir/r
enoir.promenade.jpg
[99% relevant]
31)
http://www.hol.gr/wm/paint/auth/renoir/renoir.
meadow.jpg
[99% relevant]
32)
http://www.cnam.fr/wm/paint/auth/renoir/renoir
.famille-artiste.jpg
[99% relevant]
33)
http://www.bilkent.edu.tr/wm/paint/auth/renoir/
watercan.jpg
[99% relevant]

34)
http://www.bilkent.edu.tr/wm/paint/auth/renoir/
jugglers.jpg
[99% relevant]
35)
http://www.hol.gr/wm/paint/auth/renoir/renoir.f
illes-piano.jpg
[99% relevant]
36) One of my favorite paintings, Renoir's Bal
A Bougival
http://watt.emf.net/wm/paint/auth/renoir/dancer
s/bougival.jpg (38k)
[99% relevant]
37)
http://sunsite.ms.mff.cuni.cz/wm/paint/auth/ren
oir/renoir.filles-piano.jpg (0k)
[99% relevant]

38)
http://www.atklab.yorku.ca/wm/paint/auth/toul
ouse-lautrec/alone.jpg (103k)
[98% relevant]
39)
http://www.atkinson.yorku.ca/wm/paint/auth/se
urat/grande-jatte/seurat.grande-jatte.jpg (82k)
[98% relevant]
40) Better Quality Image
http://www.npac.syr.edu/users/gcf/npacresource
s/web-db/screen12.gif (0k)
[98% relevant]
41)
http://www.npac.syr.edu/users/gcf/npacresource
s/pdb/ncube2.gif (26k)
[98% relevant]

Lycos Hit List (Ranked Order) (Site Search)

You searched all sites for: renoir
You found 1855 relevant documents from a total of 66,486,208

1) Jean Renoir
http://www.omnicorp.com/videocd/movies/reno
ir.html (14k)
[100% relevant]
2) Gallery Rodeo
http://www.bizpro.com/bizpro/grenoir2.html
(3k)
[100% relevant]
3) The Tech goes to Renoir
http://the-
tech.mit.edu/V105/N46/renoir.46a.html (10k)
[99% relevant]
4) Hotel Renoir France French Riviera Cannes
http://www.aaacom.com/hotelreservation/renoir
.htm (7k)
[98% relevant]
5) Escapades...in Paris France - Hotel Renoir -
PARIS 15 - HO
http://www.webscapades.com/france/paris/reno
ir.htm (14k)
[98% relevant]
6) The Renoir Collection

http://www.ukshops.co.uk:8000/gallery/renoir.h
tml (4k)
[98% relevant]
7) Art Room Art Gallery Pictures from Le
WebLourve Image renoir bouquet Image
http://jasmine.esu10.k12.ne.us/~lexingto/Sando
z/Art.html (6k)
[96% relevant]
8) renoir
http://www.commerce.digital.com/palo-
alto/CloudGallery/gif2/renoir28.html (1k)
[94% relevant]
9) Renoir
http://rainbow.rmii.com/~jgraham/Renoir_inde
x.html (1k)
[94% relevant]
10) Pierre Auguste Renoir
http://www.joes.com/./masters/renoir.html (1k)
[94% relevant]
11) WebMuseum: Renoir, Pierre-Auguste: Still-
Lifes
http://sunsite.unc.edu/louvre/paint/auth/renoir/sl
/ (2k)

[93% relevant]

12) Renoir Hotel
http://www.tales.com/CA/RenoirHotel/ (3k)
[93% relevant]

13) My Renoir
http://sunrise.ifmo.ru/~helia/art/indexr.html
(4k)
[92% relevant]

14) Sala Dali / Renoir
http://mes01.di.uminho.pt/Art/Museum/da_ren.
html (1k)
[92% relevant]

15) WebMuseum: Renoir, Pierre-Auguste: Nini
in the Garden
http://www.fhi-
berlin.mpg.de/wm/paint/auth/renoir/nini/ (6k)
[92% relevant]

16) WebMuseum: Renoir, Pierre-Auguste: La
Première Sortie
http://watt.emf.net/louvre/paint/auth/renoir/pre
miere-sortie/ (3k)
[92% relevant]

17) Pierre-Auguste Renoir
http://www.dap.csiro.au/~cameron/gallery/art/P
ierre-Auguste_Renoir/imindex.html
[92% relevant]

18) Lo Shampoo di Karadzic - media-event
http://www.deis.unical.it/others/usrpg134.html
(0k)
[92% relevant]

19) Pierre Auguste Renoir
http://www.polaroid.com/replica-
home/Replica/renoir.html (4k)
[92% relevant]

20) Renoir's Winter Garden Rooms/Availabilty
Chart
http://www.whistler.net/resort/accommodations
/renoir/unavail.html (3k)
[92% relevant]

21) Pierre-Auguste Renoir
http://www.elec.gla.ac.uk/%7Eabrown/painting
s/renoir/ (2k)
[92% relevant]

22) WebMuseum: Renoir, Pierre-Auguste:
Bathers

http://www.southern.com/wm/paint/auth/renoir/
bath/ (2k)
[92% relevant]

23) Auguste Renoir - Gemaelde - Kunsthalle
Tuebingen
http://www.cityinfonetz.de/aktuell/renoir/intern
et.html (2k)
[92% relevant]

24) WebMuseum: Renoir, Pierre-Auguste:
Dancers
http://archie.doc.ic.ac.uk/wm/paint/auth/renoir/
dancers/ (2k)
[92% relevant]

25) RENOIR: A Network of Excellence
http://src.doc.ic.ac.uk/req-eng/renoir/cover.html
(1k)
[92% relevant]

26) Welcome to the home page of RENOIR
RENOIR Requirements Engineering Network
Of International cooperating Research
groups,
http://web.cs.city.ac.uk/homes/gespan/projects/
renoir/cover.html (7k)
[92% relevant]

27) RENOIR: Content of Action
http://web.cs.city.ac.uk/homes/gespan/projects/
renoir/proposal.html (54k)
[92% relevant]

28) Auguste Renoir - Gemaelde - Kunsthalle
Tuebingen
http://www.cityinfonetz.de/aktuell/renoir/oeffn.
html (2k)
[92% relevant]

29) WebMuseum: Renoir, Pierre-Auguste:
Landscapes
http://yawp.giant.net/wm/paint/auth/renoir/land
/ (3k)
[92% relevant]

30) WebMuseum: Renoir, Pierre-Auguste:
Portraits
http://skynet.oir.ucf.edu/wm/paint/auth/renoir/p
ortraits/ (4k)
[91% relevant]

31) Auguste Renoir - Gemaelde - Kunsthalle
Tuebingen

http://www.cityinfonetz.de/aktuell/renoir/fuehr.
html (2k)
[91% relevant]

32) Auguste Renoir - Gemaelde - ·Kunsthalle
Tuebingen
http://www.cityinfonetz.de/aktuell/renoir/bio.ht
ml (4k)
[91% relevant]

33) Auguste Renoir - Gemaelde - Kunsthalle
Tuebingen
http://www.cityinfonetz.de/aktuell/renoir/kat.ht
ml (2k)
[91% relevant]

34) WebMuseum: Renoir, Pierre-Auguste: Les
Parapluies
http://sunsite.sut.ac.jp/wm/paint/auth/renoir/par
apluies/ (2k)
[91% relevant]

35) WebMuseum: Renoir, Pierre-Auguste: La
loge (The Theater Bo
http://mistral.enst.fr/wm/paint/auth/renoir/loge/
(2k)
[91% relevant]

36) Escapades...in Paris France - Hotel Renoir
pictures- PARIS
http://www.webscapades.com/france/paris/reno
pict.htm (5k)
[91% relevant]

37) WebMuseum: Renoir, Pierre-Auguste
http://sunsite.sut.ac.jp/wm/paint/auth/renoir/
(10k)
[91% relevant]

38) Auguste Renoir
http://research.umbc.edu/~mzhao/renoir.html
(0k)
[91% relevant]

39) WebMuseum: Renoir, Pierre-Auguste: Le
Moulin de la Galette
http://hipernet.ufsc.br/wm/paint/auth/renoir/mo
ulin-galette/ (3k)
[91% relevant]

40) Auguste Renoir - Gemaelde - Kunsthalle
Tuebingen
http://www.cityinfonetz.de/aktuell/renoir/eintr.
html (2k)
[91% relevant]

Automatic Acquisition of Object Models by Relational Learning

Maziar Palhang and Arcot Sowmya

Artificial Intelligence Department,
School of Computer Science and Engineering,
The University of New South Wales,
Sydney, NSW 2052, Australia
email : maziar, sowmya@cse.unsw.edu.au

Abstract. An intelligent visual information processing system should have the ability to understand its visual inputs. The input contents may be texts, drawings, or images. To recognise such inputs successfully, the system usually contains a priori knowledge about the class of possible inputs. This knowledge is normally hand-coded by experts. Hence, the approach is error prone, time-consuming, and requires considerable expertise. To solve these problems, researchers have proposed the use of learning methods to acquire this knowledge. This paper introduces a methodology to automatically acquire (learn) this prior knowledge (models) for a system which has the capability to recognise objects in images. Recent efforts to learn such models suffer from drawbacks. They construct models of two-dimensional objects, or use CAD designs of the object to build the model. Some have used attribute-value learners as their learning tool. Moreover, models have been often represented as graphs. Our system has the capability to learn three-dimensional object models from real images by using a *relational* learning system. Object features are first extracted, and the relations between them are found. These relations are then converted to symbolic form, and fed to FOIL, a relational learning system. FOIL produces definitions of objects which may be used during the object recognition phase.

1 Introduction

An intelligent visual information processing system should have the ability to understand the contents of its visual inputs. The inputs may be texts, drawings, or images (still or sequential). Texts and drawings are usually in binary form, for example black writing on a white background. Images may be in gray-level or colour form. The complexity of images containing objects is also higher than that of texts and drawings. Objects may be observed from different view angles and poses; also they may be occluded by other objects, or appear only partially in the image. In addition, the amount of noise is higher. Thus, recognition of objects in images is more difficult than recognition of texts and drawings.

There have been many attempts to build visual understanding systems which can recognise objects of interest from different inputs. Such systems usually contain a priori knowledge about the class of possible inputs. This knowledge is also usually provided by an expert. Hence, this approach is error prone, time consuming, and requires considerable expertise to build the systems. To tackle the *knowledge acquisition* problem, it has been proposed that *learning methods* be utilised to acquire the necessary knowledge [WK91].

In an object recognition system, the prior knowledge may be about the shape of the object, the context in which object may be found, or the function of the object. Visual systems applying shape as their knowledge are called *model-based* object recognition systems and have been used extensively by vision researchers. Surveys of model-based object recognition systems may be found in [Bin82, BJ85, CD86, SFH92, Pop94].

To represent the model and recognise the objects in images, two kinds of features can be used: *global* features, or *local* features [Gri90]. Global features denote the properties of the whole object like area, moments, etc, whereas local features represent the properties of component parts of the objects. Researchers have shown that the best way to recognise objects in images is by recognising the component parts of the objects, and the relations among them [CD86], [Gri90]. This approach is less sensitive in the presence of occlusions and noise.

Interestingly in the learning paradigm, two approaches exist to describe objects and concepts, which affect the kind of learning that is possible. These are *attribute-value* descriptions, and *relational learning* descriptions [1][Bra90]. Models employing global features can be learned by using attribute-value learning systems, since attributes describe the properties of the whole objects. However, the weakness of attribute-value formalism arises when instances have (variable) structure, and/or rules are not easily expressible by only using values of attributes [Qui90]. Since relational learning systems use relations embedded in their training set, they are best suited for learning object models based on relations among local features of objects.

Recent efforts to *learn* object models have either constructed models of two-dimensional objects, or used CAD designs of the object to build the model. Models have been often represented as graphs. Some have also used attribute-value learning systems. A system designed to work in real environments should be able to recognise three-dimensional objects. Utilising CAD designs, wireframes, and line drawings to build models makes the recognition of an object in an image difficult, because the system attempts to match the image data to idealised models. Using graphs as representation increases recognition time since graph matching is an NP-hard problem [SH81]. Attribute-value learning systems restrict the models to use global features, and their language is not expressive enough to easily describe the structure of objects. Thus, these approaches are not quite satisfactory.

---

[1] Appendix A discusses machine learning concepts and terminology

In this paper, we describe the results of an investigation into producing a visual information processing system which has the capability to acquire automatically three-dimensional object models from real two-dimensional images. Apart from attempting to solve the knowledge acquisition problem, this method has the advantage of constructing the models from images of real objects and not from idealised representations such as line drawings or wire-frames. More importantly, we have used a relational learning system as our learning tool. In our methodology, features of objects are initially extracted using standard image processing techniques. These features are then input to FOIL [Qui90], a *relational learning program*. FOIL generates definitions of objects. These definitions may be used later to recognise objects. Our research investigates the power of this tool in application to the area of automatic model acquisition.

FOIL can learn the models of objects under training based on the relations which are given to it as the prior knowledge about training (*background knowledge*). Another attraction of FOIL is the language that it uses for creating the hypothesis, that is Horn clauses. Horn clauses are a subset of first order logic, which are concise, and comprehensible to the user. Moreover, it is powerful enough to express the structure of objects in a compact form. In addition, since real images consist of considerable amounts of noise, we have selected FOIL which has good noise handling capabilities. Further, FOIL has the ability to operate with continuous numbers which some other relational learning algorithms can not handle. FOIL creates discriminatory definition of objects as well, thus making recognition faster than graph matching methods that must compare all the features of test objects with the models.

In this paper, some of the recent work on learning object models are critically reviewed first. Section 3 explains the FOIL algorithm. In section 4, our methodology comprising feature and relation extraction, the model learning approach, and related investigations are described. The following section provides recognition results obtained from the learned models. The next section discusses the advantages and disadvantages of this method, with suggested future extensions. Two appendices at the end briefly introduce the machine learning and logic programming terminologies for those not familiar with these areas.

2 Automatic Model Acquisition Systems

Among model learning systems, Connell and Brady [CB87] build an object model represented by a semantic network which incorporates the properties and relations of two-dimensional-object regions described by their smoothed local symmetries. The network is incrementally generalised to cover all variations of a shape. The system uses a modified version of Winston's ANALOGY [Win75] program as its learning algorithm. The idea in their approach is to remove a feature which is not shared by different variations of the object's shape. This system exhibits good performance when objects consist of elongated regions.

Segen [Seg85] has developed a system which constructs models of two dimensional non-rigid objects from features describing the boundaries of the objects. The features themselves are learned by an unsupervised learning method. Curvature extrema of the boundaries of a series of training images are input to the learning system. The system tries to cluster these features hierarchically such that the final clusters can discriminate among the different classes of objects. Finally, the model is represented as a descriptor list of n-ary relations among the features. This system depends heavily on good extraction of object boundaries. The method is difficult to apply to three-dimensional objects, however.

Pope and Lowe [PL93] present a system that generates models of objects from images and represents them by graphs. For each object, they construct a graph which represents the relations among the features derived by the perceptual organisation process. In a manner similar to Connell and Brady's, they try incrementally to generalise the graph when each new training image is entered into the system. Each node of the graph contains some statistical information about the feature it represents. This is in contrast to Connell and Bradys's method in which nodes represent feature attributes in symbolic form.

Zhang et al.[ZSB93] have built a system which constructs a view-independent relational model of cars from CAD wire-frame renderings. Their system analyses the wire-frame model from different viewpoints of a viewing sphere, and tries to extract view-independent relations among the features by using statistical inference approaches. These relations are represented by using a hypergraph in which edges represent the covisibility of two features, and order-three hyperedges represent the covisibility among three features. Associated with each edge of the graph, pairwise view-independent relations between features are described as logical relations.

There have been some attempts to use relational learning to construct the definitions of two dimensional objects by Cromwell and Kak [CK91], and Pellegreti et al. [PRSV94]. INDUCE [Mic80] is the common learning tool used by them. Cromwell and Kak do not make use of the relational learning capabilities of INDUCE; instead attribute value features are used. On the other hand, Pellegreti et al. do use the relational learning capability of INDUCE. However, since INDUCE does not handle noise they have added fuzzy features to their system. The other problem with this system is that segmentation parameters are hand tuned by an expert in the training phase. Moreover, the learning capability of INDUCE is limited to nullary predicates, that is predicates which correspond to propositional classes [LD94], and hence does not provide first order relational learning capability.

Another system using relational learning approach is CRG [BC94]. In CRG, the unary and binary relations between parts of objects are calculated first. The parts are labelled, then the unary feature space (U) is clustered. If any cluster uniquely represents an object, it becomes a rule for that object. Otherwise, for each unresolved cluster, another clustering step is performed in the binary feature space (UB) such that the first parts of the pairs belong to the unresolved unary cluster. Again, if a cluster can uniquely represents an object, a rule is produced for that object. Otherwise clustering continues with respect to the second parts in the unary feature space (UBU). The unary and binary feature spaces are alternatively clustered until all of the clusters are resolved or a stopping criterion has been satisfied. Designers of CRG have understood the problems with attribute-value learning systems, that is the inability to learn from relations among specific parts of objects, and they have been successful in finding a way to solve it. However, rules are restricted to numerical forms, and symbolic relations are hard to express with CRG, though not impossible. The other problem is that unary and binary feature spaces should be considered alternatively. If a binary cluster at the beginning can uniquely represent an object, then there is redundancy in clustering the unary feature space; that clustering may mislead the search. Further, if higher order relations (more than binary) are going to be considered the efficiency of the system falls down with alternative clustering of each space. In the original paper, CRG has only been applied to artificial images.

It is worth noting that graphs are the preferred representation for object models in most of these systems. Since graph matching is an NP-hard problem [SH81], this results in long recognition times. Further, apart from Zhang et al.'s system, the other systems construct models of two-dimensional objects. A system which can be used in real environments should be able to recognise three-dimensional objects, and learn their models. When three-dimensional objects are projected onto two-dimensional images, depth is lost though some cues remain. This makes model construction and object recognition for three-dimensional objects more difficult than for two-dimensional objects. Some have used attribute-value learning systems which are not powerful enough to learn and express the structure of objects. These difficulties with current visual understanding systems should be solved. Our system is an attempt to overcome some of these hurdles.

3 The FOIL Algorithm

The relational learning system that we have used is FOIL. FOIL has the ability to produce Horn clause [2] definitions of target relations based on examples and background relations. For each target relation, a series of positive and negative examples are presented. FOIL is a general to specific learning system, that is, it searches the hypothesis space from the most general description of a concept to the specific one. In general, such systems proceed to work in three steps [LD94]:

– preprocessing of the training examples,
– construction of a hypothesis defining the target concept, and
– postprocessing of the induced hypothesis.

---

[2] Appendix B contains a brief explanation of logic programming terminology. A reader unfamiliar with logic programming terminology can refer to [Hog90] for more information.

In the preprocessing step, FOIL prepares the training set consisting of positive and negative examples of the target relations. If negative examples have not explicitly been asserted, FOIL creates them using the closed world assumption[3].

There are two major loops in hypothesis construction, the *covering* and *specialisation* loops. Covering loop has the responsibility for hypothesis construction, whereas specialisation loop constructs the clauses. Specialisation loop is actually performed by the covering loop, which performs the following actions:

- finding a clause describing some positive examples,
- including the clause in the current hypothesis, and
- removing the positive examples covered by the clause from the training set.

The specialisation loop looks for the literals which should be added to the body of the clause. FOIL uses information theory heuristics to guide its search for selection of new literals. Before running FOIL, it is possible to control whether it can accept the negation of a relation as a new literal for the construction of the target relation. This option is quite useful, since sometimes lack of a relation may adequately define an idea while expressing that idea could be very difficult by merely asserting the existence of other relations.

Each of the covering and specialisation loops are controlled by *stopping criteria*. Usually the system terminates construction of clauses when all of the positive examples (*completeness criteria*), and none of the negative examples (*consistency criteria*) have been covered by the hypothesis. However, FOIL can relax these constraints so that it can handle noise.

In some situations FOIL stops clause growing, even though there are more positive examples to be covered or more negative examples to be removed. FOIL uses a heuristic that the number of bits necessary to encode a clause should not exceed the number of bits required to encode the positive examples explicitly. This idea is similar to the Minimum Description Length principle of Rissanen [Ris83]. When negated literals are allowed in the definition, the number of bits required to encode it is more than those required for unnegated literals, since an extra bit is necessary to indicate if a literal is negated or not. If a clause cannot be grown any further, FOIL may still accept this clause as valid, if it covers at least 80% of the positive examples. This parameter can be adjusted before running FOIL. Thus, the final definition may not cover some of the positive examples, or may cover some negative examples.

If $\mathcal{E}$ is the set of all training examples, $\mathcal{E}+$ the set of training examples for which the target concept $\mathcal{C}$ is true, and $\mathcal{E}-$ the set of training examples for which $\mathcal{C}$ is false, the FOIL algorithm at the outermost level or covering loop can be expressed as follows:

---

[3] In this case, closed world assumption creates negative examples corresponding to cases not explicitly asserted as positive examples

while $\mathcal{E}+$ *is not empty and encoding constraints are not violated* **do**
    find a clause characterising part of the target relation
    include the clause in the current hypothesis
    remove those tuples in the training set which are covered by the clause from
    $\mathcal{E}$
endwhile

The postprocessing step is responsible for reducing the complexity of the hypothesis. The complexity of a clause is reduced by removing those literals which do not change the accuracy of that clause. This means that, the new clause should cover all of the positive examples covered by the previous clause, but not any additional negative example. This step is performed at the end of the specialisation loop in FOIL. In a similar manner, after executing the covering loop, if it is possible to remove any of the constructed clauses without loss of accuracy, the redundant clause is pruned out.

The training file input to FOIL consists of three sections: type declarations, relation assertions, and test assertions. Type declarations define the kind of objects and features which are used as the arguments of relations. Each type can be a discrete type or a continuous type used for numerical arguments. Relation assertions consist of the introduction of each relation along with its arguments and their types. A list of tuples satisfying each relation is written under each relation. Target relations can be followed by another list of tuples which are not satisfied by the relation. However, this is optional and if they are not introduced, FOIL produces negative tuples by using the closed world assumption. Finally, to check the validity of derived rules, in the test section each target relation can be introduced along with a list of test tuples attached with a positive or negative label to indicate whether the tuple satisfies the relation or not. FOIL finds the validity of these assertions, and reports the results.

4 Methodology

Our approach tries to cover the shortcomings of the previous methods. We use first order logic for model representation, and a relational learning program for model construction of three dimensional objects. Instead of trying to recover depth, we try to find the relations which are mostly invariant and common for different view points and help to discriminate different objects. In addition, the system only tries to find features which can discriminate the objects which are in its domain of application. Therefore, the recognition time is faster compared with graph representations of models which keep all the features of objects and find a subgraph that best matches the test object.

In our system, we have used images of five kinds of three-dimensional objects: they are cubes, pyramids, mugs, cups, and plastic glasses (Fig.1). Our purpose

Fig. 1. Some of the objects used to train the system.

in selecting these objects was to have simple generic objects to test the methodology (cubes, pyramids), and other objects which are not biased towards the
methodology (mugs, cups, glasses). Images are gray level, and 320x240 pixels
wide. In the initial stages of our experiments, we have not considered all the
view points of some of the objects, especially in the case of the mug and cup
for which their handles are restricted to be visible in the left side of the image.
As seen in Fig.1, even learning and recognising this case is a difficult problem.
To consider different view points, it is necessary to supply more images from
different view points of each object to the system. This will be part of our future
investigations.

In the following sections, we describe the feature and relation extraction phase. Model learning and recognition results are described subsequently.

4.1 Feature Extraction

Before applying symbolic machine learning techniques, an image should be represented in suitable form. Since our learning technique uses symbolic representation for the input and output, we opt to represent each image symbolically. This in itself is a challenging problem [BP94], see for example [CK91], [PRSV94], [RM89], and [SL94]. It is the performance of this part that determines the success of the model learning algorithm. We must first decide which features should be extracted, and what kind of relations should be found among them such that the object can be discriminated against the other objects in the presence of noise.

First, the edges of the images are detected using the Canny edge detection algorithm [Can86]. These edges are linked and segmented into a series of straight and curved lines by the split and merge method described in [Gri90] with some modifications. Figure 2 illustrates the results of applying these processes on a mug. The relations between these edges are derived subsequently. To derive these relations, we were inspired by past research in the area specially perceptual organisation results [Low85], and heuristics reported in [Gri90], and [BL90]. The relations that our system detects are the following:

- proximity among lines and arcs,
- parallelism of near lines,
- angles between near lines in symbolic form that is, *acute, right_angle,* or *obtuse,*
- angles between two lines, two arcs, and a line and an arc in numeric form,
- swept_angle of arcs,
- connected segments denoting a closed region in the object,
- number of lines and arcs in each of these regions, and
- triple_junction of lines.

In addition, there are three other relations, *partof* expressing the ownership of a segment by an object, *regionof* expressing the ownership of a region by an object, and *belongto* denoting the ownership of a segment by a region.

In a segmented image of an object, there are many straight and curved segments. Many of these segments are noise, and therefore they should not be considered when the system tries to find the relations among segments. Otherwise, the search space of the learning algorithm becomes huge, and it cannot find enough constraints to discriminate the object from the others. Some constraints have been imposed to reduce the role of noise as much as possible when deriving the relations among the segments. For example, the ratio of the lengths of two lines (the smaller to the longer), and the ratio of the minimum distance of two lines to the length of the longer line should be greater than some value. These constraints are very important both in learning and recognition phases.

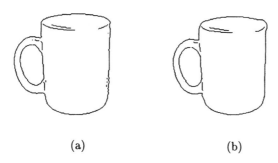

(a)   (b)

Fig. 2. Extracted edges of a mug(a), and its segmentation to straight and curved lines(b).

4.2 Model Learning

The target relations in our system are cube, pyramid, mug, cup, and glass. The relations explained in the previous section are represented in symbolic form before using FOIL, as shown in Fig. 3.

Types

No (represents continues numbers)
X (represents training objects)
Seg (represents segments)
Reg (represents regions)

Relations

partof(X, Seg)
regionof(X, Reg)
no_of_lines(Reg, No)
no_of_arc(Reg, No)
swept_angle(Seg, No)
near_lines(Seg, Seg)
near_arcs(Seg, Seg)
near_arcline(Seg, Seg)

angle_line_line(Seg, Seg, No)
arc_angles(Seg, Seg, No, No)
angle_arc_line(Seg, Seg, No)
parallel(Seg, Seg)
acute(Seg, Seg)
right_angle(Seg, Seg)
obtuse(Seg, Seg)
triple_junction(Seg, Seg, Seg)

Fig. 3. The types and relations which are symbolically produced by the system.

$$mug(A) : - regionof(A, B), no\_of\_lines(B, C), no\_of\_arcs(B, D), C <= 3, D > 3.$$
$$mug(A) : - regionof(A, B), no\_of\_lines(B, C), no\_of\_arcs(B, C), blongto(B, E),$$
$$acute(E, F), obtuse(E, G).$$

$$mug(A) : - partof(A, B), parallel\_line(B, C), obtuse(C, D),$$
$$trip\_junction(D, E, F), blongto(G, D).$$

$$mug(A) : - partof(A, B), near\_arcs(B, C).$$

$$mug(A) : - partof(A, B), near\_arcs(B, C), arc\_angles(B, D, E, F),$$
$$swept\_angle(D, G), G > 126.87.$$

Fig. 4. Output of FOIL with -n and -N options in the case of mug when trained with cup, glass, cube, and pyramid as negative examples respectively.

Experiments have been performed in two stages. Initially, the system was trained with two combinations of objects out of five, that is 10 different experiments. In each experiment, 10 images of each object were used for training, and 10 different images of each for tests [4]. We have used FOIL [5] in three modes: without considering negative literals(-n option), with negated literals permitted only for equal and less than relations(-N option), and with considering negated literals (none of the previous options). The input images contained a considerable amount of noise; however the system was able to derive the definitions successfully.

Figure 4 illustrates the induced definitions for mug when it has been trained against cup, glass, cube, and pyramid respectively. Figure 5 shows the induced definitions for cup, glass, cube, and pyramid when they have been trained against mug as negative example.

No definition has been produced for mug when trained with glass in the mode of considering negated literals. Two reasons may be deduced: firstly, in this option, the literals selected in the process of clause growing could be different from those of other options. Thus, FOIL heuristics may fail to find the correct hypothesis. The other reason as pointed out earlier is that, the negated literals need one more bit for encoding, so the maximum number of literals which are considered is less than the other two options.

To understand the induced models, consider the model of mug against pyramid in Fig 4. This definition states that an object A is a mug if it has an arc segment

---

[4] This experiment has been reported in [PS96]

[5] In these experiments, FOIL version 6.2 has been used.

$cup(A) : - partof(A, B), right\_angle(B, C), parallel\_line(B, D),$
$\qquad parallel\_line(C, E).$
$cup(A) : - partof(A, B), near\_arc\_line(B, C), swept\_angle(C, D),$
$\qquad D <= 34.6347.$

$glass(A) : - regionof(A, B), no\_of\_lines(B, C), C <= 0.$
$glass(A) : - partof(A, B), acute(B, C), right\_angle(B, D), acute(D, E),$
$\qquad blongto(F, C).$

$cube(A) : - regionof(A, B), no\_of\_lines(B, C), no\_of\_arcs(B, D), C > D, C > 3.$

$pyramid(A) : - regionof(A, B), no\_of\_lines(B, C), no\_of\_arcs(B, D), C > D, C > 3.$
$pyramid(A) : - regionof(A, B), no\_of\_lines(B, C), no\_of\_arcs(B, D), C > D, D > 0.$

Fig. 5. Output of FOIL with -n and -N options in the case of considering mug as the negative example for training.

B which is near to another arc segment C. There is also another arc segment D which forms angles E and F with B. The swept angle of D should be greater than 126.87 degrees.

In the second stage, all five objects were considered together and five different experiments were conducted [6]. The same images of objects as the first stage were used for training and testing. Each time, the images of one of the objects were used as positive examples and other images as negative examples, that is 10 positive examples versus 40 negative examples. Similar to the first stage experiments, FOIL was run in three different modes of considering literals. The system was successful in inducing the models of objects. Figures 6 and 7 illustrate the induced models derived by the system. No definition was induced for mug when FOIL was run with considering negated literals option, presumably due to the same reasons discussed earlier.

4.3 Recognition

Recognition has been performed by using the test option available in FOIL. Tables 1 to 6 illustrate the results of applying FOIL to recognise test objects in the first stage of experiments. Figures 8, and 9 also display the recognition results

---

[6] This experiment has been reported in [SP96]

$mug(A) : - partof(A, B), near\_arcs(B, C), swept\_angle(B, D),$
$\qquad swept\_angle(C, E), D > 90, E > 90, arc\_angles(F, B, G, H),$
$\qquad D <= 111.99.$
$mug(A) : - regionof(A, B), no\_of\_lines(B, C), no\_of\_arcs(B, D), D > 8, C > 4.$

$cup(A) : - partof(A, B), near\_arc\_line(B, C), near\_arcs(B, D),$
$\qquad swept\_angle(B, E), angle(F, C, G), blongto(H, C), E <= 34.6347.$

$glass(A) : - regionof(A, B), no\_of\_lines(B, C), c <= 0.$
$glass(A) : - regionof(A, B), no\_of\_lines(B, C), no\_of\_arcs(B, D), C <= D,$
$\qquad D > 3, D <= 4.$

$cube(A) : - partof(A, B), acute(B, C), obtuse(B, D), belongto(E, D),$
$\qquad obtuse(C, F), blongto(G, F), acute(D, F).$
$cube(A) : - partof(A, B), blongto(C, B), no\_of\_lines(C, D), no\_of\_arcs(C, E),$
$\qquad E <= 0, D > 4.$

$pyramid(A) : - regionof(A, B), no\_of\_lines(B, C), no\_of\_arcs(B, D), c <= 3,$
$\qquad D <= 0, partof(A, E), acute(E, F), blongto(G, E), blongto(H, F).$

Fig. 6. Output of FOIL with -n and -N options in stage2

for the second stage of experiments. The results are expressed by measuring sensitivity, specificity, and accuracy, as defined in [WK91]:

$sensitivity = no.\,of\,True\,Positives\,/\,total\,no.\,of\,positive\,tests$
$specificity = no.\,of\,True\,Negatives\,/\,total\,no.\,of\,negative\,tests$
$accuracy = (no.\,of\,TruePositives + no.\,of\,TrueNegatives)\,/\,total\,no.\,of\,tests$

The other way to perform recognition is to use Prolog. The relations found between the segments of an object should be represented as facts in Prolog format. The models should also be included in the program as rules without any change. Then, we should make a query from Prolog to find which rule is satisfied.

5 Discussion

We have developed a methodology to acquire object models from images automatically for use in a visual information processing system. Our method is

$cup(A) : -\ partof(A, B), near\_arc\_line(B, C), parallel\_line(B, D),$
$\qquad swept\_angle(C, E), E > 177.562.$
$cup(A) : -\ partof(A, B), near\_arc\_line(B, C), near\_arcs(B, D),$
$\qquad swept\_angle(B, E), near\_arc\_line(D, F), E <= 34.6347.$

$glass(A) : -\ regionof(A, B), no\_of\_lines(B, C), c <= 0.$
$glass(A) : -\ regionof(A, B), no\_of\_lines(B, C), no\_of\_arcs(B, D), C <= D,$
$\qquad D > 3, D <= 4.$

$cube(A) : -\ partof(A, B), blongto(C, B), no\_of\_lines(C, D), no\_of\_arcs(C, E),$
$\qquad D > E, obtuse(B, F), blongto(G, F), no\_of\_arcs(G, H), E <> H.$
$cube(A) : -\ regionof(A, B), no\_of\_lines(B, C), no\_of\_arcs(B, D), D <= 0, C > 4.$

$pyramid(A) : -\ regionof(A, B), no\_of\_lines(B, C), no\_of\_arcs(B, D), c <= 3,$
$\qquad D <= 0, partof(A, E), not(blongto(F, E)), near\_arc\_line(E, G),$
$\qquad not(blongto(H, G)).$

Fig. 7. Output of FOIL with considering negated literals in stage2. No definition was produced for mug.

distinct from other systems in the sense that our models are derived from real images and are applied to three-dimensional objects. The idea here is that, although many edge detection algorithms are not able to extract all of the necessary edges, there are enough clues in the extracted edges to represent the object of interest. Therefore, if we try to learn the model from the features that edge detection algorithms can actually supply us, then we do not need to estimate which edges correspond to an idealised model.

In addition, we use a relational learning program that has the advantage of learning from the relations and background knowledge, which many other learning methods cannot handle. Moreover, the rule expression language is powerful enough to represent the structure of objects, in a comprehensible way. Both numeric and symbolic relations can be expressed in the rules, unlike CRG which only supports numeric relations. The induced rules can be easily run in Prolog. This is an interesting option, since it allows us to use the symbolic processing power of Prolog. In contrast, the rules produced by CRG are not executable in Prolog in its current format, and some modifications should be performed on them before employing this capacity.

Another advantage of this method is that graph matching is not used, thus recognition is faster; since graph matching is an NP-hard problem. The average rule matching complexity of our approach is less than that of graph matching due to two reasons. Firstly, literals are matched sequentially. If one is not satisfied, other literals are not checked. This kind of matching is called *greedy* matching. Secondly, once a complete match is found further instantiations are not checked, and the process is finished, when we use the FOIL test option for recognition. If we used Prolog instead, other instantiations would be also checked, unless they were prevented. Our faster recognition time is also conceptually grounded in the generation and use of *discriminatory* rules in our system. Only those features that serve to differentiate between objects are retained in the generated rules; thus fewer number of features should be matched. In addition, the accuracy of recognition may be increased by training with more instances of each object, with the upper bound being the true accuracy value (or true error rate) of the system [WK91].

The background relations play a very important role in deriving good definitions of objects. They should be selected such that the actual arrangements of edges, and the interrelationships among them are best expressed. The higher the complexity of the object, the more powerful the relations required.

In the current implementation, our system can not handle partial and occluded views. These possibilities need to be studied further in our future research. We have experimented thus far with a few poses and views of each object. Multiple view and multiple pose models will be part of our investigations as well.

References

[BC94]   W. F. Bischof and T. Caelli. Learning structural descriptions of patterns: A new technique for conditional clustering and rule generation. *Pattern Recognition*, 27(5):689–697, 1994.

[Bin82] T. O. Binford. Survey of model-based image analysis systems. *International Journal of Robotics Research*, 1(1):18–64, 1982.

[BJ85]   P. J. Besl and R. C. Jain. Three-dimensional object recognition. *Computing Surveys*, 17(1):75–154, 1985.

[BL90]   R. Bergevin and M. D. Levine. Extraction of line drawing features for object recognition. In *IEEE 10th International Conference on Pattern Recognition*, pages 496–501, 1990.

[BP94]   B. Bhanu and T. A. Poggio. Introduction to the special section on learning in computer vision. *IEEE Trans. on Pattern Analysis and Machine Intelligence*, 16(9):865–868, Sep. 1994.

[Bra90] I. Bratko. *PROLOG PROGRAMMING FOR ARTIFICIAL INTELLIGENCE*. Addison-Wesley, 1990.

[Can86] J. F. Canny. A computation approach to edge detection. *IEEE Trans. on Pattern Analysis and Machine Intelligence*, PAMI-8(6):679–698, 1986.

[CB87]   J. H. Connell and M. Brady. Generating and generalizing models of visual objects. *Artificial Intelligence*, 31:159–183, 1987.

[CD86]   R. T. Chin and C. R. Dyer. Model-based recognition in robot vision. *Computing Surveys*, 18(1):67–108, 1986.

[CK91]   R. L. Cromwell and A. C. Kak. Automatic generation of object class descriptions using symbolic learning techniques. In *9th National Conference on Artificial Intelligence*, pages 710–717. AAAI, 1991.

[Gri90]   W. E. L. Grimson. *Object Recognition by Computer : the role of geometric constraints*. MIT Press, 1990.

[Hog90]   C. J. Hogger. *Essentials of Logic Programming*. Oxford University Press, 1990.

[LD94]   N. Lavrac and S. Dzeroski. *Inductive Logic Programming*. Ellis Horwood, 1994.

[Low85]   D. G. Lowe. *Perceptual Organization and Visual Recognition*. Kluwer Academic Publishers, 1985.

[Mic80]   R. S. Michalski. Pattern recognition as rule-guided inductive inference. *IEEE Trans. on Pattern Analysis and Machine Intelligence*, PAMI-2:349–361, 1980.

[PL93]   A. R. Pope and D. G. Lowe. Learning object recognition models from images. In *Proceedings of the 4th Int. Conf. on Computer Vision*, pages 296–301, 1993.

[Pop94]   A. R. Pope. Model-based object recognition, a survey of recent research. Technical Report 94-04, Department of Computer Science, The University of British Columbia, January 1994.

[PRSV94] P. Pellegretti, F. Roli, S. B. Serpico, and G. Vernazza. Supervised learning of descriptions for image recognition purposes. *IEEE Trans. on Pattern Analysis and Machine Intelligence*, 16(1):92–98, Jan. 1994.

[PS96]   M. Palhang and A. Sowmya. Learning object models from real images. In *First International Conference on Visual Information Systems (VISUAL96)*, pages 335–343, Melbourne, Australia, February 1996.

[Qui90]   J. R. Quinlan. Learning logical definitions from relations. *Machine Learning*, 5:239–266, 1990.

[Ris83]   J. Rissanen. A universal prior for integers and estimation by minimum description length. *Annals of Statistics*, 11:416–431, 1983.

[RM89]   R. Reiter and A. K. Mackworth. A logical framework for depiction and image interpretation. *Artificial Intelligence*, 41(2):125–155, December 1989.

[Seg85]   J. Segen. Learning structural description of shape. In *Proc. of IEEE Int. Conf. on Computer Vision and Pattern Recognition*, pages 96–99. Morgan Kaufmann, 1985.

[SFH92]   P. Suetens, P. Fua, and A. J. Hanson. Computational strategies for object recognition. *ACM Computing Survey*, 24(1):5–61, March 1992.

[SH81]   L. G. Shapiro and R. M. Haralick. Structural descriptions and inexact matching. *IEEE Trans. on Pattern Analysis and Machine Intelligence*, PAMI-3(5):504–519, 1981.

[SL94]   A. Sowmya and E. Lee. Generating symbolic descriptions of two-dimensional blocks world. In *Proc. of IAPR International Workshop on Machine Vision Applications*, pages 65–70, Kawasaki, Japan, December 1994.

[SP96]   A. Sowmya and M. Palhang. Automatic model building from images for multimedia systems. In *the Third International Conference on Multimedia Modelling*, pages x–x, Toulouse, France, November 1996.

[Win75]   P. H. Winston. Learning structural descriptions from examples. In P. H. Winston, editor, *Psychology of Computer Vision*, chapter 5. McGraw Hill, New York, NY, USA, 1975.

trained	negative object				
object ↓	mug	cup	glass	cube	pyramid
mug	-	90%	40%	100%	100%
cup	90%	-	100%(90%)	100%	100%
glass	80%	70%	-	100%	80%
cube	100%	100%	100%	-	70%
pyramid	100%	90%(100%)	100%	100%	-

TABLE 1

Sensitivity of the system by using -n and -N options. 10 positive and 10 negative objects were used as tests. The value shown in the bracket is for -N when it is different from -n.

trained	negative object				
object ↓	mug	cup	glass	cube	pyramid
mug	-	70%	90%	90%	70%
cup	50%	-	60%(70%)	90%	60%
glass	70%	80%	-	90%	80%
cube	100%	100%	90%	-	80%
pyramid	90%	70%(90%)	70%	100%	-

TABLE 2

Specificity of the system by using -n and -N options. 10 positive and 10 negative objects were used as tests. The value shown in the bracket is for -N when it is different from -n.

trained	negative object				
object ↓	mug	cup	glass	cube	pyramid
mug	-	80%	65%	95%	85%
cup	70%	-	80%(80%)	95%	80%
glass	75%	75%	-	95%	80%
cube	100%	100%	95%	-	75%
pyramid	95%	80%(95%)	85%	100	-

TABLE 3

Accuracy of the system by using -n and -N options. 10 positive and 10 negative objects were used as tests. The value shown in the bracket is for -N which it is different from -n.

[WK91]   S. M. Weiss and C. A. Kulikowski. *Computer Systems that Learn: classification and prediction methods from statistics, neural nets, machine learning, and expert systems*. Morgan Kaufmann, 1991.

[ZSB93] S. Zhang, G. D. Sullivan, and K. D. Baker. The automatic construction of a view-independent relational model for 3-d object recognition. *IEEE Trans. on Pattern Analysis and Machine Intelligence*, 15(6):531–544, June 1993.

Appendix A: Machine Learning terminology

Learning stands for acquiring knowledge from past experience. It can be performed in two ways. One approach is to obtain this knowledge by performing some experiments and without the need of an oracle. This scheme is called *unsupervised learning*. Another method is providing the knowledge with the co-operation of an oracle or a supervisor. This scheme is called *supervised learning*.

trained	negative object				
object ↓	mug	cup	glass	cube	pyramid
mug	-	90%	-	100%	100%
cup	60%	-	90%	100%	90%
glass	70%	70%	-	100%	90%
cube	100%	100%	100%	-	70%
pyramid	100%	100%	100%	-	

TABLE 4

Sensitivity of the system considering negated literals. 10 positive and 10 negative objects were used as tests. No definition was produced for mug when it was trained with glass.

trained	negative object				
object ↓	mug	cup	glass	cube	pyramid
mug	-	80%	-	90%	70%
cup	100%	-	70%	90%	80%
glass	10%	80%	-	90%	90%
cube	100%	100%	90%	-	50%
pyramid	90%	90%	70%	100%	-

TABLE 5

Specificity of the system considering negated literals. 10 positive and 10 negative objects were used as tests. No definition was produced for mug when it was trained with glass.

trained	negative object				
object ↓	mug	cup	glass	cube	pyramid
mug	-	85%	-	95%	85%
cup	80%	-	80%	95%	85%
glass	40%	75%	-	95%	90%
cube	100%	100%	95%	-	60%
pyramid	95%	95%	85%	100	-

TABLE 6

Accuracy of the system considering negated literals. 10 positive and 10 negative objects were used as tests. No definition was produced for mug when it was trained with glass.

In supervised learning, the supervisor provides some instances of a concept to be learned. Both positive and negative instances can be provided. The system should try to come up with an idea or expression which denotes all instances of that concept, ie a kind of generalisation. This reasoning from specific to general is called *induction* [LD94].

Any kind of learning needs a language for describing the objects, and a language for describing the concepts which are usually the same. There are two kinds of descriptions [Bra90]: *attribute* descriptions, and *relational* descriptions. In an attribute description language objects are described in terms of features explaining the whole objects or *global* features. Learning systems using an attribute description language are called *attribute-value learning systems*. In contrast, relational description languages describe the component parts of objects or *local* features, and relations among them. Learning system that employ a relational description language are called *relational learning systems*.

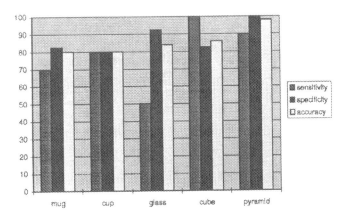

Fig. 8. Recognition results by definitions derived by -n and -N options. 10 positive and 40 negative objects were used at each training trial.

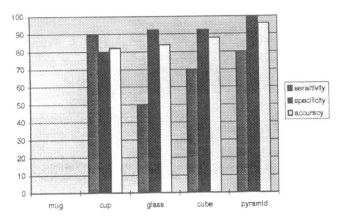

Fig. 9. Recognition results by definitions derived by considering negated literals. 10 positive and 40 negative objects were used at each training trial. No definition was produced in the case of mug.

Appendix B: Logic Programming terminology

Logic programming uses *first order predicate logic* as its language. This language consists of some rules, or a grammar.

1. In this language, the vocabulary consists of four symbols: *constant* symbols, *variable* symbols, n-ary *function* symbols, and n-ary *predicate* symbols.
2. A *term* is either a constant symbol, or a variable symbol, or an expression $f(t_1, t_2, ..., t_n)$, where f is an n-ary function symbol and t_is are terms.

3. An *atomic formula* or simply an *atom* is an expression $p(t_1, t_2, ..., t_n)$, where p is an n-ary predicate symbol, and t_is are terms.
4. If A is an atom, then A and $\overline{A}$ are *literals*. A is a positive literal, and $\overline{A}$ is a negative or negated literal.
5. A *clause* is a set of literals which denotes their disjunctions. Thus, a clause can be represented as an *if-then* rule in which negated literals are inverted and conjuncted in the precedent, and positive literals are disjuncted in the antecedent.
6. A *Horn clause* is a clause with at most one positive literal.
7. A *logic program* is a set of Horn clauses.

System Design for Structured Hypermedia Generation

Marcel Worring[1], Carel van den Berg[1], Lynda Hardman[2], Audrey Tam[3]

[1] Intelligent Sensory Information Systems
Department of Computer Science
University of Amsterdam, The Netherlands
worring@wins.uva.nl
[2] Interoperable Multimedia Systems Group, CWI, Amsterdam, The Netherlands
[3] Computer and Mathematical Sciences, Victoria University of Technology, Australia

Abstract. In this contribution we consider the design of a hypermedia information system that not only includes standard functionality of storage and presentation, but also the automatic generation of hypermedia presentations on the basis of a domain dependent knowledge base. We identify and describe the type of knowledge required and the processes involved.

1 Introduction

The usefulness of multimedia information systems hinges on the ease with which the information can be retrieved and on the speed and quality of the presentation of the information to the user. The most convenient way of interacting with multimedia information is through a hypermedia interface, where the user is guided in navigating through the large set of media items. This requires the definition of links relating the different pieces of information. This is a well known concept in hypermedia systems, but in many such systems, including HTML on the Internet, the links are embedded within the media. Recent research on hypertext models [13], hypermedia models [15] and open hypertext systems such as MICROCOSM [8] have introduced the concept of link databases in which links are stored separately from the media, using the notion of anchors. In such open environments it becomes feasible to integrate multimedia information systems and hypermedia interfaces.

With the large variety of user platforms and user requirements it is virtually impossible for an information provider to anticipate the full set of hypermedia presentations one is likely to encounter. Therefore, rather than trying to generate all possible hypermedia presentations beforehand we aim at a multimedia information system providing tools to generate presentations automatically when they are requested in a certain context by the user. To do so requires explicit knowledge about the domain. Examples of applications where such domain knowledge is present are medicine, weather, sports and news. In all of these domains, a large part of the domain knowledge is fixed whereas the media items are changing constantly.

Let us first consider an example of interaction with the proposed system. A person is consulting a database on animals and is looking at a multimedia presentation about the South Pole. At a certain point in a video on the animals living at the South Pole, the user sees a penguin, decides that more information on penguins would be interesting and clicks with the mouse on the visual representation of the penguin in one of the frames. If a link has already been created by an author, the user can follow it; however, there might be no link from the penguin to other components or anchors. Now, if the object in the video had an attribute stating that it is a penguin, we could retrieve all media items from the information system that are in some way related to penguins. This requires that we have a knowledge base describing the domain of penguins and their habitat. Now, retrieving relevant information gives us a collection of media items which are related via the domain knowledge description and possibly some stored hyperlinks. To provide for proper presentation this collection of media items should be structured automatically, combining them into coherent groups, e.g., all information on different species of penguins and one presentation on their diet. This results in a new hypermedia document that can be played at the user's hardware.

A system incorporating functionality related to the above is presented in [3]. The system is capable of automatically producing text- and/or graphics-based presentations tailored to the user's expertise, language and presentation hardware. However, both text and graphics are generated as needed; future work is planned to incorporate stored media items.

We are currently working on a system to achieve the latter functionality based on the extensible database system Monet [5] and the CMIF presentation environment [22]. In this paper we will consider some topics in the design of the proposed system. We will illustrate most concepts using video as it is the most complex and data-intensive media type. In section 2 the data model is introduced. Section 3 describes the processing steps used in the system and finally in section 4, a design for the architecture of the proposed system is presented.

2 Data model

The development of a system that automatically generates multimedia presentations is a complex task, drawing on the expertise of many disciplines. In an attempt to standardize terminology, functionality and architecture, Ruggieri et al. [24] have proposed a *reference model* for intelligent multimedia presentation systems, arguing that development, analysis and comparison of systems benefit from agreement on a reference model. In addition to basic terms, they define an *intelligent multimedia presentation system* (IMMPS) as a system that exploits knowledge sources to design multimedia presentations to achieve goals.

The reference model leaves open the data model to use. As data model, we use the Amsterdam Hypermedia Model (AHM) [15], which can be viewed as an extension of the Dexter model [13]. In the AHM, a hypermedia system consists of three layers: the *within-component layer* stores details of the content and internal structure of the components; the *storage layer* stores the hypermedia structure; the *runtime layer* stores information used for hypermedia presentation and handles user interaction. The IMMPS reference model fits into the AHM's runtime layer.

Given the complex functionality of the system, it is important to have precise definitions for the terms used for different types of information acted upon in the steps of the process. *Media items* are the raw pieces of data, e.g., a piece of video or sound. The Dexter model introduced the concepts *component* (both *atomic* and *composite*), *link* and *anchor*. Each component has a unique identifier. A composite component is a collection of atomic and/or composite (child) components. An atomic component contains *content* (a media item), *attributes* (semantic information [1]), anchors (objects embedded in the media item, such as an object in a picture) and a *presentation specification*, which describes how the component should be displayed by the system (for dynamic data, this includes the *duration*). A link connects anchors and/or components and can also be specified as a database query. (Note that anchors are *not* encoded within the media items and links are stored separately from components.)

The AHM incorporates and extends both the Dexter hypertext model and the CMIF multimedia model [6]: each atomic component is assigned a *logical channel* as presentation specification, which is an abstraction of a *physical channel* capable of playing the associated media item. Although the CMIF model allows the specification of timing constraints between components, the hierarchical structuring implicitly imposes a particular form of constraint, i.e., playing in parallel or serially. In the AHM, timing can be specified for child components relative to the parent or to a sibling component, e.g., start or end at the same time, or start a specific time after the other starts or before it ends.

We note here that the MPEG-4 project [18], if successful [2], may make it easier to identify and manage audiovisual (AV) objects. MPEG-4's goal is to establish universal, efficient coding of AV objects, of natural or synthetic origin, by defining a set of coding tools for AV objects and a syntactic description of the coding tools and coded AV objects. In the proposed syntax, each AV object has a local coordinate system (3D+Time). An AV object can be placed in a scene by the encoder or end-user via a coordinate transformation from its local coordinate system into the scene's (global) coordinate system. This coordinate transformation is part of the scene, not part of the AV object. AV objects may be composites of other AV objects.

The information on presentations in the above described format must be stored in four logical databases: the media database, the knowledge base, the link database and the component database. To achieve independence in the processing steps presented later, these databases do not have symmetric relations. The exact relations are shown in figure 1.

---

[1] Derivation of the attributes is outside the scope of the AHM. In our system, this will be handled by the annotation phase (see section 3.1): each component will receive a *semantic annotation* that is an instantiation of one or more concepts in the knowledge base.

[2] MPEG-4 is scheduled to become international standard by November 1998.

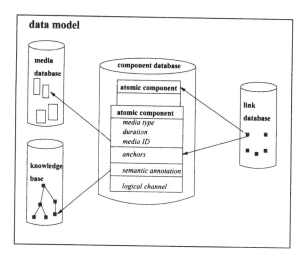

Fig. 1. *The logical databases used in the system and their relations.*

3 Processing steps

Let us go back to the example in the introduction as it indicates the information processing steps carried out by the system. In general we can divide the processing into three main steps. In the *hypermedia creation* step basically all steps are done that are carried out prior to, or at the time of entering the media items into the system. To be precise, it involves the creation of the knowledge base, insertion of the media items and giving annotations, and finally the entering of links into the link database. The other two steps are performed at run-time and will be performed in an alternating sequence. These steps are the *hypermedia presentation* (playing) of hypermedia documents and the *hypermedia generation* performed whenever the user wants to follow links other than those foreseen by the author. The different processing steps are illustrated in figure 2 and will be described in the following sections.

3.1 Hypermedia creation

Knowledge representation Domain knowledge needs to be represented in different ways for different purposes. Our interest is limited to the task of finding media items similar to another item. That is, we are concerned with the similarity of different pieces of information and are not concerned with interpreting what those pieces of information actually mean or represent. Kashyap et al. [16] approach the problem of semantic correlation of information from different media types by proposing an architecture with three levels: ontologies, metadata

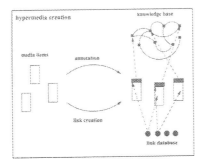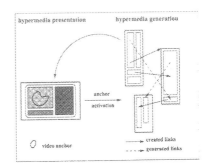

Fig. 2. *Overview of the different steps.*

and databases. Ontologies contain both domain-specific and domain-independent terms that characterize the (semantic) content of the databases, irrespective of media type. Metadata are classified as content-dependent, -descriptive or -independent information about the data (text, image, audio, video) in the databases. The ontology and metadata levels are evident in AHM components.

Porter notes that the types of features used for processing the semantics of items are of crucial importance [21]. In particular, superficial features that are about form and are independent of context and goal-of-use, e.g., size, color and material, should be distinguished from abstract features that are about function and are dependent on the context and goal-of-use, e.g., "hammer" (a tool for hitting). Superficial features can be derived from the media items through data analysis. Abstract features are much harder to obtain but might often be more useful in matching. An example of a system based purely on superficial features is the QBIC system [11] whereas in e.g. CORE [30] the distinction between the two types of features is made explicit.

Two ways of obtaining abstract features are by hand or via a domain knowledge representation. Our approach is to first create a domain knowledge representation by hand, and to assign aspects from this to the anchors within the media items by hand. This can be combined with an analysis of the raw data of the media items to obtain superficial features.

As concerns domain based annotation, work has been carried out by Davis [9] for the particular case of video. His task was slightly different to our own, but sufficiently similar to form a basis for this work. His chosen representation for domain knowledge of a collection of video sequences is based on knowledge frames, to be more specific the Framer system [12]. In broad terms this is a hierarchical frame-based structure, allowing multiple values for slots, where any node in the structure (leaf or interior) can be used for describing the persons and objects in the video as well as the activities performed by the subjects. For example, a video showing a penguin walking on an ice-floe would have the description "penguin" as a semantic attribute, which is a specialization of "bird", which is a specialization of "warm-blooded creature" etc. Another attribute used would be "standing", which is a specialization of "pose" and so on. The representation in Davis is very broad. In [27], narrower domain models are used, geared towards documentary video and news programs.

The knowledge base should also be capable of providing a similarity measure for two items. This is done by considering the hierarchical organization of the knowledge. Each semantic annotation consists of a number of attributes. The similarity between two attributes of different annotations can be defined as the number of steps one has to make in the hierarchy when moving from one concept to another. Hence, when given two annotations, a set of values is returned one for each attribute of the annotation. A zero value indicates that the match is exact and a positive value indicates that the match is inexact. Going back to the previous example, consider a picture showing a penguin lying on a beach. Both the video and the picture would have the semantic attribute "penguin", so this attribute matches exactly. The semantic attributes "lying" and "standing" have a distance of 2: one from "lying" to "pose" and one from "pose" to "standing".

Given a set of annotations corresponding to components or anchors we can define a similarity matrix or graph giving the similarity measures among all items in the set. Such a similarity matrix will be used in the hypermedia generation step. In the next section we will first discuss the annotation step.

Video annotation The task of annotating a video begins with *parsing* it into "meaningful" segments, both temporally (e.g., shots) and spatially (e.g., objects). Each of these segments can then be annotated, as the semantic content of a video is usually closely related to its temporal structure and significant moving objects. Fully automated annotation is probably too difficult, except for specific, well-defined domain areas; our system aims for semi-automatic annotation, presenting candidate segments to human annotators for confirmation, and attempting to control the variation among annotations, e.g., by using icon palettes [12]. A secondary reason for video parsing is pragmatic: in most cases, a hypermedia user would prefer to view only the relevant segment(s) of a video rather than the entire video.

Our system will be based on the following spatial and temporal segments:

- object: a connected region of arbitrary shape (which may vary over time) that appears to move as a coherent entity, e.g., a penguin. Annotating individual objects gives a more direct association of the objects with their semantics. It should furthermore be noted that the information in the knowledge base is not restricted to video, but can also be applied to related media items such as textual descriptions or audio fragments.
- shot: a sequence of pictures that appear to have been continuously filmed, e.g., consecutive pictures showing a penguin walking across the ice. Each shot will also be annotated with the type(s) of camera work (pan, zoom etc.) it contains, not only to answer queries that request a specific type of camera work, but also as semantic hints to aid in object and motion detection and in shot abstraction (see section 3.3).

- scene: a sequence of shots with the same location, e.g., a shot of diving penguins followed by shots of the penguins underwater;
- story-unit: a sequence of shots with common semantic content (a scene is a type of story-unit), e.g., shots of feeding female Emperor penguins interleaved with shots of their mates (100 km away) incubating the eggs. Most queries for specific semantic content will be answered by story-units.
- thread: a collection of scenes and/or story-units with common or related semantic content, e.g., story-units about penguins separated by story-units about seals, whales, scientists in the Antarctic etc. Threads are useful for maintaining the temporal relationships among related story-units and could be used to answer a query that is not specific enough to isolate a single story-unit.

To parse videos into these different types of segments, we will explore the use of existing methods, and also develop new techniques. Methods for detecting shot boundaries automatically are plentiful (e.g., [27, 14, 20]); work on clustering shots into story-units is well-advanced; efficiently detecting objects remains a hard problem. The segmentation problems and our proposed approaches to solving them are discussed in more detail below, but first, we briefly describe the video annotation process.

The process of annotating a video will begin by detecting shot boundaries. Each shot will be analyzed for camera work, moving objects and background, and its key frame(s) will be identified. (Key frames and other video-previewing tools are discussed in section 3.3.) Shots will then be clustered into story-units, which will be presented to the annotator for confirmation or amendment. During and after this clustering step, the annotator will be able to assign attributes to story-units, either individually or in groups (i.e., threads). To reduce variation in annotation, the attributes will be selected from a hierarchical palette, which the annotator can modify during the annotation process. Shots and objects in a story-unit will initially inherit its attributes; in the next step, the annotator will modify attributes of shots and objects, as needed. Finally, the system may suggest thread (re)groupings, based on story-unit annotations. The video annotation process is illustrated in figure 3.

Shot boundary detection: Shot-boundary detection can be done as reliably by computers as by humans [1]. Yeung et al. [31] detect shot boundaries using only reduced (approximate) DC images[3], i.e., only partially decoding the MPEG pictures, and reducing the size of the images by a factor of 64. Although methods to detect progressive shot transitions (fade, dissolve, wipe) are generally less reliable than those to detect abrupt cuts, it can be concluded that accuracies of 90-95% can be achieved with the available methods. In an interactive environment, this

---

[3] MPEG pictures are encoded in 8x8-pixel blocks. A discrete cosine transform (DCT) is applied to each block, resulting in one DC coefficient and 63 AC coefficients. The DC coefficient is just the average value of the original 64 values. A DC image contains only DC coefficients, i.e., one pixel for each 8x8-pixel block in the full-size picture.

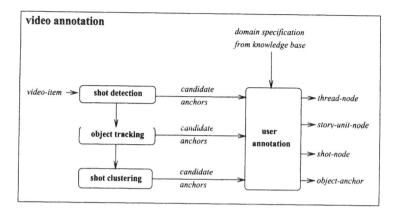

Fig. 3. *Overview of the annotation process.*

will generally be sufficient. In particular, a camera pan or zoom sequence might be misinterpreted as a gradual transition, so all detected gradual transitions should be checked during the camera work analysis step. Existing commercial and prototype software MPEG encoders use shot boundary information to optimize the allocation of bits to pictures [10], e.g., the first picture after an abrupt or gradual transition is encoded as an intra-frame (a single image, with no reference to past or future pictures). We anticipate that this practice will become commonplace in the near future; inspection of (DC images of) intra-frames will then be sufficient to detect shot boundaries during the MPEG *decoding* process. Until this happens, however, we will adopt the methods of [31].

Scene analysis: After segmenting the video into shots, sequences of shots can be grouped into semantic units - story-units and threads (although the Informedia project [28] first detects *video paragraphs*, then segments each into its component shots). Yeung et al. observe that a few minutes of video typically contain hundreds of shots. They therefore cluster sequences of shots (related by a common locale or dramatic event) into more meaningful story-units. Similarity measures on DC images and temporal heuristics enable semi-automatic detection of story-units. Image similarity measures and annotations may suggest candidates for inclusion in a thread, but inspection by the (human) annotator will be needed to ensure correctness.

Camera work analysis: Apparent motion between consecutive frames can be caused by motion of an object in the picture or by camera work (or both). Camera work analysis therefore involves distinguishing camera work from object motion; this information will be useful in the object detection step. Panning and zooming sequences can produce histogram patterns similar to gradual shot transitions, so camera work analysis is also needed to eliminate false transitions.

The basic approach to detecting a camera pan or zoom is analysis of the optical flow field: panning and zooming produce distinctive patterns of motion vectors; gradual transitions and moving objects do not (unless the object is very large relative to the image size). [2] presents a computationally efficient method for detecting camera work, based on tomography: the "X-ray" projections are the average values of each row and column in successive images. We plan to investigate the possibility of using this method in the partially-decoded domain, e.g., DC images. [25] generated X-rays from JPEG-compressed images, using only low-order DCT coefficients. Meng and Chang [19] also detect panning and zooming in the compressed domain.

Object detection and tracking: Detecting objects in a fully interactive way is a tedious task as first shots have to be defined (probably using a hierarchical magnifier as described in [27]) and then objects have to be outlined in every subsequent frame. Using computer vision techniques, the user can be aided in these two tasks. Rowley et al. [23] have trained a neural network to detect human *faces* in images containing frontal views of faces (with both eyes visible and open). In [7] the use of video objects as anchors is proposed. Their method of defining anchors aids the user in defining objects by using interpolation. However, this is purely based on computer graphics and no use of the video data itself is made. Hence, the resulting video objects have an inaccurate representation.

We intend to use an object tracking framework similar to [4]. In this framework, a contour is parameterized with a small set of parameters using B-splines. Based on the video data found locally around the contour, the object is tracked through the sequence using predictive filtering. For our purposes, we will extend the framework to take into account color edges rather than intensity edges. This might be combined with the estimation of dominant and multiple motion models to separate the fixed (background) layer from moving objects and to differentiate camera motion from object motion [11]. In [19], moving objects are detected in some types of MPEG-encoded video, using motion vectors and DC coefficients; however, DC image analysis is inadequate for detecting small object movements, as each DC coefficient is the average value of an 8x8 block of pixels.

Link database creation Although we aim at automatic generation of links, authors have the option of creating or adding to a link database. For links based on information not explicitly coded in the knowledge base, this is even essential. Adding links that can be derived from the knowledge base should be done in close conjunction with the hypermedia generation step described in the next section. Adding those to the link database might speed up the processing, but adding them to the link database explicitly is not essential.

3.2 Hypermedia generation

Whenever the user selects a subject of interest, by selecting an anchor in a media item, for which more information should be provided, the semantic attributes associated with the selected anchor are recorded. A call is made to the database to select items that are similar to the given set of attributes [4]. This will yield a set of media items as well as a similarity matrix describing their relations (see section 3.1).

The set of media items should be presented to the user in a structured way as a hypermedia presentation. Here we have to decide which items will be grouped into composite components and how they will be connected by links. This is done on the basis of a set of heuristics. Heuristics for semantic grouping can be based on the matching criteria in [17]:

- goal-directed: group components that involve the same goal;
- salient-feature: group components that match most important features or largest number of important features;
- specificity: group components that matches features exactly over those that match features generally;
- frequency preference: group components that are matched frequently;
- recency preference: group components that are matched recently;
- ease-of-adaptation: group components for which the features are easily adapted to new situations.

The above criteria can be mapped directly to the distances defined in the similarity matrix or their dynamic behavior. Example composition and linking heuristics not based on the semantics are:

- create the smallest number of composites;
- create the smallest number of links between composites
- don't allow incompatible media types (e.g. 2 videos together).

The weighting for the different criteria depends on how the different approaches work in practice, and may even be put in the hands of the end user e.g. to give preferences for an overview of a subject area, or an in-depth search.

3.3 Hypermedia presentation

In the above generation step, a complete hypermedia presentation description is derived. At this point it does not yet include the actual media items, but a logical channel has been assigned to each media item. As indicated before, a logical channel represents a physical channel capable of playing the media item. Hence, when the hypermedia presentation is sent to the client, logical channels have to be mapped to the physical channels available. When this mapping is performed, the client informs the database server of the physical channel properties, e.g., resolution for a picture channel.

---

[4] In the ideal situation there would be some sort of memory, so that the user's previous selections can be stored and the associated attributes used to contribute to the information used in the database search.

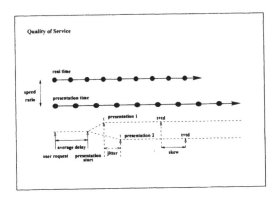

Fig. 4. *Quality of service.*

A key issue for acceptance of a multimedia information system is the quality of service provided by the system. The parameters that determine the quality of service are depicted in figure 4. Ideally real time equals the presentation time. The *ratio* between real time and the presentation time is an important quality factor. *Average delay, jitter* and *skew* represent relative timing delays between user requests and simultaneous presentations. The last factor, the *utilization*, describes the ratio between the data volume used for the presentation and the data volume available.

From this description it is clear that the quality of service is timing related. Consequently, this aspect has a great impact on the system design as a whole. As the multimedia data used for a presentation may be too voluminous to be stored in the client, the database must be designed to offer the quality of service. In other words, it must have a real-time kernel.

To keep a specific quality of service it might be required to reduce the utilization such that all of the above measures are kept within acceptable limits. This can for example be achieved by sending images at a reduced resolution. This adaptation can also be initiated by the client when for example a window in which a media item is presented is resized. So apart from sending information on the properties of the physical channels also the required quality of service should be communicated. On the basis of these measures the database can start sending the actual media items to the client in the appropriate format and with the highest quality possible within the constraints. The whole process is shown in figure 5.

Video presentation For delivery of video from the database server to a client workstation, users will be offered two options: (1) the server decodes and sends the pictures to the client or (2) the server sends the MPEG stream to the client for local decoding, either in hardware or software. These options can be combined with quality-of-service parameters, such as reduced picture rate or resolution. In addition, the client and/or server might buffer sequences of decoded pictures (in physical or virtual memory) if there is enough storage.

The first option requires a very high bandwidth network [5] to provide the highest quality of service and places a heavy load on the server's processor(s) and/or storage (depending on the number of pictures buffered in the server). The second option requires a client workstation with reasonable processing and storage capabilities.

All three - network bandwidth, processing power and storage capacity - are increasing rapidly and becoming more affordable. However, network bandwidth fills up almost as soon as it becomes available, so the first option cannot always be depended on for timely delivery of decoded pictures to the client. On the other hand, individual users often have access to workstations with fast processors and large amounts of storage, and workstations are more readily upgraded than are networks or database servers. Hence, the second option may prove to be more viable. The client software for accessing the video database server would include the MPEG decoder. There would be a switch to use the client workstation's hardware MPEG decoder, if it has one.

Video abstraction and representation: Many queries will retrieve several relevant video clips (shots, story-units or threads). These should be presented to the hypermedia user in a compact, yet informative, format that enables them to decide which clips to view in full. Several techniques have been proposed for automatically deriving an abstract of the content of a video or video segment, and presenting this information visually and concisely. Initially, we will evaluate the following video representations for computational efficiency and conciseness.

- Key frames: one or a few pictures are chosen to represent the video or video segment; these can be displayed as thumbnail (e.g., DC) images to further reduce the amount of data transferred. The selection algorithm might be purely positional - e.g., the first, middle and last pictures in a shot - or it might be based on similarity measures and frequency - e.g., this segment contains many pictures similar to this - or on camera work - e.g., the first and last pictures of a zoom. The Informedia project [28] combines clues from image analysis and keyword prominence analysis to identify a key frame for each shot in a video paragraph (story-unit), and to select one of these to represent the entire paragraph.
- Mosaic (salient still) [11]: several pictures in a shot are combined to create a single still image that retains much of the original content and context while dramatically reducing the amount of data (e.g., a 64KB mosaic of a 22MB panning shot of Yosemite Valley is available from QBIC's WWW page *http://www.almaden.ibm.com/cs/video/*). Mosaics are easily created from the results of dominant motion estimation, which we plan to use for object detection (see section 3.1). Because this technique separates moving

---

[5] Typical video picture rates are about 30 pictures per second. A decoded full-color 256x256 pixel picture occupies 256 KB. Sending 30 decoded 256x256 full-color pictures per second to a client workstation requires a network bandwidth of 60 Mbps.

objects from the background, it can also be used to create a *dynamic* mosaic, with the objects moving against a completely static background mosaic. A mosaic is an alternative to a key frame for a shot; although it may be possible to create mosaics of some *scenes*, most story-units would require more than one mosaic.

- Scene transition graphs [31]: the story-line of an entire video is represented as a directed graph. each node is a cluster of visually similar and temporally close shots, represented by a key frame; edges indicate the temporal flow of the story. *Cut edges* partition the graph into story-units. Since our system is most concerned with representing story-units, we will be interested in the degree of clustering possible, i.e., the ratio of the number of shots to the number of nodes in a story-unit. For some types of video (e.g., situation comedies), this ratio can be quite high.

- Skim video [26]: "significant" images and words are selected from the video segment and accompanying audio to create a compact synopsis (e.g., 1100 frames of the documentary "Destruction of Species" can be represented by a 78-frame skim video). Natural language processing is applied to the transcript to identify the most important keywords and phrases and the time-corresponding frames are examined for scene changes, camera work and relevant objects. Additional clues are obtained from numerous heuristics based on widely-used film production practices. Skim videos provide an efficient filtering mechanism to the hypermedia user, if the static representations are inadequate for differentiating the retrieved video clips.

4 System architecture

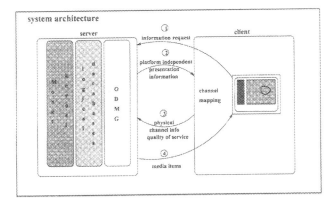

Fig. 5. *Overview of the layered architecture of the multimedia information system (or server) and the communication with the client in the presentation of hypermedia.*

The limitations for storing multimedia information in relational systems are well known. The kernels of these systems simply do not provide the hooks for achieving the fine control required in meeting the real time constraints. Object-oriented systems have the advantage that they enable the expression of multimedia data operations, such as image and video algebra [29]. Unfortunately, real-time behavior is not achievable with these systems.

Extensible databases provide the required level of control to implement multimedia databases. They allow extension of a small fixed database kernel with application specific data types and operations. Our system is based on Monet [5], an extensible main-memory database system. Monet uses a flexible and efficient decomposed storage model and offers database triggers, a type extension mechanism and a set of binary relational algebra operations. The latter have predictable performance, which is important in achieving a certain quality of service.

The basic media types can be implemented using the type extension mechanism of Monet. These types include video, audio, images, links, anchors and the spatial and temporal relations used for presentation. At the application interface level an Object Oriented interface to these types is provided based on the ODMG data model. This has the advantage that a seamless interface is provided for applications written in any language. Currently, bindings for C++ and Java exist.

The image, video and temporal types have been implemented and the audio type is under construction. Video pictures can be converted into full-size or reduced DC images; images can be processed by image processing operations, similarity measures and detectors. Work has begun on the object tracking system for video annotation. The annotation and retrieval mechanisms will be implemented as ODMG applications.

5 Conclusion

We have considered the design of a multimedia information system in which hypermedia presentations can be generated automatically. In the system, we have identified four logical databases: a knowledge base, a media database, a component database and a link database. The processes acting upon this information can be divided into three steps. In the *hypermedia creation* step, the logical databases are populated. In this step, each component is semi-automatically assigned a semantic annotation. The *hypermedia generation* step is based on heuristics using a similarity function for grouping and linking components. Finally, the design of the hypermedia system architecture is such that real-time adaptive *hypermedia presentation* can be achieved.

References

1. P. Aigrain, H.J. Zhang and D. Petkovic, Content-based representation and retrieval of visual media: A state-of-the-art review. *Multimedia Tools and Applications*, 3, pages 179–202, 1996.

2. A. Akutsu and Y. Tonomura, Video tomography: An efficient method for camerawork extraction and motion analysis. *Proc. ACM Multimedia Conference*, 1994.

3. E. André and T. Rist, Coping with temporal constraints in multimedia presentation Planning. *Proc. ECAI 96*, 1996.

4. A. Blake et al., A framework for spatiotemporal control in the tracking of visual contours. *International Journal of Computer Vision*, 11(2):127–145, 1993.

5. P. Boncz and M.L. Kersten, Monet: an impressionist sketch of an advanced database system. *Proc. BIWITT'95*, 1995.

6. D.C.A. Bulterman, G. v. Rossum and R. v. Liere, A structure for transportable, dynamic multimedia documents. *Proc. USENIX*, pages 137–155, 1991.

7. V. Burrill, T. Kirste and J. Weiss, Time-varying sensitive regions in dynamic multimedia objects: a pragmatic approach to content based retrieval from video. *Information and Software Technology*, 36(4):213–223, 1994.

8. H. Davis, W. Hall, I. Heath, G. Hill and R. Wilkins, MICROCOSM: An open hypermedia environment for information integration. *Proc. ECHT*, 1992.

9. M. Davis, *Media streams: representing video for retrieval and repurposing*. PhD thesis, MIT, 1995.

10. A. Dev, Personal communication, 1996.

11. M. Flickner, H. Sawhney, W. Niblack, J. Ashley, Q. Huang, B. Dom M. Gorkani, J. Hafner, D. Lee, D. Petkovic, D. Steele, and P. Yanker, Query by image and video content: the QBIC system. *IEEE Computer*, 28(9), 1995.

12. K. B. Haase, FRAMER: a persistent portable representation library. *Proc. ECAI 94*, 1994.

13. F. Halasz and M. Schwartz, The Dexter hypertext reference model. *Communications of the ACM*, 37(2):30–39, 1994.

14. A. Hampapur, R. Jain and T. Weymouth, Digital video segmentation. *Proc. Second ACM International Conference on Multimedia*, pages 357–364, 1994.

15. L. Hardman, D.C.A. Bulterman and G. v. Rossum, The Amsterdam hypermedia model: Adding time and context to the Dexter model. *Communications of the ACM*, 37(2):50–62, 1994.

16. V. Kashyap, K. Shah and A. Sheth, Metadata for building the MultiMedia Patch Quilt. In *Multimedia Database Systems: Issues and Research Directions*, S. Jajodia and V.S. Subrahmaniun, Eds., Springer-Verlag, 1995.

17. J. Kolodner, Judging which is the "best" case for a case-based reasoner. *Proc. Case-based reasoning workshop*, 1989.

18. MPEG Convener, Description of MPEG-4, *http://drogo.cselt.stet.it/mpeg/mpeg-4_description.htm*.

19. J. Meng and S.-F. Chang, Tools for compressed-domain video indexing and editing. *SPIE Conference on Storage and Retrieval for Image and Video Database*, Vol. 2670, 1996.

20. K. Otsuji and Y. Tonomura, Projection detecting filter for video cut detection. *Proc. First ACM International Conference on Multimedia*, pages 251–257, 1993.

21. Porter et al., Concept learning and heuristic classification in weak-theory domains. *AI Journal*, 1990.

22. G. van Rossum, J. Jansen, S. Mullender and D. Bulterman, CMIFed: a presentation environment for portable hypermedia documents. *IEEE Multimedia*, 1993.
23. H. Rowley, S. Baluja and T. Kanade, Human face detection in visual scenes. CMU Technical Report *CMU-CS-95-158R*, 1995.
24. S. Ruggieri, M. Bordegoni, G. Faconti, T. Rist, P. Trahanias and M. Wilson, The Reference Model for Intelligent Multimedia Presentation Systems: 1st Draft. Proc. ECAI 96 Workshop *Towards a Standard Reference Model for Intelligent Multimedia Systems*, 1996.
25. F. Salazar and F. Valéro, Analyse automatique de documents vidéo. IRIT rapport de recherche *95-28-R*, Université Paul Sabatier, 1995.
26. M.A. Smith and T. Kanade, Video Skimming for Quick Browsing Based on Audio and Image Characterization. CMU Technical Report *CMU-CS-95-186*, 1995.
27. S.W. Smoliar and H. Zhang, Content-based video indexing and retrieval. *IEEE Multimedia*, pages 62–72, 1994.
28. H.D. Wactlar, T. Kanade, M.A. Smith and S.M. Stevens, Intelligent access to digital video: Informedia project. *IEEE Computer*, 29(5), pages 46–52, May 1996.
29. R. Weiss, D.D. Andrzej and D.K. Gifford, Content-based access to algebraic video. *Proc. International Conference on Multimedia Computing and Systems*, pages 140–151, 1994.
30. J.K. Wu, A.D. Narasimhalu, B.M. Mehtre, C.P. Lam and Y.J. Gao, CORE: a content based retrieval system for multimedia information systems. *Multimedia systems*, 3:25–41, 1995.
31. M. Yeung, B.L. Yeo and B. Liu, Extracting Story Units from Long Programs for Video Browsing and Navigation. *Proc. International Conference on Multimedia Computing and Systems*, 1996.

Springer
and the
environment

At Springer we firmly believe that an international science publisher has a special obligation to the environment, and our corporate policies consistently reflect this conviction.
We also expect our business partners – paper mills, printers, packaging manufacturers, etc. – to commit themselves to using materials and production processes that do not harm the environment. The paper in this book is made from low- or no-chlorine pulp and is acid free, in conformance with international standards for paper permanency.

 Springer

Lecture Notes in Computer Science

For information about Vols. 1–1247

please contact your bookseller or Springer-Verlag